GW00545579

Ethnicity & Conflict
in the Horn of Africa

EASTERN AFRICAN STUDIES

*forthcoming

Ethnicity & Conflict in the Horn of Africa

Edited by

KATSUYOSHI FUKUI

Professor in the Department of Cultural Anthropology
Kyoto University

JOHN MARKAKIS

Professor of African Studies
In the Department of History & Archaeology
University of Crete

James Currey
LONDON

Ohio University Press
ATHENS

James Currey Ltd
54b Thornhill Square
Islington
London N1 1BE, England

Ohio University Press
Scott Quadrangle
Athens
Ohio 45701, USA

Available in North-Eastern Africa from

The Book Centre
Addis Ababa University
P.O. Box 1176
Addis Ababa
Ethiopia

Fountain Publishers
P.O. Box 488
Kampala
Uganda

The Nile Bookshop
P.O. Box 8036
Khartoum
Sudan

Department of National Guidance
Asmara
Eritrea

British Library Cataloguing in Publication Data

Ethnicity and Conflict in the Horn of
Africa. — (Eastern African Studies)
  I. Fukui, Katsuyoshi II. Markakis, John
  III. Series
  305.896

ISBN 0-85255-226-2 (cased)
      0-85255-225-4 (paper)

Library of Congress Cataloging-in-Publication Data
Ethnicity & conflict in the Horn of Africa / edited by Katsuyoshi
  Fukui, John Markakis.
      p.   cm. — (Eastern African studies)
  Includes bibliographical references and index.
  ISBN 0-8214-1080-6
    1. Africa, Northeast — Politics and government — 1900-1974.
  2. Africa, Northeast — Politics and government — 1974-
  3. Africa, Northeast — Ethnic relations. I. Fukui,
  Katsuyoshi, 1943-   . II. Markakis, John. III. Title:
  Ethnicity and conflict in the Horn. IV. Series: Eastern
  African studies (London, England)
  DT367.8.E88 1994
  305.8′009676 — dc20   93-41409
                                                    CIP

Typeset in 11/12 pt Baskerville by Colset Pte Ltd., Singapore
Printed and bound in Great Britain
by Villiers Publications, London N4

Contents

PART I

Conflict on the Margin

List of Maps

List of Figures

List of Tables

Preface

The studies included in this volume were initially presented to the Symposium on 'Ethnic Conflict in Northeast Africa,' sponsored by the Taniguchi Foundation and organized by the National Museum of Ethnology at Osaka, 27 March–13 April 1991. This was the fourteenth symposium sponsored by the Taniguchi Foundation and the Senri Foundation. The first of these, held in 1977, also at Osaka, had a related ethnology theme — 'Warfare Among East African Herders' — and three of its participants — Fukui, Turton, Baxter — also took part in the fourteenth symposium. There is, therefore, thematic and participant continuity between the two occasions, and the publication edited by Fukui and Turton, *Warfare among East African Herders* (1979), serves as a point of reference for this volume.

All the participants in the 1977 symposium were anthropologists with a special interest in mobile pastoralism in East Africa. This interest was also represented in the 1991 meeting with several papers. In addition, the latter occasion included historians and political scientists, as well as anthropologists with other interests. What brought them together was concern for the people of the Horn of Africa, where entire communities have been shattered by unending violent conflict, the cause of which is commonly said to be ethnic divisions. A desire to shed light on the ambiguous connection between ethnicity and conflict was shared by those who participated in the symposium, and ensured consistency among their contributions.

The hosting of the symposium in Osaka and the participation of four Japanese scholars testify to the growing academic interest in that country concerning Africa. Generous support from the

Taniguchi Foundation under its Executive Director, Mr Toyo-
saburo Taniguchi, the National Museum of Ethnology under its
Director General, Dr Tadao Umesao, and the Senri Foundation
made possible both the meeting at Osaka and the publication of
the contributions. Fukui, the symposium organizer, worked tire-
lessly with his colleagues to ensure its success. Dr Tadao
Umesao's kind invitation enabled Markakis to spend three
months in 1992 at the National Museum of Ethnology, a time
devoted to the editing of this volume in collaboration with Fukui.
It is owing to Markakis' tough work that this volume has seen
the light of day smoothly. The administration and staff of the
Museum offered invaluable assistance in the completion of this
task, as did Ms Yuko Matsumoto, who performed secretarial
duties.

Finally, we would like to record a word of deep thanks, on
behalf of the contributors in this volume, for the Grant-in-Aid for
Publication of Scientific Research Result in the Ministry of
Education, Science and Culture in Japan.

Osaka

K. Fukui
J. Markakis

Notes on Contributors

Tim Allen is lecturer at the Open University, London. He is a social anthropologist who has done research in southern Sudan and northern Uganda among the Acholi and Madi, and has published articles on both groups.

P.T.W. Baxter retired from the department of Social Anthropology, University of Manchester, in 1989. He began his Oromo research among the Boran of northern Kenya in the early 1950s and subsequently worked among the Arssi in Ethiopia. He has also carried out research in Uganda and Ghana. He has written extensively on Oromo culture and on the development of pastoral people. He is an editor of the following books; *Age, Generation and Time* (1978), *Property, Poverty and People* (1990), *When the Grass is Gone: Development Intervention in African Arid Lands* (1991) and *Voice, Genre, Text: Anthropological Essays in Africa and Beyond* (1991).

Katsuyoshi Fukui was associate professor at the National Museum of Ethnology in Japan until March 1993, and is now professor in the Department of Cultural Anthropology at Kyoto University. He has studied pastoral, agro-pastoral and swidden societies in Japan and East Africa, including southern Ethiopia and Sudan, since 1964. He has written *Tsubayama: A Swidden Village* (1974) (Japanese), *Cognition and Culture: Ethnography of Colour and Pattern Among the Bodi* (1991) (Japanese), and is co-editor of the following publications: *Warfare among East African Herders* (1979), *Explorations of Pastoralism: Ecology, Culture and History* (1987) (Japanese), *What is the Ethnic Group?* (1988) (Japanese).

Wendy James lectures in the Institute of Social and Cultural Anthropology at the University of Oxford, and is a Fellow of St Cross College. Her area of interest is the borderland along the Sudan–Ethiopia frontier, where she has carried out research. She has taught for five years at the University of Khartoum, and was a visiting scholar in the Institute of Ethiopian Studies at the University of Addis Ababa. She has published two books about the Uduk: *'Kwanim Pa': The Making of the Uduk People* (1979), *The Listening Ebony* (1988); and co-edited *The Southern Marches of Imperial Ethiopia* (1986).

Eisei Kurimoto is associate professor in the National Museum of Ethnology at Osaka. He is a social anthropologist who has conducted extensive research, beginning in 1978 among the Pari in southern Sudan and the Anuak in western Ethiopia. He has published numerous articles on the history, economy and political systems of these people.

Yoshiko Kurita is a research fellow in the National Museum of Ethnology at Osaka. Her field of study is the dynamics of nation-building in the Third World, and her area of interest covers Egypt and Sudan. She was research associate in the Institute of African and Asian Studies at the University of Khartoum during 1985–1987. She has published articles on the emergence of Sudanese nationalism.

John Lamphear is professor in the Department of History, University of Texas at Austin. He has carried out research on the history of the Jie and Turkana in East Africa, and has numerous publications on this subject, including *The Traditional History of the Jie of Uganda* (1976) and *The Scattering Time: Turkana Responses to Colonial Rule* (1992).

John Markakis is professor of African studies in the Department of History and Archaeology, at the University of Crete. The Horn of Africa is his area of interest, where he has followed social and political developments for the past 25 years. He has lived and worked in Ethiopia, and carried out research in Sudan, Somalia and Kenya. Among his publications are *Ethiopia: Anatomy of a Traditional Polity* (1974), *Class and Revolution in Ethiopia* (1978), *National and Class Conflict in the Horn of Africa* (1987), *Military Marxist Regimes in Africa* (1986) (co-edited), *Conflict and the Decline of Pastoralism in the Horn of Africa* (1992) (edited).

Hiroshi Matsuda is lecturer at St Agnes Junior College, at Takatsuki. He has studied small agro-foragers, Koegu and Karo, in southern Ethiopia since 1986.

M.A. Mohamed Salih is associate professor in social anthropology, senior research fellow at the Scandinavian Institute of African Studies, Uppsala, and leader of the research programme 'Human Life in African Arid Lands'. He carried out extensive research among pastoral communities in the Sudan, Nigeria and Ethiopia. He is the editor of *Family Life in the Sudan* (1987), *Agrarian Change in the Central Rainlands; Sudan* (1987), *Ecology and Politics* (1989), *Pastoralism and the State in Africa* (1990), *Pastoralists and Planners; Indigenous Knowledge and Pastoral Development in Northern Nigeria* (1992) and *The Least Developed and the Oil-Rich Arab Countries* (1992).

David Turton is a Senior Fellow of the Granada Centre for Visual Anthropology at the University of Manchester, where he was formerly Senior Lecturer in the Department of Social Anthropology. He has been conducting research on the Mursi of south-western Ethiopia since 1969, and has published numerous articles on their response to ecological change, drought, famine and war. He was editor of the anthropological journal *Man* from 1984 to 1986, has co-edited *Warfare Among East African Herders* (Senri Ethnological Studies 3, 1979) and *Film as Ethnography* (MUP, 1992), and collaborated with Granada Television in making five films on the Mursi. He is a Research Associate of the Overseas Development Institute (London) and editor of its journal *Disasters*.

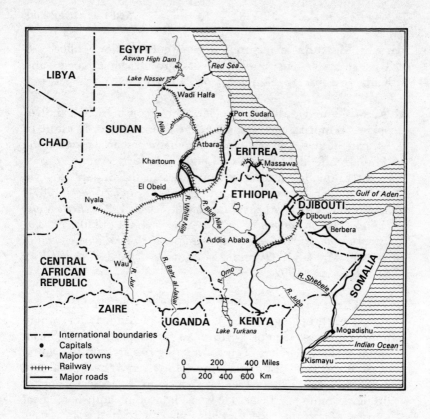

Map 1   The Horn of Africa

xiv

Introduction

KATSUYOSHI FUKUI
& JOHN MARKAKIS

The Horn of Africa is the area bounded by the Red Sea, the Indian Ocean, the Nile basin, and the East African highlands. It is a vast area with a richly variegated physical environment, to whose requirements the inhabitants of the region adapted themselves with great ingenuity. The cultural landscape of the region is also immensely varied, as is shown in the contributions to this volume. Variety notwithstanding, the people who share the region have much in common. A sizeable but diminishing section of the Horn's population are pastoralists occupying a distinct ecological niche, and their material and social culture though varied in form is similar in essence. That culture is now under intolerable stress throughout the region, and the pastoralists are involved in a violent struggle for survival, also depicted in several contributions to this volume. The majority of the region's inhabitants are cultivators whose existence, like that of the pastoralists, is jeopardized by drought, famine and violent conflict. Impoverished and powerless, they are victimized by all sides. The truth of the African saying, 'When elephants fight, the grass suffers,' is vividly illustrated in this volume with case-studies of cultivators caught in the maelstrom of war fought within and across state borders. This is another distressing aspect of the conflict that joins the people of the region in common misfortune, as war spills across state borders and people flee across frontiers in search of refuge.

Conflict has been endemic in this region for two decades. In their introduction to *Warfare among East African Herders* (1979) Fukui and Turton noted that intertribal fighting among pastoralists in this region was exacerbated in the 1970s by the

1

worse incidents of drought and famine in living memory, and the easy availability of firearms, which were now coming into common use. Much worse was in store for the region in the 1980s, when drought became the rule and famine reached biblical proportions. War spread to agricultural regions, and was fought on many levels simultaneously — between states, regions, ethnic groups, clans and lineages. Thanks to sophisticated weaponry generously supplied by patrons from abroad, warfare was waged on high technological levels far above the region's native capacity, and the antiquated Austrian Mannlicher rifle, the weapon of the 1970s, was now replaced by the Kalashnikov. Such escalation changed the nature of war just as anthropologists were coming to grips with this subject, and some of them found the groups they were studying facing extinction.

There are few areas or communities in the Horn fortunate enough to have avoided direct involvement in the manifold conflict. The selection of case-studies in this volume covers a broad spectrum of recent experiences by a variety of groups in different parts of the region. They range in size from the Oromo in Ethiopia, who number perhaps 20 million, to the Koegu in the same country who number less than 500. Some of them, like the marginal groups of the Omo valley, are involved in classic confrontations with their immediate neighbours over land. However, the nature of the conflict has changed even there, and a group can be literally decimated in one engagement. Other groups are drawn into larger regional confrontations, which provide a broader setting for the continuation of local disputes. Larger and more advanced groups, like the Dinka and the Oromo, are involved in conflicts at the level of the state, and for goals that include autonomy and even independence.

What purpose is served in putting such disparate groups under the same analytical spotlight? It is not merely to demonstrate the all-embracing nature of the conflict in this region, although that is an important part of the story. Rather, one purpose is to illustrate the variety of motives and goals involved in what is simply and obscurely labelled 'ethnic conflict'. This variety is best demonstrated in the sharply focused studies of small groups contributed by anthropologists. A contrasting purpose is to depict the common context — historical, material, political — within which motives and goals are defined and pursued, and this emerges most clearly in the more general treatment of the larger groups.

Conflict in what might be called the contemporary tribal zone, since it lies at the margin of the state's effective range of authority, is set apart by at least one peculiar feature: its motives and goals are unrelated to the state, although the latter can significantly influence the course and outcome of the conflict — for example, by controlling the supply of firearms. Studies of conflict at the margin are presented in the first part of this volume. In contrast, with regard to motives and goals, the state is the common point of reference in conflicts involving groups large enough to compete at the centre for state power. Studies of conflict at this level are presented in the third part. Often, smaller groups are drawn into confrontations at the state level which are not directly relevant to their own motives and goals but which they seek to exploit for their own parochial purposes. Case-studies of this kind are included in the second part.

Like the conflict itself, the purpose of this work is manifold. Rejecting the Hobbesian explanation for social conflict, as indicated by Turton in his essay, the contributors delve into the motivation of those who engage in it. As is to be expected, given the many differences among the groups studied, conclusions vary, though without being fundamentally contradictory. The impact of violent conflict on social and cultural institutions and values is another theme pursued by the contributors to this volume. The destructive aspect of war is predictable. Even so, the impact of widespread and protracted warfare depicted in this volume, waged without defined front lines or distinctions between combatants and non-combatants, is stunning.

The impact, however, is not unambivalent. A contrasting theme emerges from the accounts of peoples' creative responses to the hazards posed by conflict. These concern not merely survival, but also social and cultural adaptation to new circumstances. The adoption of new technologies of warfare is the most obvious response. More significantly, this may be followed by social adaptation to new circumstances created by conflict. The coalescence of clans and lineages into larger political units with unified leadership, usually labelled 'tribes', is such an adaptation familiar to social anthropologists. Indeed, 'tribalization' is said to have occurred centuries ago in the 'tribal zone' as a response to pressures from expanding European imperialism (Ferguson & Whitehead, 1992: 12–16). In this volume, Lamphear describes this process in connection with the Jie and Turkana in the mid-nineteenth century. Turton suggests that war is essential to the creation and maintenance of Mursi political unity. Also in this volume, Allen points to a contrasting phenomenon, that is, the weaving of networks of social interaction that span 'tribal' lines between the Acholi and Madi, which are relied upon to mitigate the impact of 'tribal' conflict between these two groups.

3

Most parties to the conflict in the Horn wage sophisticated propaganda battles, deploying a variety of ideological weapons. Nationalism, socialism, religion and ethnicity are commonly used. The first three have a universal appeal, designed to transcend the parochial attraction of the fourth, and have been used for that purpose by those who control the post-colonial state in this region. As it turned out, ethnicity proved by far superior as a principle of political solidarity and mobilization, and emerged as the dominant political force from the wreckage of the post-colonial state. Therefore, it would seem that the 'ethnic' label usually attached to conflict at all levels in this region is not altogether inappropriate.

The conundrum ethnicity represents as a concept and tool of social analysis is well known. It is a term, someone wrote, 'that invites fruitless definitional arguments among those professional intellectuals who think they know, or ought to know, what it means' (Tonkin *et al.*, 1989: 11). Its application in a multitude of conflict situations compounds confusion, which is why Horowitz (1985: xi) complains 'there is too much knowledge and not enough understanding' about ethnicity. At the centre of the confusion is the hazy perception of the 'ethnic group' itself. Aside from the old primordial (Shils, 1957; Geertz, 1967) and the new socio-biological (Van den Berghe, 1981) schools of thought on this subject, it is generally agreed that the ethnic group is a social construct and, therefore, subject to change. Its fluid, chameleon-like character defies precise definition and limits its value as a category for analysis.

A long, earnest discussion took place during the 1991 Osaka symposium, at which the papers included in this volume were presented, and it was not without misgivings that the participants consented to the use of the term 'ethnic', which they deemed to have little analytical value, in conjunction with the type of conflict they had studied. The anthropologists, who were the majority, considered it impossible to define ethnic identities on the basis of genealogical or cultural criteria, because, once the ideological screen of common origin is pushed aside, a complex pattern of fusion and fission among groups is revealed which, if it follows any discernible rule, it is to enhance a group's chances for survival.

Discussions on the definition of ethnicity often conclude that the term need not be defined for scholarly work to proceed. In his contribution to this volume, Turton also argues that it is not necessary to start by defining ethnic identity, because 'an ethnic group is not a group because of ethnicity, but because its members engage in common action and share common interests' (p. 17). These are operational criteria to be applied by the researcher to collective behaviour in competitive or conflict situations, and the approach is the reverse of the usual one that begins with a priori definition of the 'ethnic group'. Once the group is identified on this basis, then the ethnic construct can be matched with it to see how it fits. As indicated below, this is not to deny that the construct itself possesses a force of its own. A group's cohesion, however, derives from its members' perception of shared interests, and in the case of the Mursi according to Turton, these are focused on a particular territory, the occupation of which appears to be the foundation of Mursi identity. In Turton's interpretation of Mursi ideology, their ethnic identity is temporal and likely to dissolve into its clan components once this territory is lost. Furthermore, in an advance on the 'tribalization' thesis, Turton suggests that war is not simply a means by which an existing 'tribe' defends its territory, but rather it is the essential means by which such political superstructures have been created and are maintained among the Mursi and their neighbours in the Omo valley. In this sense, ethnicity is not the cause of war, but the reverse.

In his discussion of the Mela, neighbours of the Mursi, Fukui argues that shared culture cannot create a group, unless its members share the 'we consciousness', which is contrasted to the consciousness of 'they'. These perceptions are not fixed, because some who were 'they' in the past are now 'we', and the reverse is also probably true. In his re-creation of Mela ethnogenesis, Fukui unravels a complex pattern of fusion and fission of groups which is designed to ensure clan survival and hegemony. In his analysis of Mela conflict, Fukui finds an equally complex pattern of confrontation, involving a number of groups with varied historical and cultural affinities, as well as economic relations, *vis-à-vis* the Mela. Ethnic, that is, genealogical and cultural, factors are important in defining this pattern, but they are not the only ones that seem to have a role in determining the incidence and intensity of conflict. In essence, Fukui sees conflict as the catalyst in the process of Mela ethnogenesis, and as a mechanism for adjusting population movement to territory. In his study of the Koegu, Matsuda believes he found this miniscule group in the process of 'drifting' across the ethnic boundary, and presumably redefining its identity by repositioning itself between its neighbours. Low-intensity conflict mediated this process and acted as the balancing mechanism of inter-group relations.

Allen in his study of Acholi–Madi relations describes what he calls 'inside' and 'outside' spheres of moral and social interaction, which cut across conventional 'ethnic' lines. Thus, while at one level the dividing line of the conflict can be perceived by the people themselves to correspond with the Acholi–Madi 'ethnic' divide, at another, less visible level the same people interact positively in networks that cut across 'tribal' lines. Indeed, such networks are relied upon in times of conflict to mitigate its consequences. Like Fukui, Allen found that clan and lineage ties are the threads out of which the networks comprising the 'inside' sphere are woven. This supports Turton's suggestion 'not only that clans are older than many of the political divisions they cut across, but that they are seen as the "stuff" of social life or "natural" by the people themselves' (p. 20). Both Turton and Allen agree with Schlee (1985: 19), who argues that 'a clan is not simply a sub-unit of a "tribe", because it can be represented in more than one "tribe"'. Inter-ethnic clan relationships, Schlee found, are relied upon in times of stress (1989: 7).

What is deduced from the study of marginal groups is that ethnic/tribal identities are essentially political products of specific situations, socially defined and historically determined. Turton and Fukui point to the functional role of conflict in defining and maintaining group boundaries which serve to delineate 'ethnic identity'. Turton, Fukui and Lamphear also point to the role of conflict in creating and maintaining political superstructures, that is, 'tribes'. In other words, seen in historical perspective, ethnicity and its representative structures ('tribes') emerge as the consequence rather than the cause of conflict.

Bringing the spotlight of history to bear on ethnicity — 'collocation' it was called by the editors of *History and Ethnicity* (Tonkin *et al.*, 1989) — is a recent and promising development. For one thing, it has expanded the scope of enquiry into the pre-colonial period, as Lamphear's essay demonstrates. Whenever possible, historically minded anthropologists, a new breed, trace the process of ethnic identity construction and reconstruction into the past, and the results are often illuminating. They suggest, according to one scholar who refers to East Africa, 'that the construction and deconstruction of tribal identities were features of history . . . before there was any major direct European influence on the ordering of identity there' (Willis, 1992: 193–4). Amselle (1990), who has conceptualized the *logique métisse* of structural fluidity and the politics of identity formation in Africa's past, is mostly critical of Western cultural anthropology for its static perception of ethnic identity, especially in the colonial setting.

Nevertheless, as Amselle recognizes, identity formation in the colonial setting becomes subject to new pressures and limits. A key factor introduced in this period is the administrative imperative of grouping Africans according to 'tribal' categories based on a variety of criteria, which included geography, language, names, political relationships, etc. The tendency is to create new fixed identities and to freeze existing ones. Allen contends that 'both the Acholi and Madi ethnic labels were colonial creations' (p. 123). This is a reference to the names assigned by colonial authorities to an assortment of groups for purposes of administrative convenience. However, as time passed and circumstances changed, the label came to designate a level of social interaction which can also function as a group in conflict situations. Africans found it was convenient, if not advantageous, to belong to a recognized 'tribe' when dealing with the colonial state. The 'invention of tribes' in the colonial setting, therefore, is not simply an administrative expedient employed by alien rulers, but also a native response to a drastically altered socio-economic and political environment. For this reason, Allen cautions against the dismissal of ethnic/tribal labels, on the grounds that they do represent social reality, despite the genealogical and cultural lacunae in their make-up.

The gestation of this reality in the colonial setting is a notion argued persuasively by many scholars, including Young (1976) and Nnoli (1989). Most consider the colonial urban setting to be the cradle of contemporary ethnicity, a phenomenon commonly regarded as the political manifestation of group competition that began in the colonial state. There seems to be a consensus that the coalescence which gives rise to 'tribes' and 'ethnic identities' occurred as a response to novel pressures in a changed environment, in which basic units — clans, lineages, villages — could not cope. If ethnicity, then, is essentially a political phenomenon of recent provenance, ethnic conflict must be examined in the context of the contemporary state.

In *Warfare among East African Herders* (1979) there is little mention of the state. The fact that the state's presence was lightly felt in the pastoralist regions of the Horn — the contemporary 'tribal zone' — until then, and that the herders carried on with their bloody feuds without regard to its authority is the main reason why the state does not appear as an actor in that collection. The fact that the narrow focus of social anthropology did not encompass the role of the state was another. An opening in this respect was made in the *Southern Marches of Imperial Ethiopia* (James & Donham, 1986). In contrast, the state's visible presence is evident in all the essays of the present volume. The state does not simply affect warfare in the tribal zone by its presence, or merely intervene in conflicts between third parties. The state itself is both the arena and a major contestant, when it is not the very object of violent conflict.

What has happened to propel the state into the centre of conflict? To begin with, the tribal zone does not exist any more, in the sense it can be said to have existed even in the anthropologist's imagination. Concern for territorial integrity, political security, smuggling and banditry led the post-colonial state in the Horn of Africa to establish a presence in the periphery of its domain, if only through military means. Furthermore, drought and famine in recent years have destroyed the last vestiges of self-sufficiency of most groups, and made them dependants of aid organizations operating under state control. However, these developments account for the heightened presence of the state, not its manifold involvement in war with its subjects. In order to account for the latter, we need to consider the nature of the state in the Horn of Africa.

This is the theme of Markakis's contribution to this volume. He points first to the expansionist trend associated with the modern state in this region, which began with the colonial partition of the Horn and continued in the post-colonial period. The state incorporated regions that were never fully integrated even administratively into its structure. In this periphery, inhabited by a *mélange* of alien and alienated groups, the state was able to maintain only a military presence. With memories of past autonomy still fresh, and lacking meaningful ties to their present rulers, some indigenous people engage in conflict in an attempt to regain autonomy. As Kurimoto says in this volume of the Pari, one reason for their aggressive actions is 'their wish to remain autonomous without government' (p. 100).

Another feature of the state in this region is what Mazrui (1975) calls 'ethnocracy', meaning the monopolization of state power by certain ethnic groups, and the consequent exclusion of the rest. The ruling groups have a proprietary attitude towards the state, and what they promote as the 'national' identity is the mirror image of their own ethnic ego. Consequently, the process of 'national integration' promoted by the state verges on assimilation. The target groups of this process often react by invoking their own cultural attributes in opposition, as Baxter describes in the case of the Oromo. Cultural oppression, then, is another source of confrontation, and tends to make ethnicity the ideological catalyst of the conflict.

In most instances, exclusion from state power correlates with exclusion from access to material and social resources controlled by the state, a correlation most evident in the periphery. This tends to perpetuate and aggravate disparities which have ecological and historical antecedents. Given the dominant role of the state in the production and distribution of material and social resources, it is not possible to redress such disparity without access to its power. Therefore, the struggle for scarce resources is waged on the political level, and the state is the focal point of it. Markakis notes that the areas of the Horn most lacking in development are also the ones where conflict has flourished.

To sum up, the state is the point of reference for an analysis of the conflict at several levels. At one level, the conflict is a struggle for recognition and power between those who control the state and those that seek a share of state power, or, alternatively, autonomy and even independence. At another level, it is a struggle for scarce resources, in which the state appears both as a protagonist and as the prize. At yet another level, it is a resistance struggle against a state-directed process of deracination of subordinate groups. By definition, in the 'ethnocratic' state there is a correlation between the patterns of social, economic and ethnic stratification. In this context, where cultural ('ethnic') differences coincide with socio-economic and political divisions, ethnicity inevitably becomes the ideological essence of the conflict.

In the same context, the process of 'tribalization' accelerates, as illustrated by several contributions to this volume. Baxter's account of the Oromo is illuminating. Not a compact group, they comprise what Lamphear calls in a different context a 'cultural confederation'. Finding themselves in a situation that demands ethnic political solidarity, not found in Oromo tradition, Oromo intellectuals strive to 'create' a national identity by invoking shared cultural elements, such as language. Likewise, Allen notes the reinforcement of Acholi ethnic identity through the propagation of a conjectured historical tradition. The regionalist movements discussed by Kurita also seek to forge political solidarity among groups which can best be described as 'cultural confederations', by emphasizing shared culture as well as interests. In contrast, the Uduk described by James, a marginal group that strives desperately to keep a low profile, have an ethnically defined political identity imposed on them by circumstances entirely beyond their control, and by external agents, that is rival forces battling for control of the state, missionaries and relief agencies.

Enough has been said to make the point that the 'ethnic' label invests the parties to the conflict with a corporate essence, presumably deriving from genealogical and cultural factors, that simply does not exist. As indicated, ethnicity is the ideological form, not the substance, of the conflict, and like all ideologies it is not a cause but a symptom of social disorder. The reasons for its contemporary prominence must be sought in the situation that produced it. Like all ideologies, ethnicity aims to reduce complex phenomena into simple and related propositions in order to promote political mobilization. Those who respond to its appeal constitute the 'ethnic group' at a specific conjuncture. They are not, by any means, all those who would presumably qualify under the 'ethnic' criteria mentioned above. Nor are their motives uniform and their goals the same, as the ethnic ideology might imply.

The range of variation in motivation is wide. In the discussion at the Osaka symposium, the familiar divergence between the materialist and socio-cultural perspectives inevitably surfaced. The exposition of the former by Markakis highlights group competition for scarce resources and state intervention in this process. While rejecting this perspective, Turton marks the centrality of territory in the calculus of conflict, and Fukui refers to the demographic dimension of it. Indeed, the main variables of the materialist category — environment, demography, technology, political economy — appear in nearly all contributions as empirical factors linked to motivation.

Other factors, not as obvious, were identified. It was noted earlier that the conflict is fought at several levels simultaneously, ranging from lineage to state. Very often these levels overlap, and the question of motivation then becomes quite complex, as some of the studies in this volume illustrate. Kurimoto unravels an intricate pattern in the case of Pari adherence to the rebel cause led by the Sudan People's Liberation Movement (SPLM), and the contrasting attitude of their closest neighbours. Among the factors involved is the antagonism inherent in the Pari age system between the ruling age grade and the youth. Mohamed Salih discusses the Dinka perception of the SPLM, in which they are the dominant group, and the apparent contradiction between Dinka traditional ideology with its parochial focus, and the SPLM's radical and universalistic aspirations for a new Sudan. Kurita adds several twists to this theme in her treatment of regionalist movements in Sudan. She notes the manipulation of regionalist popular aspirations by the leadership of regional movements — earlier in order to consolidate its local bases of power, and more recently in order to integrate itself into the ruling class at the centre. She underlines the irony of the latter trend coming at a time when the central government, seeking local support in its battle for survival, is in effect restoring the tribal pattern fashioned during the colonial period.

The analytical virtues of this collection will interest the specialist. The insights it offers into the chemistry of the conflict will interest the expanding polyglot community of peacemakers, aid workers, and development experts who confront the consequences of the conflict in the Horn of Africa. For the layman whose attention has been drawn to the unending human drama in this region, it offers a collated picture of uncommon suffering and destruction composed of many images, often drawn by the people themselves. Extreme as it may seem, the odyssey of the Uduk people, recounted here in their own words, is the tragic fate of many millions in this region. Beyond gaining the reader's sympathy, it is hoped this volume will enhance his or her understanding of what is the real nature of 'ethnic conflict' in the Horn of Africa.

References

Amselle, J.L. (1990) *Logiques métisses: anthropologie d'identité en Afrique et ailleurs.* Paris: Payot.

Ferguson, B.R. & Whitehead, N.L. (1992) *War in the Tribal Zone.* Santa Fe, New Mexico: School of American Research Press.

Fukui, K. & Turton, D. (eds) (1979) *Warfare among East African Herders.* Osaka: National Museum of Ethnology.

Geertz, C. (1967) The integrative revolution. In C. Geertz (ed.), *Old Societies and New States.* Chicago, Illinois: University of Chicago.

Horowitz, D.L. (1985) *Ethnic Groups in Conflict.* Berkeley: University of California Press.

James, W. & Donham, D. (1986) *The Southern Marches of Imperial Ethiopia.* Cambridge: Cambridge University Press.

Mazrui, A. (1975) *Soldiers and Kinsmen in Uganda: the Making of a Military Ethnocracy.* Beverly Hills, California: Sage Publications.

Nnoli, O. (1989) *Ethnic Politics in Africa.* Dakar: Codesria.

Schlee, G. (1985) Interethnic clan identities among Cushitic-speaking pastoralists. *Africa,* **55** (1).

—— (1989) *Identities on the Move: Clanship and Pastoralism in Northern Kenya.* Manchester: Manchester University Press.

Shils, E. (1957) Primordial, personal, sacred and civil ties. *British Journal of Sociology,* **8**.

Tonkin, E., Macdonald, M. & Chapman, M. (1989) Introduction. In E. Tonkin *et al.* (eds), *History and Ethnicity.* London: Routlege.

Van den Berghe, P. (1981) *The Ethnic Phenomenon.* New York: Praeger.

Willis, J. (1992) 'The making of a tribe: Bondei identities and histories. *Journal of African History,* **33** (2).

Young, C. (1976) *The Politics of Cultural Pluralism.* University of Wisconsin.

CONFLICT
ON THE MARGIN

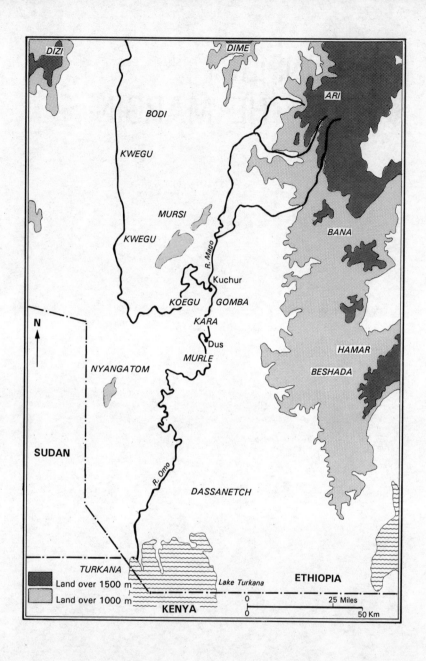

Map 2   Ethnic groups in the lower Omo valley, Ethiopia

14

1 Mursi Political Identity & Warfare: The Survival of an Idea

DAVID TURTON

Since 1970, the Mursi, who live in the lower Omo valley of south-western Ethiopia, have suffered a series of calamities comparable, in terms of human suffering and general social disruption, to those which affected large areas of north-east Africa at the end of the nineteenth century and the beginning of the twentieth. Then it was rinderpest, smallpox, drought, famine and the expansion of the Ethiopian state which threatened their survival. Over the past 20 years it has been drought and famine, growing demographic pressure on subsistence resources, and the spread of automatic weapons into the Omo valley from Uganda and Sudan (Turton, 1977, 1988, 1989).

These last developments represent the most recent and, in Mursi eyes, most severe threat to their continued existence as an autonomous political entity. One incident in particular brought them face to face with the imminent prospect of a world without Mursi. In February 1987, their south-western neighbours, the Nyangatom (also called Bume in Ethiopia and Dogiro in Kenya), who had recently obtained Kalashnikov automatic rifles from Sudan, launched a massive attack on the southern Mursi, killing several hundred people (possibly 500), mainly women and children, in one day. Immediately afterwards, the Mursi evacuated the entire southern part of their territory. When I visited them in December 1987, they were confidently expecting a second Nyangatom attack within the next three months. Unless they could arm themselves with automatics, they said, they would be driven from their land entirely and have to find refuge where they could in the highlands, on either side of the Omo valley. Although they would survive there as individuals in scattered enclaves, and

15

although their clan names would persist, the 'Mursi' would have disappeared.

I took this to mean that those who survived this dispersal would no longer identify themselves as Mursi, although they would, apparently, continue to identify themselves as members of named clans. Mursi identity, it seemed, was problematic in relation to clan identity. It was not given in nature but had to be humanly created and deliberately maintained. My aim here is to clarify the notion of Mursi identity, and to explore the role of warfare in creating and maintaining it. I begin by explaining why I prefer to call it political rather than ethnic.

Political versus ethnic identity

Political identity and ethnic identity are terms often used interchangeably because both refer to the identity an individual can find through membership of a collectivity. (I use the term collectivity to include both groups and categories.) When they are used to designate the collectivities themselves, however, ethnic and political carry different implications. The key difference is that the first implies a mode of recruitment while the second implies a mode of organization.

In his account of the 'ethnic origins' of European nations, Anthony Smith identifies six 'key elements of that complex of meanings which underlie the sense of ethnic ties and sentiments for the participants' (1986: 24). One of these, which he calls 'the *sine qua non* of ethnicity', is 'myths of origins and descent'. Another is 'association with a specific territory', a form of words chosen to take account of cases where the 'ethnic' (group) has been dispersed from its homeland.

Ethnie do not cease to be *ethnie* when they are dispersed and have lost their homeland; for ethnicity is a matter of myths, memories, values and symbols and not of material possessions or political power, both of which require a habitat for their realization . . . [P]oetic and symbolic qualities possess greater potency than everyday attributes; a land of dreams is far more significant than any actual terrain. (p. 28)

The usefulness of the ethnic label, both in political rhetoric and popular discourse, is based on the assumption it embodies that mere consciousness of shared origins is enough to constitute a group. This in turn enables it to be applied to groups which are, in reality, very different from each other, both organizationally and in terms of the behaviour of their members; or which may not be groups at all in any meaningful sense of the word, but rather categories (Cohen, 1969: 4).

The disadvantages from the point of view of sociological analysis are comparable to those which Scheffler identified long ago in his critique of descent theory. (1966). The mere presence of a descent construct (recognition of a tie to a common ancestor) in the minds of members of a group does not, Scheffler points out, tell us much about the nature of that group. We have to go on to specify how the construct is related to group activities. One of the ways in which it may be so related is as a principle of recruitment, but we should begin, logically and empirically, with the group as an operational entity. A 'descent group', in other words, is not a group because of 'descent' — a mental construct — but because its members do certain things together.

My favourite illustration of the kind of difficulties into which descent theorists were led by their failure to appreciate this simple point is the following passage from Goody's account of the LoWiili of north-western Ghana, in which he wrestles with the 'limiting case' of the 'matrilineage' (1967):

This group is known by a technical term but has no specific name. It conforms to none of the usual criteria of a corporate group. It is non-localized. It is not a property-holding group. Its members never meet together, nor do representatives of segments, and it is therefore not an assembling group ... Though limited in its functions and vague in its conceptualization, it nevertheless constitutes a social group in the accepted sociological sense ... The existence of a technical term itself indicates a consciousness of unity. (p. 85)

In other words, it is a group simply because there exists a technical term for a genealogical connection through women.

The same kind of clarification which Scheffler introduced into the discussion of descent and descent groups seems to me to be called for in the discussion of ethnicity and ethnic groups. The point is not to deny the reality and importance of the 'ethnic construct', but to question the usefulness of treating it as the logical prerequisite and sufficient condition for the existence of a group. An ethnic group, in other words, is not a group because of ethnicity but because its members engage in common action and share common interests. Having identified the group on the basis of these 'operational' criteria, it is then a matter for empirical investigation to determine how the 'ethnic construct' is related to it — as principle of recruitment, for example, or simply as symbolic expression of unity and solidarity.

I have made the focus of this paper the political, rather than ethnic identity of the Mursi, because I am concerned with the organization of collective action, within a territorial framework, and because I wish to stress that it is this, rather than a tradition

17

of common origin, which makes them a group in the first place. It would be pointless to ask whether the Mursi do or do not constitute an ethnic group, but it is instructive to consider how the two criteria of ethnicity quoted above from Smith — 'myth of origins and descent' and 'association with a specific territory' — might apply to them. For this it is useful to return to their own prediction that, were they to be dispersed from their present territory, the Mursi would disappear but their clan identities would persist.

There are around a dozen clans (*kabicho*, sing. *kabi*) which are named exogamous categories of the population, based on putative descent from a common ancestor. The Mursi 'myth of origins' is an account of how five of these clans (Komorte, Bumai, Juhai, Kagisi and Garakuli) originated at a place called Thaleb, somewhere to the south-east, and how they migrated in an anticlockwise direction into their present territory, 'finding' and forming affinal alliances with other clans *en route*. These 'original' clans therefore are seen as the historical core of the population, but they are not exclusive to the Mursi; the same clan names are found amongst the Chai and Tirma (collectively known as Surma) to the west of the Omo (Abbink, 1991: 8–9).

The decisive event in creating a specifically Mursi identity was the movement of members of these clans from the west to the east bank of the Omo, sometime during the first half of the nineteenth century. That this event was decisive is attested by oral history and borne out by linguistic evidence. The Mursi and Surma speak mutually intelligible languages, but that of the Mursi differs phonetically from the others in ways consistent with it having been the last to diverge from the common stock. That the migration occurred less than 200 years ago is clear from genealogical information — specifically, answers to the question, 'Which of your ancestors was the first to be born on the east bank of the Omo?'

Mursi informants openly admit, with no hint of moral discomfort, that they took their present territory from its previous inhabitants, the Bodi, who retreated north of the River Mara (see Map 2). But the area evacuated by the Bodi was much larger than that which the invaders initially occupied around Kurum, in the south-western corner of present Mursi territory. It was not until the 1930s that Mursi began to cultivate along the River Mara, making it their *de facto* northern boundary, and it was not until 1975, after two more wars with the Bodi, that the Mara became the *de jure* boundary between the two groups (Turton, 1988). This progressive spreading out from Kurum, which is now regarded as the historical centre or 'stomach' of Mursiland, seems to date from the 1890s, a decade which saw the arrival in the lower Omo valley of not only of the first European explorers, but also the occupying forces of Emperor Menelik's expanding state of Abyssinia, and a disastrous rinderpest epidemic, which had already devastated large areas of the Ethiopian highlands and Sudan (Pankhurst & Johnson, 1988).

An account of Mursi origins, therefore, can take two forms. On the one hand, it can focus on the journey of five 'original' clans from a place of origin called Thaleb, which cannot be identified by either the Mursi or anyone else with any actual place, but which is, in Smith's phrase, a 'land of dreams'. On the other hand, it can focus on the relatively recent and continued occupation of an 'actual terrain', Kurum, and the subsequent and relatively easily documented 'colonization' of the area between Kurum and the River Mara.

Indulging for a moment in speculation, one can imagine Kurum, the present historical and symbolic 'centre' of Mursiland, as a future 'land of dreams'. Imagine a dispersal of the present Mursi population; clan identities survive and new territorially based units, equivalent to the now dissolved Mursi, are created around core populations drawn from those clans. Perhaps Kurum will then become for those units what Thaleb is for the present Mursi. But it will not remain the territorial base of a specifically Mursi identity. Perhaps this imagined scenario can be seen as a repeat performance of the historical events which lay behind the 'myth of origins' just outlined. For this we need only to see the predicted disaster of flight before an enemy armed with automatic weapons as equivalent to some earlier disaster which may have dispersed a population (not a Mursi population) from a place now remembered as Thaleb.

The point I wish to emphasize is that Mursi identity is linked essentially to the occupation of an 'actual terrain' and not to the supposed origin of certain Mursi clans in a 'land of dreams'. The following are evidence of this: (i) it is not only Mursi clans who claim this origin; (ii) members of clans who do not claim this origin are nevertheless fully Mursi; (iii) dispersal from their present territory is, in the eyes of the people themselves, tantamount to the disappearance of the Mursi; and (iv) the belief that their clan identities would survive such dispersal. This is why I prefer to think of Mursi identity as political rather than ethnic and of 'the Mursi' simply as a territorially based political unit. The label 'ethnic' would seem to be more appropriately applied to clan identities, which are not territorially based and which do not involve collective action, save in ritual contexts.

19

In his work on interethnic clan identities in northern Kenya, Gunther Schlee (1985; 1989) has drawn attention to the fact that clan identities cut across ethnic — I would prefer to call them 'political' — divisions and are often much older than those divisions.

> Clans, and more so subclans, are thought of as natural in the sense that their members have specific innate physical, ritual and mental qualities . . . they are also believed by some people to be universal . . . quite a number of clan identities which are socially relevant today must be older than 400 years, and older than some present day ethnic [political] divisions. It is these clan identities which have remained stable . . . and that provide us with a valuable key to the history of this area. (1985)

Whatever the implications of this for the historian, Schlee ends his article with some observations which are highly pertinent to the anthropologist interested in the 'social construction' of group boundaries.

> Normally we define a geographical or social unit at the beginning of our study: we study such-and-such an institution among the So-and-so, and we define the So-and-so even before we go out into the field. Ethnic categories may thus become straitjackets for our thought . . . More important, ethnic categories are used as a privileged grid of classification which blinds us to the other categories by which people identify themselves or others. Might it not be better to start with a radical application of the concept 'network' than from established social units? (p. 33)

Substituting my terminology for Schlee's, what we are faced with here is the suggestion not only that clan identities are, as a matter of empirical fact, older than many of the political divisions they cut across, but that they are seen as 'given' or 'natural' by the people themselves. In other words, relationships based on clan identities are seen as the 'stuff' of social life, out of which relatively impermanent and fragile political divisions are constructed.

If groups such as the Mursi are treated, to all intents and purposes, as 'given in nature', then the conflict which is seen to define their boundaries is also given in nature: it is simply the way in which independent political groups must relate to each other in the absence of an overarching political structure. But, if a network of relations based on clanship and other identities is treated as primary, conflict begins to look like one of the means by which independent and mutually opposed political units are temporarily 'carved out' from this 'underlying' sociality in the first place. In the next section I apply this line of reasoning to the Mursi case. In doing so I am indebted not only to Schlee's work on clan identities in northern Kenya, but also to Simon

Harrison's (1989) interpretation of warfare at Avatip, on the
Sepik River in Papua New Guinea.

Political identity and warfare

What seems to have happened in the anthropological study of war
is that armed conflict between tribal groups has been artificially
isolated from encompassing state structures and yet analysed on
the basis of an explanatory model, the purpose of which is to
legitimize the state form of political organization. The main
assumption of this model, formulated most famously by Thomas
Hobbes, is that a propensity for conflict, and violent conflict in
particular, is a fact of human nature which it is the purpose of
the state to keep in check. The fundamental problem of political
organization at the state level is the suppression of violence — or,
better, defining it as illegitimate.

This Hobbesian view of aggression and warfare was modified
but not reversed by the Durkheimian tradition in social anthropology. For Durkheim, the group is also the source of peace and
order through the moral authority it exerts over the individual.
This, of course, was an explanation of social order specifically
designed for societies defined as a residual class — namely,
those lacking the centralized authority structures characteristic of
states. The central problem of structural-functional anthropology
became that of social control. Although cultural variation in
the incidence and form of warfare required explanation, the
institution of war itself did not. It was simply the inevitable consequence of a lack of overarching mechanisms of social control —
in other words, of the state. Thus has anthropology bolstered the
Hobbesian project: the legitimization of the state form of political
organization.

One can go further in identifying a Hobbesian bias in the
way anthropologists have represented 'tribal' warfare. Perhaps
the most widespread approach to be found in the literature is
the materialist one. This has been described by Brian Ferguson
(1984: 23) as focusing on 'war's relation to the practical problems of maintaining life and living standards'. More recently,
Ferguson has identified three 'mutually reinforcing premises' of
the materialist approach: that 'causal primacy' is given to the
'infrastructure'; that 'there may be competition between and
selection among groups'; and that 'wars occur when those who
make the decision to fight estimate that it is in their material
interest to do so' (1990: 28–30). These propositions seem to boil

down to the single assumption that warfare is the result, in one way or another, of competition between groups for scarce resources. This in turn is based on two other, unspoken, assumptions: that competition is a fact of nature which does not, therefore, need to be accounted for, and that groups exist independently of the relations between them. The materialist explanation of warfare, in other words, only works if the same assumptions are made about groups as Hobbes made about individuals.

These assumptions are so evidently linked to a specifically Western understanding of what it means to be human and of the relationship between the individual and society (Howell & Willis, 1989: 10–12) that they must be highly suspect as the 'premises' of any attempt to define, let alone explain, war as a universal human phenomenon. But there are also empirical grounds for doubting the usefulness of treating groups such as the Mursi and their neighbours as Hobbesian individuals writ large. For not only are they, both to themselves and to the outside observer, the products of relatively recent population movements, but they also form today a regional system of economically interdependent contiguous local groups (Turton, 1991).

The suggestion that groups are defined by the relations between them is hardly new in anthropology. Over 20 years ago, Frederich Barth pointed out that, in contrast to 'the simplistic view that geographical and social isolation have been the critical factors in sustaining cultural diversity', ethnic boundaries 'do not depend on an absence of social interaction and acceptance, but are often the very foundations on which embracing social systems are based' (1969: 9–10). The idea that exchange serves to create groups rather than to link pre-existing ones has also proved applicable in both the New Guinea and the African contexts. Roy Wagner (1967) argued that the patrilineal clans of the Daribi were the product of the gift transactions of their members. Wendy James (1978) has explained the 'sudden' appearance of matriliny among the Uduk of the Sudan–Ethiopia borderland as the result of the 'suspension' of marriage transactions upon which the existence of patrilineal groups depends. And I have argued that 'it would be circular to interpret the payment of bridewealth [among the Mursi] as compensating a group of agnates for the loss of a sister or daughter' when it is the payment of bridewealth which makes them a group 'in the first place' (Turton, 1980: 73).

Harrison, in his account of warfare at Avatip, on the Sepik River in Papua New Guinea, has extended this line of reasoning to include both exchange and warfare. His argument is that warfare and peaceful exchange are simply two different, but not opposed or mutually incompatible, ways of creating boundaries between groups, of creating groups 'in the first place'. It has often been argued that exchange is functionally equivalent to warfare in Melanesia, in the sense that it acts as a surrogate for the latter. What Harrison emphasizes, for Avatip, is that both exchange and warfare are forms of ritual, and therefore social, action which serve to define and create groups, and that 'peaceful' exchange is not seen as opposed to, controlling, or substituting for the 'asocial' activity of warfare:

> warfare was not a kind of by-product or residuum of their political independence, as though they could take that independence for granted from the start, but the means used purposefully by men to construct a political identity for their community in the first place, not just as a physical population secure from extermination but, more basically, as a conceptual entity free from the normative claims of outsiders. (1989: 595)

The Mursi have, in their own eyes, faced the possibility of extermination in the last few years, specifically since the massacre of around one-tenth of the population by the Nyangatom in February 1987 (Turton, 1989). But there is another and more 'basic' sense in which they are threatened; through a loss of confidence in the centrality and power of their indigenous institutions. Such a loss of confidence could happen simply through increasing contact with the Ethiopian state, an alien political structure over which they have no control, and in relation to which they have no means of making themselves 'count' as an autonomous unit. This alien structure is the source of keenly felt needs and alternative values which the indigenous institutions cannot define, let alone satisfy.

What is at stake, then, when talking about the disappearance of the Mursi, is not simply their capacity to provide for their own physical survival within a defined territory, but also, and more fundamentally, the capacity of their institutions to go on defining the values and satisfying the needs which give meaning and purpose to social existence. This line of reasoning implies that social institutions are not ends in themselves but the means by which, together, people define their values and realize them in concerted, collective action. It also implies that political identity is a product rather than a cause of social action. Following Harrison (1989) I suggest that, for the Mursi and their neighbours, warfare is not a means by which an already constituted political group seeks to defend or extend its territory, but a means by which the very idea of it as an independent political unit, free from the normative claims of outsiders, is created and kept alive.

This hypothesis accounts well enough for the part played by

23

warfare and its ritual resolution in defining the changing territorial relationship between the Mursi and their northern neighbours, the Bodi, over the past 100 years (see Fukui in this volume).
It is clear that, as distinct political units, these peoples are as
much products of their periodically hostile relations with each
other, as they are of their relations with the physical environment (Turton, 1979, 1988). The same hypothesis accounts for the
way in which the Mursi responded to the Nyangatom attack of
February 1987.

The Nyangatom, one of the 'Karamojong cluster' of peoples
who speak the same language as the Turkana, are concentrated
in the Nakua area along the Kibish River, which here forms
the boundary between Ethiopia and Sudan. Tornay (1981)
calls this the 'pastoral region' and its inhabitants the 'pastoral
Nyangatom', to distinguish them from those who live permanently at the Omo River and depend almost entirely on cultivation. During the 1970s, the Nyangatom were at war with most
of their neighbours and lost nearly 10 per cent (400–500 people)
of their population as a result, mainly at the hands of the
Dassanetch (Tornay, 1979). Relations between the Nyangatom
and the Mursi were also hostile during this period, but the conflict
between them remained at the level of retaliatory killings; a few
on either side died (Tornay, 1979: 105). At other times, there
appears to be what might be called a watchful peace between
Nyangatom and Mursi, with some economic exchange between
individuals; for example, Mursi pots for Nyangatom grain, or
Mursi grain for Nyangatom goats. These contacts are regular and
close enough for Mursi living from Kurum southwards to understand, and occasionally speak, some Nyangatom.

Since 1984, the Nyangatom have become increasingly well
armed with automatic rifles and are now conscious of being 'king
of the tribes' in the lower Omo area (Tornay, 1992). One of
the major events in the Nyangatom rise to dominance was the
February 1987 attack on the Mursi. This was sparked by a particularly provocative Mursi killing, a few weeks earlier, of six
Nyangatom who were staying as guests in a Mursi settlement at
Gowa, on the Omo north of Kurum (Alvarsson, 1989: 54). After
this incident the Nyangatom planned a large-scale attack, using
automatic weapons.

According to one account I was given, the Mursi living south of
Gowa were warned that a retaliatory raid was being planned, but
were told that it would not be directed at them. They were
advised — treacherously according to my informant — to evacuate their settlements and congregate further west, towards the

Omo–Mago junction until after the anticipated attack. On 21 February, a Nyangatom war party crossed the Omo at the Kara village of Dus, moved northwards up the east bank of the Omo, turned westwards to cross the Mago and attacked these Mursi — mainly women and children — who had sought safety by gathering together in the bush (Alvarsson, 1989: 56). Only the roughest estimate can be given of the number who died. The Mursi told me I could get some idea by imagining a crowded marketplace in the district capital, Jinka, but it must have been several hundred.

This event upset the normal 'tit for tat' of Mursi–Nyangatom warfare, not only because of the large number of Mursi casualties and because most of them were women and children, but also because it proclaimed a drastic technological imbalance between the two groups, which, four years later, at the time of my last visit (January 1991), showed no sign of being eliminated. The Nyangatom had gone from strength to strength, being able to obtain Kalashnikovs for as little as four to seven head of cattle. Their main source of supply appeared to be the Toposa, fellow members of the Karamojong cluster living in Sudan, who had in turn been supplied by the Sudan government as part of its policy of arming local 'militias' to fight the Sudan People's Liberation Army (Tornay, 1992). The Mursi had no access to automatic weapons, and had so far not been able to acquire them in significant numbers through their established links with arms dealers in the Ethiopian highlands, to the east of the Omo valley.

Immediately after the massacre, the Mursi abandoned the southern part of their territory. When I visited them, 10 months later (December 1987), they were expecting another onslaught from the Nyangatom which, they predicted, would force them to abandon the rest of their territory. There was no doubt that the Mursi wanted an end to a situation of great insecurity, which was having serious adverse consequences for economic production. Most serious of all was the fact that they had abandoned their flood-retreat cultivation sites along the banks of the Omo from Kurum southwards. (These were not reoccupied until the 1989–90 dry season.) But the only way the Mursi could see of ending this insecurity was through a counter-attack, comparable to the one the Nyangatom had launched against them. This meant that it would have to be a *kaman*, a daylight attack involving a large number of men, rather than a *luhai*, a night-time or early morning raid by one or two (Turton, 1991: 167–8). Most important of all, the Mursi war party would have to be armed with at least some automatic weapons.

25

From what I was told, it was not the physical impact these weapons would have on the Nyangatom that mattered, but what possession of them by the Mursi would symbolize. The Mursi I spoke to in December 1987 seemed ready to mount a 'return match' — they used the analogy of 'home' and 'away' duelling contests between Mursi territorial sections — even if they had as few as 10 automatic rifles. When I objected that this would mean, in the long run, many more Mursi than Nyangatom deaths, I was told that this did not matter; the surviving Mursi would still be able to make a secure peace. It was not a simple matter, then, of the Mursi taking physical revenge on the Nyangatom, by inflicting an equivalent blow to the February massacre. What was at issue, it seemed, was a symbolic, not an actual, equivalence, whether of war casualties or weapons. This suggests that the activity of warfare itself, and not just the joint rituals with which it concluded, can be seen as a common ritual language, a system of shared meanings by which groups make themselves significant to each other and to themselves, as independent political entities.

Rather than speaking, as I did above, of the Mursi making peace with the Nyangatom, it would be more accurate to speak of them re-establishing the relationship they enjoyed before the 1987 massacre, which was certainly not one of peace. What the massacre had destroyed was not peace, but a relationship of mutual respect between two politically autonomous and independent groups. For the Mursi, the intensification of the conflict with the Nyangatom would represent the restoration of the previous political order, not its breakdown. As at Avatip:

Their imagined antithesis of political order is not an imagined state of total violence, a collapse of all social restraint in a war of all against all. Rather, escalation is a positive constitutive process, in which each stage calls for a greater intensity of action . . . and is always seen, therefore, as under the actors' control. (Harrison, 1989: 592).

What, in their own eyes, threatened the survival of the Mursi as a political group was not that so many people had been killed in the Nyangatom attack of February 1987, or that many more were likely to be killed in future attacks but that, having no access to automatic weapons, they had lost control, at least temporarily, of the 'constitutive process' of escalation.

The expected second Nyangatom attack did not materialize and, under pressure of hunger, the Mursi, who had evacuated the left bank of the Omo south of Gowa after the massacre, returned to cultivate there in the 1989–90 dry season. Still without automatic weapons and still feeling highly insecure, they only stayed long enough to take in the valuable flood harvest, a pattern that was repeated the following year. Was the situation, then, slowly returning to normal? Or, rather, were the Mursi slowly and fatalistically accepting the inevitable and adapting themselves to a new political relationship with the Nyangatom, one of subordination?

An event which occurred at Kurum in January 1991 suggested otherwise. This was the long overdue creation, by means of a three-day ritual, called *nitha*, of a new male age set. The set, which was given the name Geleba, was the first to have been created since 1961. By becoming a member of an age set a man moves from the grade of *teru* to that of *rori* and, simultaneously, from that of *lusi* (boy) to that of *hiri* (adult). Depending on the length of time since the last *nitha*, some of the new *rora* may be in their 40s, with wives and children of their own and therefore already treated, in domestic as well as public life, as *de facto* adults. The age span of the Geleba set was 15–45 years. Each of the three main territorial sections into which the Mursi are divided — Ariholi, Gongulobibi, Dola — holds its own *nitha*, in that order, Ariholi taking the lead because its territorial base is Kurum, the 'stomach' of the country. It was the Ariholi *nitha*, then, which took place at Kurum in January 1991; the other two sections held theirs about six months later. Because I had been monitoring the preparations for the *nitha*, which was delayed for several years, I was sufficiently confident of the timing of the Ariholi ritual to take a film crew from Granada Television in Manchester to Kurum to film it (Woodhead, 1991a, b).

The main events of the *nitha* took place in and around a specially constructed enclosure of branches with a tree at its centre and two openings, one opposite the other. The enclosure was built around a young tree, about six feet tall. The reason for the choice of this highly unimpressive tree was that it had a long life ahead of it. It would grow and flourish as, it was hoped, would the members of the new age set, who were thus identified not only with the tree but also with the place where it was rooted. The place where an important ritual is held is identified with the group, as the group is with the place. For example, rituals which mark the end of periods of hostility between the Mursi and their northern neighbours, the Bodi, act as boundary markers in the gradual encroachment by Mursi on Bodi territory, converting *de facto* Mursi occupation into *de jure* ownership (Turton, 1979).

By holding the *nitha* at Kurum, under the eyes of the Nyangatom as they sported their Kalashnikovs on the opposite bank of the Omo, the Ariholi Mursi were, among other things, making a symbolic defence of this 'actual terrain', which they still

27

considered unsafe for permanent reoccupation, but on the continued occupation of which their Mursi identity depended. In the future, if the Mursi claims to *de jure* ownership of Kurum were contested, they could point to the fact that the Geleba age set had been created there — and to the tree where the main events of the *nitha* had taken place.

There the story would have ended, had I not received information while revising this article for publication which suggests an even closer and more direct link between the *nitha*, the 1987 massacre and the preservation of Mursi identity. The information came from Jean Lydall who, with her husband Ivo Strecker, had recently returned from a visit to the Hamar, neighbours of the Mursi, whom they have known for over 20 years. They had been told that in March 1992 the Mursi had launched a large-scale attack on the Nyangatom, the delayed response to the 1987 massacre. The Nyangatom suffered heavy casualties, and some of the survivors were now living as refugees amongst the Kara and Hamar. The Mursi were now seen as a threat also by the Hamar who, in May, were removing their cattle from the Omo, south of the Mago junction, for fear of Mursi raids. The information is scanty but the source is reliable. It seems worthwhile, therefore, to attempt an interpretation of it, even though this will need to be checked and possibly modified in the light of further fieldwork. The main question which arises is how to explain this apparent reversal in the military fortunes of the Mursi.

The main question which arises is how to explain this sudden reversal in the military fortunes of the Mursi. At the time of my last visit in January 1991, they still considered themselves to be in serious danger from the Nyangatom, due to the lack of automatic weapons. They had not been able to acquire any from the government despite frequent appeals, their access to supplies coming from the west was still blocked by the Nyangatom, and the highland traders who were their traditional source of firearms were unwilling or unable to supply them with automatics.

Exactly a year later, Serge Tornay found the Nyangatom in what seemed an impregnable position and clearly unconcerned about the possibility of attack from the Mursi or any other group.

During the 1991–92 dry season the Nyangatom were at peace with their neighbours. In December and January they were harvesting bumper crops of sorghum, both from river banks and irrigated fields. The political atmosphere was nothing less than euphoric . . . It was said that no taxes would be levied (by the new government of the Ethiopian Peoples Revolutionary Democratic Front [EPRDF]) and that political and economic autonomy would not be questioned any more. Being heavily armed, . . . safe from starvation and with a rapidly growing population, they had many reasons to feel confident in their future. (1992, p. 17)

Tornay wisely adds that this optimism may have been exaggerated, since misfortunes would surely return in due course. But presumably neither he nor the Nyangatom would have predicted a major Mursi attack coming just two months later.

It is easy enough to explain why the Mursi attack came in March. The flood retreat crop from the Omo cultivation areas would have been harvested and safely stored, and the population which had occupied the Omo banks during the dry season (mainly women, girls and children) would have returned to the relative safety of the eastern grazing areas. The Omo would still be easily fordable in several places and, if the local rains had already started, the overcast skies and cool conditions would have made it easier for the war party to survive with only the water they were able to carry. But why this March? Two events of the previous year, one national and one local, probably account for this.

The national event was the fall of the government of Mengistu Haile Mariam in May 1991, when the rebel forces of the EPRDF entered Addis Ababa. This was followed by the disbanding of the former government's army and police force, which must have caused a flood of automatic weapons to come on to the market, and the virtual disintegration of the administrative and judicial system in the south of the country. In these circumstances it became possible for the Mursi to obtain Kalashnikovs in significant numbers through their established links with highland arms dealers.

The local event was the forming of the Geleba age set. The reported attack would certainly have been the responsibility of members of the new set, a large proportion of whom may have taken part in it. The members of a new age set seek to make a historical name for it by performing some daring, arduous or otherwise memorable feat, and circumstances had conspired to give members of the Geleba set just such an opportunity at the outset of its existence. In fact, the reported attack came at the earliest feasible moment in the life of the new set, which was not fully formed until the Dola section, the most populous, held its *nitha* in July or August 1991.

The possession of some automatic weapons was clearly an important factor in the decision of the Mursi to launch this attack, almost five years after the Nyangatom attack of February 1987. In view of what they told me in December 1987, however, it is

29

hardly likely that they would have felt it necessary to be as well armed as the Nyangatom, and they surely were not. If the connection suggested in this article between political identity, warfare and ritual activity has any merit, what does seem to have been crucial is the ritual transformation of the men who were called upon to carry out the attack. That is, until they were formed into an age set, they were not able to make this reply, in the sense that their action would not have communicated the appropriate and intended message both to themselves and to the Nyangatom.

References

Abbink, J. (1991) The deconstruction of 'tribe': ethnicity and politics in southwestern Ethiopia. *Journal of Ethiopian Studies*, **24** (November).

Alvarsson, J. (1989) *Starvation and Peace or Food and War? Aspects of Armed Conflict in the Lower Omo Valley*. Uppsala: Research Reports in Cultural Anthropology, University of Uppsala.

Barth, F. (1969) Introduction. In F. Barth (ed.), *Ethnic Groups and Boundaries: the Social Organisation of Culture Difference*. London: George Allen & Unwin.

Cohen, A. (1969) *Custom and Politics in Urban Africa: a Study of Hausa Migrants in Yoruba Towns*. Berkeley: University of California Press.

Ferguson, R.B. (1984) Introduction: studying war. In R.B. Ferguson, (ed.), *Warfare, Culture and Environment*. Orlando, Florida: Academic Press.

—— (1990) Explaining war. In J. Haas (ed.), *The Anthropology of War*. Cambridge: Cambridge University Press.

Goody, J. (1967) *The Social Organisation of the LoWiili*. Oxford University Press.

Harrison, S. (1989) The symbolic construction of aggression and war in a Sepik River society. *Man* (NS) **24**.

Howell, S. & Willis, R. (1989) *Societies at Peace: Anthropological Perspectives*. London: Routledge.

James, W. (1978) Matrifocus on African women. In S. Ardener (ed.), *Defining Females: The nature of Women in Society*. London: Croom Helm.

Pankhurst, R. & Johnson, D.H. (1988) The great drought and famine of 1888–92 in northeast Africa. In D.H. Johnson & D.M. Anderson (eds), *The Ecology of Survival: Case Studies from Northeast African History*. London: Lester Crook.

Scheffler, H. (1966) Ancestor worship in anthropology: or, observations on descent and descent groups. *Current Anthropology* **7** (5).

Schlee, G. (1985) Interethnic clan identities among Cushitic-speaking pastoralists of northern Kenya. *Africa*, **55**.

—— (1989) *Identities on the Move*. Manchester: Manchester University Press.

Smith, A.D. (1986) *The Ethnic Origins of Nations*. Oxford: Basil Blackwell.

Tornay, S. (1979) Armed conflict in the lower Omo valley, 1970–76: an analysis from within Nyangatom society. In K. Fukui & D. Turton (eds), *Warfare among East African Herders*. Osaka: Senri Ethnological Studies, No. 3, National Museum of Ethnology.

—— (1981) The Nyangatom: an outline of their ecology and social organisation.

In M.L. Bender (ed.), *Peoples and Cultures of the Ethio-Sudan Borderlands*. East Lansing, Michigan: Michigan State University.

—— (1992) More chances on the fringe of states? The growing power of the Nyangatom, a border people of the lower Omo valley, Ethiopia (1970-1992). Paper presented at the workshop on 'Human and Ecological Consequences of Military Conflicts in Africa.' Bergen: Centre for Development Studies.

Turton, D. (1977) Response to drought: the Mursi of south west Ethiopia. In J.P. Garlick & R.W.J. Keay (eds), *Human Ecology in the Tropics*. London: Taylor and Francis.

—— (1979) A journey made them: territorial segmentation and ethnic identity among the Mursi. In L. Holy (ed.), *Segmentary Lineage Systems Reconsidered*. Belfast: Papers in Social Anthropology, Vol. 4, Queen's University.

—— (1980) The economics of Mursi bridewealth: a comparative perspective. In J.L. Comaroff (ed.), *The Meaning of Marriage Payments*. London: Academic Press.

—— (1988) Looking for a cool place: the Mursi, 1890s–1980s. In D.H. Johnson & D.M. Anderson (eds), *The Ecology of Survival: Case Studies from Northeast African History*. London: Lester Cook.

—— (1989) Warfare, vulnerability and survival: a case from southwestern Ethiopia. *Cambridge Anthropology*, **13** (2).

—— (1991) Movement, warfare and ethnicity in the lower Omo valley. In J. Galaty & P. Bonte (eds), *Herders, Warriors and Traders: Pastoralism in Africa*. Boulder, Colorado: Westview Press.

Wagner, R. (1967) *The Curse of Souw: Principles of Daribi Clan Definition and Alliance in New Guinea*. Chicago, Illinois: Chicago University Press.

Woodhead, L. (1991a) *The Land is Bad*. Disappearing World series, Granada TV, Manchester (film, 52 minutes, colour).

—— (1991b) *Nitha*. Disappearing World series, Granada TV, Manchester (film, 52 minutes, colour).

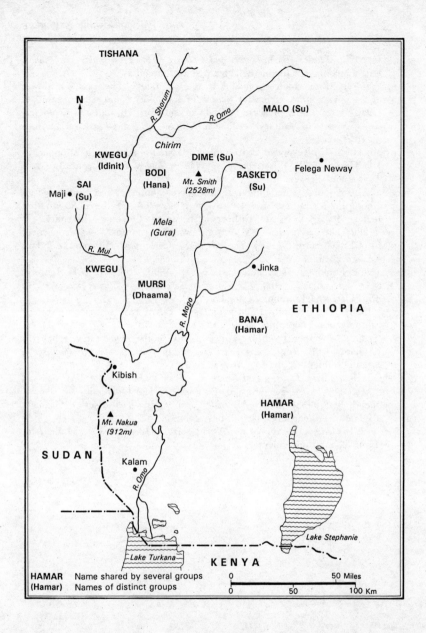

Map 3   Distribution of the Bodi

32

2 Conflict & Ethnic Interaction: The Mela & their Neighbours

KATSUYOSHI FUKUI

There have been a lot of arguments concerning the definition of the ethnic group. Most of the relevant studies focus on classification and typology in an attempt to provide a universal definition. For example, in a typical effort, Isajiw (1974) lists more than 10 cultural attributes, including language and religion, as the basis for ethnic group classification. However, shared cultural attributes cannot form an ethnic group, unless its members also share what Ri (1985) calls the 'we consciousness'. It is quite natural that the consciousness of 'they' is a prerequisite for the existence of 'we'. These two kinds of consciousness are not permanently fixed in contradistinction. It is clear for our own knowledge of ethnogenetic processes that 'we' sometimes involves those who were once 'they' but were incorporated.

The question, then, is how 'they' are incorporated into what becomes the 'we' with a modified composition. Under what circumstances does such a process occur? I presume the answers to these questions may reveal some fundamental elements in the nature of ethnogenesis. To begin with, we must deal with the issue of ethnic boundaries that divide 'us' from 'them'.[1] In this chapter, I will try to account for the formation and transformation of ethnic boundaries in the case of the Mela-Me'en (Bodi) in the Omo valley of south-western Ethiopia (Map 3). Particular attention is paid to conflict, because it is among the most important aspects of ethnic group interaction in this region, one which can affect group identity as well as territory (Otterbein, 1973).

Consciousness of 'we' among the Mela-Me'en

The Mela population of about 2500 live scattered in a wooded savanna area covering more than 2000 square kilometres. Linguistically they belong to the Surma group of the eastern Sudanic branch in the Nilo-Saharan language family. The Mela are one of seven sections of the Me'en ethnic cluster. Of these seven, the Mela and Chirim are collectively called Bodi by outsiders, while the other five are called Tishana.[2] The Mela raise cattle and goats, and also cultivate sorghum and other crops. Cattle are particularly important, not only in their economy, but in the ethos of their society and world view. It is not too much to say that they cannot perceive their existence without cattle. Cattle are also the object of interethnic raiding and are the direct cause of most conflicts in which the Mela are involved (Fukui, 1979).

The Me'en are the largest unit sharing 'we consciousness'. When they say 'we, the Me'en', the implication is that other groups in the vicinity are regarded as enemies and despised. In a different context, it can connote human in contrast to animal, though I experienced this only once during my stay with the Mela. When I was doing research in folk classification of animals, a man said to me: 'We, including you [the author], are Me'en [human beings],' in contrast to wild beasts. However, consciousness of shared identity hardly ever unites all the Me'en in practice. Reviewing oral tradition for the past few hundred years, I found not a single occasion when the Me'en took action in unison.

Sections of the Me'en sometimes form alliances against other ethnic groups. There were occasions when the Mela and the Chirim united in interethnic clashes. This sort of alliance can break down easily. In 1976, while I was in the region, the Mela were about to attack the Chirim on account of a dispute over the distribution of cattle obtained in a joint raid.[3] This shows that relations among Me'en sections are complicated and fragile. Each section has its own history and relationships with neighbouring ethnic groups, and a different pattern of fusion and fission resulting from conflicts with them.

The Mela are the largest unit in which the 'we consciousness' translates into collective action. While they are divided into two territorial units called Hana and Gura, each with its own chief (*komorut*), the Mela have a very strong corporate identity and constitute a solid group in conflicts. By analysing the historical process of Mela formation, it is possible to identify certain basic ethnic group characteristics.

First, however, mention should be made of Mela's relations

with the Ethiopian state. Although they live within the boundaries of that state, the Mela have little consciousness of Ethiopian identity. Largely because of their geographical isolation, they have had few contacts with the state in the past 100 years. But they did come to realize its power to oppress and learned to be submissive.[4] The execution of the leader of a Mela rebellion a generation ago was a lesson for them. About 20 years ago, a police station with 30 men was set up in Melaland to maintain security, but ethnic conflicts continued despite its presence. More recently, famine relief supplies have reached the region under the auspices of the Ethiopian government. Nevertheless, the Mela still have little grasp of the nature and magnitude of the state to which they belong.

Conflict and the Mela

Violent conflict is a dominant feature of Mela life. During my stay with them, the Mela were said to have killed several hundred people belonging to other ethnic groups. From a Mela perspective there are two types of ethnic conflict (Fig. 1). One is between groups of equal status. Enemies of this type are called *baragara* (enemy) and are similar to the Mela in their subsistence economy and the pivotal role of cattle. Included in this category are their Mursi neighbours to the south, who are also Surma-speakers, and the Hamar, who are Omotic speakers and live to the south-east beyond an uninhabited plain about 50 kilometres wide. The Hamar are an eternal enemy, and between them and the Mela there are no means of settling conflicts and making peace. The Mela do not journey to Hamarland to attack, but when attacked by the Hamar they put up a good fight. The last battle between the two took place in 1961, when the Mela allied with the Mursi to repel the Hamar. The Mursi are an occasional enemy, and in their clashes with the Mela women and children usually are not harmed. They have a tradition of conflict resolution, and once peace is restored the Mela and the Mursi visit each other and exchange cattle. During 1973–5, the annual toll in lives taken in Mela–Mursi conflict was about 15.

Conflict with agricultural peoples on the highland is of a different kind. The Mela show no mercy to the people who are collectively called Su, and who are not regarded as *baragara* because they are not of equal status. Whole settlements of Su have been wiped out in Mela attacks, with minor losses for the attackers. Such one-sided and large-scale violence prompted an

35

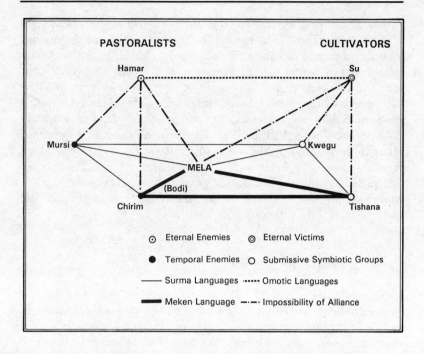

Figure 1 Group interaction and the Mela

American linguist, H. Fleming, working with the Dime, a Su group, in the late 1960s, to appeal to the Ethiopian government to save the latter from annihilation.[5] As a result, eight Mela leaders were imprisoned, but the Mela continued attacking the Su in different areas.

Group relations and conflict

The Mela call their enemies *baragara* and their allies *nganiya*. In order to see what factors determine in which of these two categories a neighbouring group is likely to fall, I shall compare types of relationship and affinity between groups, ranging from commonality of language to peace-making ceremonies. For example, the linguistic relationship between the Mela and the Su is the lowest, for they belong to different language families; their cultures also differ considerably; Mela culture being centred on cattle, while the world of the Su is crop cultivation, including ensete. However, the Mela have historical links with two Su groups. According to tradition, the chiefly lineage of both Mela territorial units, Hana and Gura, came from the Sai 10 generations ago, and even now the Mela chiefs visit the Sai chiefs to perform a ritual. Oral tradition also has it that another Su group, the Gerfa, was once conquered by the Mela.

Concerning intermarriage, the Mela have no such link with the Mursi, the Hamar-Banna or the Su, including the Sai. Concerning their chiefs, the Hana and the Gura chiefly lineages split only five generations ago. In this respect, the connection between the Mela and the Kwegu derives from the fact that, having been conquered by the Bodi once, the Kwegu are still regarded as their clients (*gaima*), although the actual relationship is one of symbiosis. Among the Mela, territory is divided among chiefs, and no trespassing is normally allowed between groups — save between the Hana and the Gura, and then only among individuals.

Between groups that do not share a territory there is a stretch of uninhabited land, which may be called a natural barrier and whose size seems to correspond with the frequency of conflict. Thus, a small barrier of this kind separates the territories of the Mela and the Chirim. Young cattle-herders in Hana go to the Chirim border in order to find good grasses and to have a cattle camp there. There is a stretch of uninhabited land 10–20 kilometres wide between the Mela and the Mursi, and this widens when there is conflict and the Mela try to distance themselves from the enemy. It almost disappears when they are on friendly terms. The width of the no man's land between the Mela and the Hamar is about 50 kilometres.

The possibility and nature of alliances are another indicator of group relations that have a bearing on conflict. For instance, the Mela and Mursi form temporary alliances only against the Hamar. Although they both make war against the Su, they never operate jointly. Another indicator is the treatment of women and children in war. In Mela–Mursi clashes women and children are not harmed, unless they interfere in the fighting. In contrast, women and children are not spared in fighting between the Mela and the Hamar, or the Mela and the Su, with the exception of the Sai and Gerfa.

Mechanisms for conflict resolution are yet another indicator. In cases of homicide between Hana and Gura, the two sections of the Mela, the issue is settled by paying compensation in cattle. It is not as easy to settle such an issue between the Mela and the Chirim. Homicide involving Mela and Mursi can evolve into a blood feud and even into war. However, there are also a search for resolution and a mechanism for concluding peace. There is no such mechanism between the Mela and the Hamar. Conflict with Su living near Melaland can be resolved, but only government intervention can settle conflict with Su who live farther away. Finally, there is the peace-making ceremony. This is performed when the prospects for peace are good, and the sacrifice of a white ox is its main feature.

It would seem from the above that there is a correlation between commonality of clan, intermarriage and bond links on the one hand, and conflict on the other. Clan commonality expresses an element in the historical formation of groups, while their present link is represented by intermarriage and bond links.[6] Among groups with such connections, conflict, when it occurs, is subject to resolution, and alliances are formed against a common enemy. It appears also that groups which share a language are able to perform peace making ceremonies. In contrast, the Mela have no means of seeking peace with the Hamar, whose language is completely different, without the intervention of a third party. The same holds true for most of the Su.

Conflict is unlikely to develop between the Hana and the Gura, although they are now under different chiefs. Thus, even though it consists of two distinct political units, the Mela (Hana–Gura) is the largest unit within which conflict does not occur. Bodi is the collective name for the Mela and the Chirim, as I explained before, and outsiders see them as one ethnic group sharing a language and culture. Nevertheless, the Chirim are a Mela enemy, something which may be explained by the fact that they have a low clan commonality. The traditional enemies of the Mela, they say, are the Chirim, the Mursi and the Hamar. A common feature of all three is that they are all pastoralists. Mela's enemies share the same world with them. In their strategy of conflict, the Mela always strive to maintain a balance of intergroup relations. For example, at the end of 1975 they performed the peace-making ceremony to end a war against the Mursi, and in February of the following year they launched a large scale attack against the Su.[7]

Historical background of the Mela

The data included in this section are derived mainly by tracing the location of tombs of clan ancestors mentioned in oral tradition. Clan elders are well informed about the location of burial places of their ancestors, and tracts of land are named after some natural feature or cultural association.[8] By matching movements referred to in tradition against such place-names, it is possible to trace the course of Mela territorial expansion. Although pseudo-historical statements may be included in this account, nevertheless it can serve as the basis for reconstructing Mela history, as Buxton (1963) also assumed in connection with the Mandari. Present-day Mela (Hana and Gura) comprise three population strains which have been assimilated over the years. These are: (i) the earlier indigenous population; (ii) the Saigesi and other clans whose ancestors are believed to have conquered the present territory of the Mela; and (iii) groups of people who immigrated into the territory over the years.

The indigenous population is said to have included the Idinit (Kwegu), the Oimulit and the proto-Mela. The Kwegu were engaged in hunting–gathering over a larger area than they occupy today. Two of their clans, the Solgut (Kudhun) and the Gali, merged into the present Mela. The Oimulit raised cattle and goats on the plain, before they were driven by the ancestors of the Saigesi to the Hamar country, and are said to be the ancestors of the Hamar. Only a few Mela are knowledgeable about the Oimulit, who are said to have merged into the Mela. One the other hand, most Mela are well informed about the proto-Mela, or the 'true Mela' (Mela *chim*). They consisted of three clans: Mineguwa, Ajit (Elma) and Kilingkabur. The Mela say the present Melaland belonged to them. The Mineguwa's seasonal movements took place between a place called T'eba during the rainy season and Mungur in the dry season, both of which are located between Gura and Mara. The Ajit (Elma) moved between Wora near the Elma River during the rainy season and Buchuwa at the junction of the Elma and Mago rivers in the dry season. When the ancestors of the Saigesi conquered these areas, the Kilingkabur fled to Hamar and Karo territory, while the other two clans, Mineguwa and Ajit, merged with them.

The first Saigesi invaders were led by a man called Delkaro, son of a chief called Dobulkama from Sai near Maji. They moved into the Mara area at the present northern boundary of the Mursi territory in search of pasture for their cattle. At that time, Mara belonged to the Kwegu, and the Mursi lived in a place known as Lukui in the lower part of the Omo. The Kwegu attacked the Saigesi and killed Delkaro, whose followers belonged to four clans: Timbach, Gilgu, Limech and Golme. They buried Delkaro at a spot called Lechelugu, and a bull with a *seroji* (mixed colour) hide was slaughtered. There was no chief for one year following the death of Delkaro. The following year, Dobulkama from Sai became chief, only to be rejected soon afterwards by the group.

39

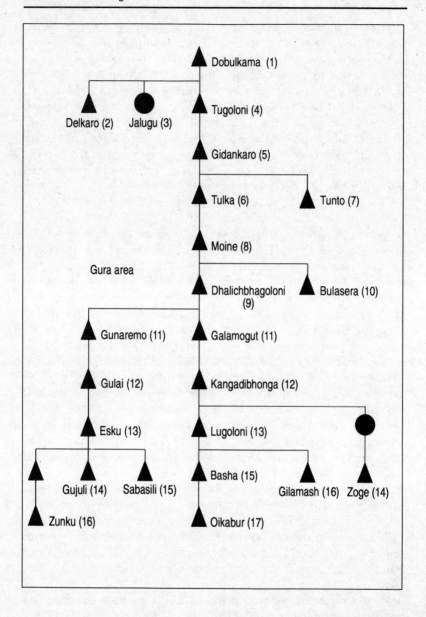

Figure 2   Genealogy of Mela komorut *(Saigesi clan)*

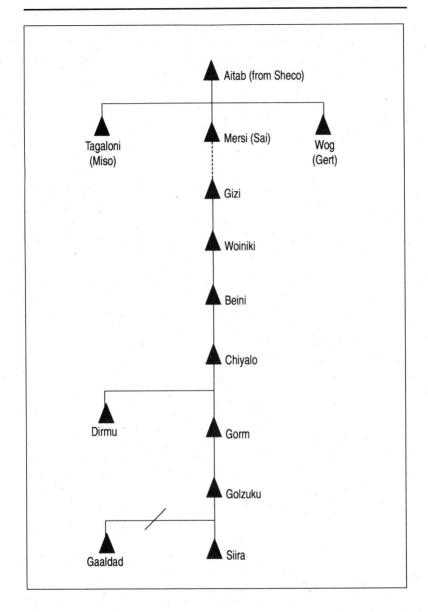

Figure 3   Genealogy of Sai komorut *(Saikiyasi clan)*

Then Delkaro's younger sister, Jalugu, was installed as chief. She and her group stayed at Lechelugu for three years and at Kologa for four years. There were constant disputes among them. Before long, Delkaro's half brother, Tugoloni, came from Sai, and there was talk of making him chief, but he refused. Jalugu tried to move into Mara with her followers and drowned in the Omo River during the rainy season.

Those who stayed in Lechelugu were often attacked by the Kwegu, and asked Dobulkama of Sai for help. After three days, he arrived with his younger brother Gartaso. Dobulkama advised them to return to Sai, but Tugoloni refused, and decided to settle in the Mara area along with Gartaso, their families and their livestock.[9] There they were joined by those who had stayed behind in Lechelugu, as well as by two clans, Gula and Marka, who came from Sai. On the fourth day after they arrived, they slaughtered an animal to install Tugoloni as chief (*komorut*). Seven days later, they attacked the Kwegu in Mara, Hana and Sigidan in the northern Omo valley. They killed some, and captured others, whom they exchanged for cattle with the Gabiyo-Me'en to the west of the Omo. The descendants of the Kwegu, who became clients (*gaima*) of Tugoloni, remain in Sigidan to this day.

Gartaso died of sickness at Talba towards the lower part of Hana. Tugoloni and his group attacked the Mursi and moved into Zingei on the lower part of the Mara River. Then he moved to Oso (Saala) in the middle section of the Mago River, and then to Tutubach in Gura. He finally died at Dhaama in the Hana area, and his tomb made of large stones is at a place called Chobur near Dhaama. The descendants of the Saigesi (Ulkui) continue to pay visits there to make offerings of cow's milk and blood, tobacco and coffee at the tomb of their ancestor Tugoloni. Tugoloni's eldest son, Gidankaro, succeeded him. After his installation, Gindakaro, who had been born at Oso, moved to Tekawoch in Gura and then to Ch'ao near the Oso, and died of sickness at Chamowa in Gura. Tulka, his eldest son, succeeded him and was killed by foreign raiders in the Oso. His younger half-brother, Tunto, succeeded and moved to Gorku in the Hana area. He had six wives, though his period in office was short, and he died at Jomeli at the lower end of the Hana River.

Tulka's eldest son, Moine, was installed as *komorut* and moved to Kanchuwa in the Hana area and then to Kelechuchu in the same area. His burial place is not known. Dhalichbhagoloni, Moine's eldest son, was born at Moizui in the Hana area. After he succeeded his father, he moved to Jakuku and Delmagoloni and finally died at a placed called Selo; all these places are located in the Hana area. He is said to have been a great *komorut* with five wives. His descendants are called Biologu, after the name he bore as a young man. After Dhalichbhagoloni's death, his younger brother, Bulasera, succeeded him, but his period in office was short. He was succeeded by Galamogut, Dhalichbhagoloni's eldest son, who moved near Dildi to the west of Bol (Gerfa), which is the southernmost village in Dimeland. His older half-brother, Gunaremo, fought against him and became *komorut* of the Gura area, thus splitting the group into two sections. The Gura *komorut*-ship has been retained by Gunaremo's agnatic line to the present day. Galamogut died at a place named Lalanyu between Hana and Gura. As his eldest son had died previously of sickness, his second son, Kangadibhonga, succeeded, and later moved to Alumu in Chirim country and raided for cattle. Afterwards, he moved to a place called Suluchu near Sigidan in the Kwegu area, and eventually was killed by Esku, who later succeeded to the Gura *komorut*-ship.

Religious and kinship strategies for merging populations

The oral tradition cited above forms the basis of present-day Mela ideology. The office of *komorut* passes through the agnatic line, but only sons born from five particular clans qualify for installation. These clans are Timbach, Mineguwa, Ajit, Gali and Gerfa. Among these only one, Timbach, originated in Sai, having migrated with Delkaro, the first Saigesi invader. The others are clans whose ancestors belonged to peoples conquered by the Saigesi. Two of them, Mineguwa and Ajit, belong to the group called 'Mela *chim*' ('true Mela'). A fourth, Gali, is one of the clans of the Kwegu, and the Gerfa belong to the Dime group of hill farmers. Girls belonging to these clans decorate themselves with the same red necklace, called *gala*, that the *komorut* wear.

The position of mothers and sons relative to the office of *komorut* is illustrated in the case of a recent *komorut* in Hana. His first wife belonged to the Ajit clan, one of the clans that qualify for office, but she died after giving birth only to a daughter. Had she given birth to a son, he would have become *komorut*. His second wife belonged to the Dombuloch clan, ancestors of which had migrated from Sai, and her son was rejected by the Hana people. His third wife belonged to Ajit, and the *komorut*, named Oikabur, was her eldest son. He was installed as *komorut* in January 1974, but died in 1976. His younger full brother succeeded him and is *komorut* now. The fourth wife belonged to

43

Gulach, a Chirim clan; therefore, her son, though older than Oikabur, did not qualify for office. The fifth wife belonged to Gali, another clan that qualified for office, and her son was nominated to become *komorut* before Oikabur, but died soon afterwards.

The Mela still identify with Sai, the ancestral land of the Saigesi clan, which played a central role in their history. After the installation of a new *komorut*, he and his followers travel to Sai near Maji to perform a ritual together with the chief of the area, who himself claims descent from the same line as the *komorut* of Melaland. Interestingly, a headman of the Kwegu also participates in the ritual. They slaughter a male calf and purify each other with its blood. Cows are presented to the Mela, and the Kwegu headman, who is called the *gaima* of the *komorut*, drives the cow back to Melaland.[10] When they reach the *komorut*'s compound, they slaughter another male calf and purify the necklace stones they brought from Sai. Cows brought back from Sai are called *bheliyach*, and their milk is used in rituals to confer fertility on humans, animals and plants. The *komorut* sprays such milk over his cattle every morning, and over his followers during rituals held on special occasions — for example, when they are preparing for a fight.

The undercurrent of population movements

It is obvious that an ethnic group is not a separate and impervious unit, but one that is in a constant state of flux in relation to its neighbours, merging with one, separating from another, over the course of time. Such population movements are reflected in the group's historical consciousness and ideology. Whether the Saigesi conquest is a real historical event or merely a myth, it is the corner-stone of Mela ideology. It explains why the putative descendants of those who are believed to have come to conquer Melaland continue to return to the 'home country' to demonstrate their historical lineage. The cows they bring back reaffirm not only their ethnogenesis, but also their subsequent integration and expansion into the Mela.

Of course, conflict is not waged for its own sake, but for desired objectives. For the Mela, the principal objective is control of territory, but this is not simply a process of straightforward expansion. It may be comparatively easy to dislodge a few individuals from their land, but it is much harder to displace an entire population from its territory when the groups are evenly matched militarily. It is better to compromise with one's opponent from a position of strength after a series of attacks.[11] The Mela strategy seems to be not simply territorial conquest, but to impose on opponents the status of *gaima* (client) and incorporate them by means of affinal kinship links.[12]

The conclusion of a Mela–Chirim conflict offers an illustration of this process. They fought for two years, nearly two generations ago, when Zoge, the present *komorut*'s grandfather's cross-cousin, was chief. The Chirim were forced to flee to Nyomonitland, beyond the Omo, where they stayed for three years. One evening a Chirim *komorut* came to the compound of the father of the present Hana *komorut*, who had succeeded Zoge in the mean time, and said: 'Now our conflict is over. I offer one of my daughters to you. I will be your *gaima*.' Afterwards, many Chirim came to cultivate the fields of the Hana *komorut*, and stayed for about three years.

Once another group is merged into the Mela as a client, the Mela do not attack it. The ethnic groups whom the Mela do not attack are the Sai, the Kwegu and the Gerfa. The Sai are one of the Su groups, from where the *komorut* ancestors are said to have migrated, as noted above. The Kwegu were the original inhabitants of Melaland and were conquered by the Mela, becoming Mela clients later. The Gerfa are a subgroup of the Dime, who live in the eastern mountainous area. According to Mela oral history, they also were conquered by the Mela, and have now become their clients. The Gerfa people sometimes join Mela attacks on the northern highlanders, as do some of the Kwegu. Though both the Kwegu and the Gerfa are sedentary groups, they join the Mela in attacks against other sedentary highlanders, in return for patronage and protection. The Mela trade their livestock products for the agricultural produce of the Gerfa. The Gerfa thus play an indispensable role for the daily subsistence of the Mela, especially in critical times.[13] The repeated attacks in the past 30 years by the Mela against the other Dime cultivators may indicate that the objective of the recurring conflict is to reduce the latter to the same client status as the Gerfa and Kwegu. Raiding for cattle, therefore, is only one aspect of the conflict. Another, it can be said, represents the undercurrent of Mela expansion and an element in the process of their ethnogenesis.

Notes

1 That is, from the group, not the individual, point of view (Barth, 1969).
2 Bodi is the name given to the two subgroups of the Me'en on the east bank of the Omo, the Mela and Chirim, by the neighbouring agricultural people and the Ethiopian authorities. The Me'en themselves do not use this name.
3 Field research was done during thirteen months between 1973 and 1976, and for some weeks in 1989 and again in 1991.
4 Hana was divided into four *kebele* (administrative districts) when I visited there in 1989, but there seemed to be little government influence in the area.
5 Personal communication from Professor H. Fleming, whom I met in 1984 at the Eighth International Conference of Ethiopian Studies, in Addis Ababa.
6 The Mela held a peace-making ceremony with the Mursi at a place within Mursi territory called Zinninya, which is on the southern side of Mala River, and slaughtered a white male calf. The ceremony was arranged through the Mursi's approach to a friend in Gura called Golondoli. After eight months the Mursi came to Melaland to slaughter another white male calf for peace-making.
7 The Mela attacked the Su several times in February and March 1976.
8 The historical background of the Mela is detailed in Fukui (1988).
9 I heard almost the same story about Tugoloni when I visited Sai in 1989. Sai people call the Mela *mela-kiyasi* and themselves *sai-kiyasi*.
10 I got the same information in Sai, but the former *komorut*, called Oikable, had died without visiting Sai. His younger brother, who succeeded him, visited Sai for the special ritual after he was installed in Hana.
11 Turton (1979), on the other hand, sees a territorial movement in Mursi–Bodi relations, as does Tornay (1979) regarding population movements in the lower Omo.
12 When I visited the Mela in 1989 and 1991, I found they had expanded into the eastern mountainous area that was originally Dimeland. But the hill farmers had not yet offered any girls to the *komorut*, although they had provided him with beer and labour to cultivate his fields.
13 Most of pastoral peoples in the lowlands have a symbiotic relationship with some highland agricultural people.

References

Barth, F. (ed.) (1969) *Ethnic Groups and Boundaries: the Social Organization of Culture Differences*. Boston: George Allen & Unwin.

Buxton, J.C. (1963) *Chiefs and Strangers: a Study of Political Assimilation among the Mandari*. Oxford: Clarendon Press.

Fukui, K. (1979) Cattle colour symbolism and inter-tribal homicide among the Bodi. In K. Fukui & D. Turton (eds), *Warfare among East African Herders*. Osaka: Senri Ethnological Studies, no. 3, National Museum of Ethnology.

—— (1988) The religious and kinship ideology of military expansion among the Bodi (Mela). In T. Beyene (ed.), *Proceedings of the Eighth International Conference of Ethiopian Studies*. Addis Ababa: Institute of Ethiopian Studies.

Fukui, K. & Turton, D. (eds) (1979) *Warfare among East African Herders*. Osaka: Senri Ethnological Studies, no. 3, National Museum of Ethnology.

Isajiw, W.W. (1974) Definitions of ethnicity. *Ethnicity* **1** (2).

Lamphear, J. (1976) *The Traditional History of the Jie of Uganda*. Oxford: Clarendon Press.

Otterbein, K.F. (1973) The anthropology of war. In J. Honigman (ed.), *Handbook of Social and Cultural Anthropology*. Chicago: Rand McNally.

Ri, K. (1985) Ethnicity and modern society: an approach to political sociology. *Shisou* **4**, (Japanese).

Tornay, S. (1979) Armed conflicts in the lower Omo valley, 1970–1976: an analysis from within Nyangatom society. In K. Fukui & D. Turton (eds), *Warfare among East African Herders*. Osaka: Senri Ethnological Studies, no. 3, National Museum of Ethnology.

Turton, D. (1979) War, peace, and Mursi identity. In K. Fukui & D. Turton (eds), *Warfare among East African Herders*. Osaka: Senri Ethnological Studies no. 3, National Museum of Ethnology.

3 Annexation & Assimilation: Koegu & their Neighbours

HIROSHI MATSUDA

The lower Omo valley is home to about a dozen known groups that claim distinct ethnic identities (see Map 2, p. 14). Given the constant flux in the inter-group relations that shape temporal ethnic identities, it is never possible to know exactly how many there are (Table 1). The fluidity of interethnic relations is illustrated in the case of the Koegu, whose existence was anything but obvious when I first visited their area in 1986. My interest at the time was focused on the Kara, and I spent some months in the village of Dus, which I thought was exclusively populated by the Kara. At one point, I visited the village of Kuchur, 30 kilometres to the north, where I was told Kara also lived, and I detected no difference between the people there and those at Dus, only that the people at Kuchur referred to themselves as Karo.

After my return to Japan, a linguist (Hieda, 1991) who had visited the same region alerted me to the existence of the Koegu, who lived among the Kara, and I returned to the region in 1988 intending to study the relationship between these two groups.[1] My plan was to see this relationship from the vantage-point of the Kara; therefore, I went to stay at Kuchur. As I was to discover, this was a Koegu village with only two Kara families in it. Dus, on the other hand, had a mixed population of Koegu and Kara. The two groups were closely integrated in a relationship I call annexation, and the name Karo was used as a common designation. While I was there, this relationship broke down amidst conflict. As the distance between the Kara and the Koegu widened through violence, the latter moved closer to the powerful Nyangatom, a former enemy of both Kara and Koegu. This new

Table 1 Ethnic groups in the lower Omo valley

Self-name	Name given by others	Language group	Population	Subsistence E.	Reference
Koegu	Muguji	Surma (N-S)	500	A·P·H·G·F	Matsuda 1991: 17–32
Kwegu	Nyidi	Surma	200	A·P·H· G·F	Turton 1986: 148–171
Kwegu	Yidi	Surma	400	A·P·H·G ·F	Turton 1986: 148–171
Me'en (Meken)	Bodi	Surma	3,000	A·P	Fukui 1979: 147–177
Mun/Muni (pl./s.)	Mursi	Surma	5,000	A·P	Turton 1976: 533–561
Omo Murle	Ngarich (Murle)	Surma	200	A·P·F	Tornay 1981b: 33–60
Nyangatom	Bume	Nilotic (N-S)	5,000	A·P·G	Tornay 1981a: 91–117
Kara	Karo	Omotic (A-A)	1,000	A·P·H	Matsuda 1991: 17–32
Gomba	Gomba	Omotic	50?	A·P·H	Matsuda 1991: 17–32
Hamar	Hamar	Omotic	15,000	A·P	Lydall 1976: 393–437
Beshada	Beshada	Omotic	?	A·P	Lydall 1976: 393–437
Bana	Bana	Omotic	11,000	A·P	Bender 1976: 1–23
Dassanetch	Geleb	Cushitic (A-A)	15,000	A·P·F	Almagor 1978

Note: 1 The Gomba speak Kara, and the Beshada speak Hamer now.
2 Populations are approximately estimated.
3 Abbreviations are as follows:
N-S; Nilo-Saharan Super family; A-A; Afro-Asiatic Super family, A; Agriculture, P; pastoralism, H; hunting, G; gathering, F; fishing.

relationship seemed to be a step in the direction of assimilation of the Koegu by the Nyangatom.

The Koegu–Kara clash differs in four respects from the usual conflict among pastoralists in the lower Omo. Firstly, there is no memory of earlier conflict between the two groups. Secondly, it does not involve cattle-raiding, since the Koegu have no cattle and depend on cultivation, fishing, hunting and gathering. Thirdly, territory is not involved, since the Koegu are not seeking to expand. Fourthly, this is not a conflict between two separate political entities, but rather a division of the Karo into two rival ethnic groups. In this essay, I will seek to clarify the reasons for the division and the role of conflict in balancing interethnic relations.

During my stay in the lower Omo region, from August 1988 to March 1990, I stayed for 12 months in Kuchur, where 350 out of 500 inhabitants were Koegu. I also spent a few weeks each in other Koegu hamlets, as well as in Kara and Nyangatom settlements. I followed closely the process of the conflict, which continued after I left. I sought the views not only of the Koegu people, but of the Kara and Nyangatom as well. I attended meetings held in and outside the area. Local government officials were concerned about the conflict, and I discussed it with them, and also consulted some of their records. Kara was the language most often used on such occasions, while Koegu was used less frequently because even Koegu coming from outside the region did not understand this language, nor did the Nyangatom.

Koegu: people of the forest and river

The Koegu belong to the Surma group of languages. Because they are called Muguji by the Kara, they appear by that name in several ethnographic studies (Bryan, 1945: 196; Bender, 1975: 37, 1976: 10, 467; Turton & Bender, 1976: 535; Lydall, 1976: 393; Turton, 1986: 273). They are one of the smallest groups in the lower Omo, and remain among the least known. Their number in the area of my research did not exceed 500. There are other smaller Koegu groups living among the Bodi and the Mursi, which have little or no contact with the group I describe here. One reason for the Koegu's low profile is their habit of introducing themselves to outsiders as Karo, the name they share with the Kara. They were ordinarily in the shade of the Kara.

Their settlements are scattered in the riverine forest along the Omo River. Four to seven families cluster in small hamlets, and acquire their food and commodities within the space of a few kilometres. However, when I was among them in 1988, about 350 people congregated around the village of Kuchur, near the junction of the Omo and its tributary the Mago, because they feared an attack by the Mursi, their northern neighbours. Another group of about 150 Koegu lived in the village of Dus with the Kara, and a few more families lived in Labuk, another Kara village four kilometres south-east of Kuchur.

More than 70 per cent of the food consumed by the Koegu in Kuchur consisted of agricultural products obtained from river-bank cultivation (Matsuda, 1988). The main crop is sorghum. Some maize is also planted in the flood plain after the land dries. The seed and leaves of cow-peas and green grams are mixed with hard porridge of sorghum. Though they have two or three grain harvests in a year, they do not produce enough for their subsistence. Fishing is a crucial activity for the Koegu, and fish becomes their main food in the off-crop season. Techniques for preserving fish, such as drying and smoking, are not used. This is partly because it is easy to catch fish with harpoons in shallow pools during the rainy season. Men and children often go there to spear fish when the pools begin to dry. They sometimes spend a night there and eat many fish, but they seldom bring a catch back home. They also fish with hook and line in the main course of the Omo, but many people do not have hook and line. The hand-to-mouth nature of the Koegu economy is revealed in their fishing activity — that is, immediate obtaining and immediate consumption.

Honey-gathering is important in two aspects: economic and spiritual. Grown men set beehives on trees, the number of which sometimes is more than fifty for each person. They can get honey two or three times a year after the flowering season. The total is 40 to 80 kilograms for each person, quite enough for a year's consumption of a family. Honey is eaten with porridge of sorghum. Some honey is sold for money in markets, though the Koegu rarely go to town. Honey is given to trade partners in neighbouring groups, and some people brew honey wine for guests. To treat elders and close friends to a party like this is considered to be a good custom. The elders invited to the party bless the host by blowing wine through their mouth on his face. It is said that the more urine a guest discharges in the house, the more honey there will be in the host's beehives the following season.

In his discussion of the symbiotic relationship between a group of Koegu and the Mursi, Turton (1986) regards the hunting skills of the former as an important factor in that relationship, in the sense that the Koegu are valued by the Mursi as a source of ivory and leopard skins. Indeed, the Koegu at Kuchur are regarded by their neighbours as having an uncanny knowledge of the forest and the animals living there, as well as for their skill in hunting and trapping them. However, the value of their knowledge and skills has diminished because the sale of ivory has been banned by the Ethiopian government, and the Koegu hunt animals for food with old rifles. I recorded only 12 incidents of animal shooting in a period of 79 days. Given the size of Kuchur's population (350), this is not enough to qualify the Koegu as hunters.

Wild plants are used more in the production of material culture than for food. Except for some iron parts used in utensils and tools, the Koegu make all their utensils from the products of the forest. The largest and most unique product of the Koegu is a dug-out canoe made from the trunk of the wild fig-tree. The Koegu also make clay pots for cooking. Canoes and pots are important items in Koegu trade with their neighbours along the Omo, the Kara and the Nyangatom.

A conspicuous feature of the Koegu economy that sets this group apart from its neighbours is that they have no cattle. The people in Kuchur own a few goats and sheep, but they entrust them to the care of their kinsmen in Dus, who are more inclined to herding. The Koegu economy and way of life and their sense of economic values contrast sharply with those of their pastoralist neighbours. This contrast is the underlying reason for the unique social position of the Koegu in the lower Omo, which is described in the next section. In this connection, I would like to stress the role which fishing and hunting–gathering groups have played in the regional economy. According to Sobania: 'For all the pastoralists of the Lake Turkana basin, the hunting, gathering and fishing communities in their midst represented a possible refuge upon which the impoverished and destitute members of their societies could fall back' (Sobania, 1988: 45).

The case of the Koegu is somewhat different. The Koegu are not simply a refuge for the neighbouring pastoralists in times of crisis. Rather, the Koegu move in and out of close relationships with their neighbours, depending on the change of natural and social conditions. This is a process of group interaction in the Lower Omo, where very small groups and the larger pastoralists have coexisted; a process that also affects ethnic identity formation. At the time of my study, the relationship of the Koegu with the pastoralists was shifting from what I call 'annexation' by one group, the Kara, towards 'assimilation' by another, the Nyangatom. The shift, I believe, represents the Koegu main strategy for survival, as well as the pastoralists' approach towards the small fishing, hunting and gathering groups such as the Koegu (Matsuda, 1991).

Koegu and their neighbours

The Kara, a group that numbers about 1000, were formerly more like brothers of the Koegu rather than neighbours. In fact, a bond partnership between families of both groups was often compared to brotherhood by themselves. Both groups believe that the Koegu are the original inhabitants of the Omo area, and that the Kara immigrated to this place later. The Kara have the following oral tradition of how they came to stay at the riverain area.

In former days, the people of the Kara lived in the mountainous area where the Bana live now. One day an ox was missing and a man followed its footprints. He discovered the big water [Omo River]. This is the place which they call Keske now [near Dus]. Because he found it a good place to plant sorghum, he went back at once to his village and had a talk with the villagers. Then, all the villagers decided to move to this place. Though the Muguji [Koegu] had already settled there at that time, they did not plant sorghum. So the Kara taught cultivation to the Muguji.[2]

These two groups are not distinguished from each other by appearance, body ornaments, clothing, hair-style, economic activity or anything else. While the Kara persist in regarding themselves as pastoralists, they have no cattle, only a few goats and sheep, and subsist mainly by cultivation. The two groups lived in the same hamlets, spoke to each other in Kara and fought together against outsiders. The partnership called *belmo* in Koegu and *bel* in Kara characterized their merger into one political unit under the name Karo. Exchange of gifts made the partnership strong and enduring. For example, if a Koegu gave sorghum or honey to his Kara *belmo*, the Kara gave a goat, sheep, cotton cloth, coffee or bullets to his Koegu partner. There was no fixed time or rate of exchange, but they remembered well when and what was given and received. Firearms were also given to the Koegu in this way. A Koegu elder told me:

Some years before, the Kara loaned rifles to the Koegu and we shot elephants and leopards with it. The Koegu gave ivory and leopards' skins to the Kara *belmo*. After that, the rifle was given to us in return for those gifts. The rifles which the Koegu have now are obtained like this.[3]

53

I would like to note that *belmo* is not a relationship of equity. From the Koegu side, not only goods but also labour power were offered to their Kara partners. For example, the Koegu slashed fields and watched over birds for their partners in the farming season. The Kara did not reciprocate. Moreover, since the Kara claimed possession of all the arable land along the Omo, the Koegu presumably had only the right to cultivate their partners' land. Obviously, the Kara were dominant in this sense.

Taboos and disdain demarcated the respective positions of the two groups more distinctively than the economic aspects mentioned above. Not only intermarriage, but sexual contact between them was taboo. They believed their flesh might rot if they had sexual intercourse. For the same reason, it was pro-hibited to drink water, sorghum beer or honey wine from the same bowl. This meant they never enjoyed drinking together in a circle, though they lived in the same hamlet. In addition, the Kara called the Koegu 'stinking people' who usually ate fish, and 'poor people' who had no cattle. The Kara expressed even stronger feelings of contempt, saying, 'The Muguji are baboons'. I would describe the relationship between the Koegu and the Kara as one of annexation of the former by the latter. The two groups were regarded as one by outsiders. Their spatial territories overlapped. They acted as one group against enemies. The ethnic boundary between them, however, was rigidly maintained through taboos and disdain, and they never amalgamated into one ethnic group.

The Nyangatom are an agro-pastoral group numbering about 5000 people, living on the western side of the Omo. The influx of automatic rifles in the 1980s triggered a series of clashes in the region, which resulted in a chain reaction of group displace-ment in the Omo basin. The heavily armed Turkana drove the Nyangatom eastward, and the latter in turn, having obtained arms from the Toposa, forced the Dassanetch (pop. 15,000) and the Mursi (pop. 5000) to cross from the western side of the Omo to the east. Nyangatom society is described in detail by Tornay (1979, 1981a). I shall briefly mention their changing relationship with the Koegu.

The Koegu and Kara fought together against the Nyangatom until 1988. According to Tornay, the Nyangatom clashed three times with the other two in the 1970s (1979: 97). Though they were enemies, however, the Koegu were strongly influenced by the Nyangatom. I shall mention here just a few instances of this. During my stay in Kuchur, three Koegu girls got married to the Nyangatom. In all three cases, these girls were carried off from

Table 2 Koegu songs

Language	Number
Koegu	5
Kara	14
Nyangatom	58
Baña	9
Hamar	2
Mursi	13
Dassanetch	12
mixed	5
Total	118

Note: See (Matsuda 1992: 59).

the village and taken to their husbands' relatives. It was after some weeks that the negotiation for a bride price started with the girls' relatives. It seemed to me that the Koegu parents were pleased with their daughters' marriages to the Nyangatom. I did not observe the reverse, that is, Koegu men marrying Nyangatom women. Possibly, this is because the bride price of the Koegu is much lower than that of the Nyangatom. A Koegu man pays one rifle and some goats and sheep to the bride's relatives, while the Nyangatom man continues to pay cattle, goats and sheep for the rest of his life.

Such intermarriage is not a recent development. In fact, Koegu and Nyangatom used to live together earlier in Kopriya. One of the territorial sections of the Nyangatom, named Ngikumama, was closely associated with the Koegu, and some Nyangatom of this section are said to speak Koegu even now. All of the Koegu in Dus and the male adults in the Kuchur group were fluent speakers of Nyangatom. They said they learned it from the Nyangatom as boys, when they were working as herdsmen.

Another aspect of Nyangatom cultural influence is seen in the dances and songs of the Koegu. I recorded 118 songs which they sing in dancing. Fifty-eight of these were sung in the Nyangatom language, while only five were sung in Koegu (Table 2). Most of the Nyangatom songs were sung in dances where the youths jump high in Nyangatom fashion. The subject of most of these songs was cattle. On the other hand, most of the Koegu songs were about animals and birds (Matsuda, 1992). I collected 12 age-set names at Kuchur in 1989. Six of these were the same as Nyangatom age-set names which Tornay noted in his paper (1981a: 166–7). The order of these six names was nearly identical to that of the Nyangatom. However, Tornay states that among other Nyangatom territorial sections (he collected them in the Kibish area) names do vary to some extent. We may therefore assume that the Nyangatom and the Koegu have a similar age system. It is possible that the culture traits of the Nyangatom were introduced to the Koegu by way of the Kara. Nevertheless, I have no doubt that these cultural similarities promoted Koegu assimilation by the Nyangatom.

In addition to intermarriage, language and other cultural affinities, the Koegu began to develop bond partnerships with the Nyangatom during the conflict with the Kara discussed below. The Koegu also call their Nyangatom bond *belmo*, but it is a different relationship from their bond with the Kara. The Nyangatom are not owners of cultivating fields, nor do they exact labour from the Koegu. Moreover, apparently there is no taboo or disdain towards the Koegu on the part of the Nyangatom. Thus, while the Koegu and the Kara have a vertical super-ordinate relationship, the Koegu and the Nyangatom have a horizontal co-ordinate relationship. Moreover, while the Koegu have maintained the ethnic boundary that separates them from the Kara, they seem to want to remove the boundary that distinguishes them from the Nyangatom. That is why I see this relationship as potential assimilation, and distinguish it from the relationship the Koegu had with the Kara, which I see as annexation.

The Kwegu and their neighbours

The name Kwegu — spelled with a *w* rather than an *o* — appears in some ethnographic and linguistic works (Bender, 1976: 37; Muldrow, 1976: 606), but little is known about them. Turton's (1986) study offers a glimpse of their social organization and relationship with the Mursi. According to him, about 200 Kwegu live in Mursi territory and another 400 live among the Bodi, north of Kuchur. The Mursi (pop. 5000) are cattle herders with a strong pastoralist ethos. They move from pasture-land to the riverain area, which is infested by tsetse-flies but suitable for cultivation. Seasonal movement is indispensable to their way of life and to their identity as herders. Consequently, the Mursi depend on the technology and knowledge of the Kwegu to live in the riverain area. For example, the Kwegu hunt elephants and leopards, make and use fish harpoons and dug-out canoes, control canoes during the dangerous rainy season, etc. As in the case of the Koegu–Kara relationship, the Kwegu and Mursi ethnic boundaries are maintained through taboos on marriage and other social distinctions. The Kwegu do not depend economically on the Mursi, but they need strong patrons to protect them from other Mursi.

Turton defines the Kwegu–Mursi connection as a patron–client relationship which is a means of domination, and speculates that it was formed initially to provide the Mursi with ivory and animal skins. His conclusion is that the ethnic identity of the Kwegu has been formed through their relationship with the Mursi. Domination connotes essentially a political, that is, a power relationship, while the Koegu–Kara connection is more than that. I prefer to call it annexation, meaning that one group joins another in a closely united but subordinate capacity.

What differences, if any, are there between the Koegu–Kara and Kwegu–Mursi cases, and what do such differences reveal? To begin with, while the Kara also regard themselves as herders, they do not own cattle, only some goats and sheep, and they live in the riverain area throughout the year. They have fully adapted to the environment of river and forest. All the men keep beehives in the forest, and are able to control a canoe on the swollen river. In short, Kara economic dependence on the Koegu became negligible, and their relationship lost its material substance and became a mere shell. It is not surprising, therefore, that it could easily disintegrate, as it did recently. Very little is known of the Kwegu who live among the Bodi. Fukui's essay in this volume provides some information (p. 33).

Koegu-Kara conflict

In October 1988, at Jinka, the capital of South Omo Administrative Region, a Kara student told me the Kara were quarrelling with the Koegu in Dus, and that the Kara had ordered the Koegu living in Dus to move to Kuchur. I heard later that leaders of the two groups had quarrelled over the distribution of goods brought to them by aid organizations and the government of Ethiopia. This was the immediate cause for the conflict whose course is described below.

On 10 December 1988, a Nyangatom man was shot dead by a Dassanetch at Kundama, in Kara territory along the Omo. The killing took place in the sorghum field of a Kara leader, who was the killer's bond partner. The Kara let the Dassanetch escape in order not to be caught by the Nyangatom. That night, hundreds of Nyangatom warriors assembled in Kadakuchin, a

57

small settlement on the bank opposite Kundama, to plan an attack against the Kara. The Koegu in Kuchur who heard this news took refuge immediately in the forest on the east side of the Omo, fearing the Nyangatom would attack them as well. This shows how the Koegu identified with the Kara. However, the Nyangatom attacked neither the Kara nor the Koegu.

In May 1988, the Nyangatom had been raided by the Turkana and were forced to evacuate the area along the Kibish River, which was important to them for cultivation and grazing. The Nyangatom moved their camps eastward to the Omo, and many of them were staying in Kadakuchin with their herds when that incident occurred. While I was in Kadakuchin, the Nyangatom told me they intended to drive the Kara out of the Omo area. For the Nyangatom, the Kara were not a potential partner for coexistence. The latter also regarded themselves as pastoralists, and the two groups had a serious fight in the 1970s. (Tornay, 1979: 97). It appears the Nyangatom intended to ally with the Koegu and occupy the riverain area by displacing the Kara. On their part, the Koegu needed the support of a strong ally in an armed conflict against the Kara. Thus, the Koegu and the Nyangatom both had good reasons to form the close relationship described below.

On 9 February 1989, the Koegu and the Nyangatom held a big feast in Kuchur to celebrate their alliance. In the evening, about 70 Nyangatom came to Kuchur and began to dance with the Koegu girls. Honey wine was prepared for the Nyangatom guests in some houses. On 10 February, trouble occurred in Dus, and the news reached Kuchur within the day. A Koegu had attacked a Kara with a knife, and was himself shot by the Kara. The feast in Kuchur converted to a meeting to plan reprisals. All the villagers and visitors got ready to fight under the leadership of a Nyangatom elder. The Koegu and the Nyangatom seemed to further strengthen their solidarity after this day. Many Nyangatom came to visit the bond partners they had made in Kuchur during the feast. They brought sacks of sorghum and maize loaded on donkeys. In contrast, the break between the Koegu and the Kara became definite after the incident of 10 February. The last Kara family left Kuchur before the feast.

In June 1989, the administrator of Hamer *awraja* (district) came to Murle (45 kilometres south of Kuchur), and talked with the leaders of the Koegu, the Kara and the Nyangatom about the trouble. According to the administrator, whom I interviewed later, the following agreement was concluded. The Koegu who had been living in Dus were to move to Kuchur. The area higher than Labuk was to be Koegu territory, while the Dus area, lower than Labuk, belonged to the Kara. However, the Koegu from Dus did not move to Kuchur, but established a new settlement in Galgida two months later. Galgida is 10 kilometres downstream of Dus, and near the Nyangatom border. The reason why the Dus group did not move to Kuchur was that there was no arable land there to be distributed to them. Moreover, the Dus group had increased the relative importance of pastoralism in their economic life while living with the Kara, and this made them hesitate to move to Kuchur. Kuchur was more suitable to the original way of life of the Koegu, which depended on fishing, honey-collecting and river-bank cultivation.

We have to take into consideration also the viewpoint of the local administration. Kara territory consisted of two *kebele*, the smallest administrative unit in Ethiopia. One was the Dus *kebele*, which included the habitat of all the Kara and the Dus Koegu group. The other was the Labuk *kebele*, which included the Kuchur group of the Koegu. Both *kebele* were in the Hamar *awraja*. The administrator of the *awraja* suggested to the people that the arrangement be changed to comprise the Dus *kebele* with all the Kara in it, and the Kuchur *kebele* with all the Koegu, so that the two groups would be separated administratively. The Koegu did not agree, believing that if they were grouped into one *kebele* they would get less from the government in terms of aid, and particularly firearms and ammunition. Moreover, the Koegu hoped to be included in Kurraz *awraja* where the Nyangatom belonged. The Koegu always complained that the administrator of Hamar *awraja* was a native Hamar, and favoured the Kara because of their close links with the Hamar.

The Koegu from the Dus group moved to Galgida after all. This shows they preferred unification with the Nyangatom, rather than a distinct political unit of all the Koegu. The Dus group would move again in December 1989 from Galgida to Ukuule, which is in the midst of the Nyangatom territory. In the first half of 1989, the conflict between the Koegu and the Kara was not very serious. There was plenty of rain in 1988, and there was a wide arable flood plain at the beginning of 1989. In contrast, the rainy season of 1989 — March to May — was poor. Consequently, there was a tense atmosphere between the groups on the reduced flood plain when the cultivation season started in October.

On 12 November, a Gomba man living in Labuk came to Kuchur to see the field which he had cultivated the previous season. He wanted to cultivate his field again. Because the

Gomba are regarded as part of the Kara by the people in Kuchur, the man was thrashed with a stick by a Koegu in front of the village. Some elders intervened and settled the quarrel; however, tension between the two groups reached a new peak. A Koegu man from Labuk came to Kuchur to report that the Kara in Labuk threatened to burn Kuchur. In Kuchur, people decided to send women and children to the forest the same day, and they sent a messenger to the Nyangatom villages to ask for help. After sunset, they held a meeting and war-dances outside the village. The Kara did not attack Kuchur, because they knew the power of the Nyangatom, who were armed with automatic rifles. Some Nyangatom warriors came to stay permanently at Kuchur after this incident.

On 23 December, a Koegu elder was thrashed by some Kara in his field between Labuk and Kuchur. After the elder fled to Kuchur, the two groups had an exchange of shooting that lasted the whole day. A young Koegu was wounded in the leg in this fight. Two days later, some Koegu from Kuchur, including women and children, on their way to Galgida to seek refuge, were attacked by Kara at Laapa, inside Nyangatom territory. One Kara was shot dead. The Dus group now left Galgida and moved to Ukuule, further inside Nyangatom territory. Two months later, the people of Kuchur decided to leave their village until the next cultivation season. They departed, leaving most of the harvest of that season in the fields and granaries. Some went to Kopriya, 20 kilometres west of Kuchur, and the rest to Lorutuk, 40 kilometres south. Both places are in Nyangatom territory.

Conclusion: the drifting ethnicity of the Koegu

Group coalitions of the type described here play an important material and political role in the survival strategies of the inhabitants of the lower Omo and, as Sobania (1988) notes, elsewhere as well. As suggested in the case of the Koegu and the Kwegu, another function served by the ties formed between such minor groups and their larger and more powerful neighbours might be to reinforce the ethnic identities of both partners. These relationships are based on the 'consent', as Turton (1986: 158) put it, of the minor group to be stigmatized and subordinated. In return, the subordinate groups receive protection. Such a relationship can last only as long as the underlying reasons for it exist. The Koegu–Kara union disintegrated because it no longer had a *raison d'être*. By contrast, the developing Koegu–Nyangatom union resulted from the need of the Nyangatom pastoralists to find a partner in an area where they had recently moved in large numbers, and the permanent need of the Koegu for protection.

I would like to reconsider from this point of view some factors which caused the disruption of the Koegu–Kara relationship.

1 There was a reciprocal dependence based on the bond partnership between the two groups. It was functioning well and stabilized their connection while ivory was an important item in local trade in the Lower Omo. The Koegu received protection from the Kara against other groups, such as the Nyangatom and the Mursi. After the ban on hunting elephants, the *belmo* partnership lost its substance.

2 The Koegu and the Kara had a common enemy in the Nyangatom, at least till the 1970s. The situation changed after the Nyangatom obtained automatic rifles and the military balance shifted accordingly. The Kara could no longer defend the Koegu against the Nyangatom.

3 The Dus group of the Koegu, who were no longer regarded as foragers, began to graze their goats and sheep on the west side of the Omo, while the Kara did the same in the east. An element of competition now entered their relationship, which also involved arable land.

The long-standing relationship between the Koegu and the Kara was broken, but this does not necessarily mean the Koegu were asserting their identity independently of ties with any group. Their alliance with the Nyangatom was consolidated through the conflict, but this was not the first close contact between the two groups. They had been associated with each other for a long time, and their new relationship was formed in this historical context. Assimilation, as I have called the Koegu–Nyangatom relationship, was thus strengthened and promoted through the conflict. This relationship appeared to be a step in a process leading to the Koegu becoming part of the Nyangatom.

Notes

1 Research upon which this paper is based was supported by the International Research Programme of the Ministry of Culture, Education and Science of Japan. The study was included in the projects on 'Comparative Studies on Agro-Pastoral Societies in Semi-arid Africa: Northeast Africa', in 1986, and 'Comparative Studies on the Systems of Subsistence Economy in North-East Africa: Folk Models and their Application', in 1988–9. Fieldwork was undertaken under the auspices of the Institute of Ethiopian Studies, Addis Ababa University. I am grateful to Dr Katsuyoshi Fukui, leader of the projects, and Dr Taddesse Beyene, Director of the Institute of Ethiopian Studies, for support and advice.

61

2 Recorded in an interview with Lale Aila, an elderly Kara at Dus, on 11 February 1987.
3 Recorded in an interview with Aiko, a middle-aged Koegu at Kuchur, on 4 July 1989.

References

Almagor, U. (1978) *Pastoral Partners: Affinity and Bond Partnership among the Dassanetch of South-west Ethiopia.* Manchester: Manchester University Press.

Bender, M.L. (1975) *The Ethiopian Nilo-Saharans.* Addis Ababa.

—— (1976) Introduction. In M.L. Bender (ed.), *The Non-Semitic Languages of Ethiopia.* East Lansing, Michigan: Michigan State University.

Bender, M.L., Bowen, J.D., Cooper, R.L. & Ferguson, C.A. (eds) (1975) *Language in Ethiopia.* London: Oxford University Press.

Bryan, M.A. (1945) A linguistic no-man's land: the Sudan–Ethiopia border. *Africa,* **15** (4).

Hieda, O. (1991) *Koegu Vocabulary, with a Reference to Kara.* Kyoto: African Study Monographs, suppl. 14, Kyoto University.

Lydall, J. (1976) Hamer. In M.L. Bender (ed.), *The Non-Semitic Languages of Ethiopia.* East Lansing, Michigan: Michigan State University.

Matsuda, H. (1988) Riverbank cultivation in the lower Omo valley: intensive farming systems of the Karo, southwestern Ethiopia. *Africa-Kenkyu* (Journal of African Studies) **32** (Japanese).

—— (1991) 'Annexation' and 'assimilation' of ethnic groups: inter-ethnic relations around the Koegu, southwestern Ethiopia. In *Africa-Kenkyu,* **38** (Japanese).

—— (1992) The dance among the Koegu of Ethiopia: identity and interethnic relations of the forager. *Bulletin of the National Museum of Ethnology* **17** (1) (Japanese).

Muldrow, W. (1976) Languages of the Maji area. In M.L. Bender (ed.), *The Non-Semitic Languages of Ethiopia.* East Lansing, Michigan: Michigan State University.

Sobania, N. (1988) Fishermen herders: subsistence, survival and cultural change in northern Kenya. *Journal of African History,* **29** (1).

Tornay, S. (1979) Armed conflict in the lower Omo valley, 1970–1976: an analysis from within Nyangatom Society. In K. Fukui & D. Turton (eds), *Warfare among East African Herders.* Osaka: Senri Ethnological Studies, no. 3, National Museum of Ethnology.

—— (1981) The Nyangatom: an outline of their ecology and social organization. In M.L. Bender (ed.), *Peoples and Cultures of the Ethio-Sudan Borderlands.* East Lansing, Michigan: Michigan State University.

Turton, D. (1986) A problem of domination at the periphery: the Kwegu and the Mursi. In D. Donham & W. James (eds), *The Southern Marches of Imperial Ethiopia: Essays in History and Social Anthropology.* Cambridge: Cambridge University Press.

Turton, D. & Bender, M.L. (1976) Mursi. In M.L. Bender (ed.), *The Non-Semitic Languages of Ethiopia.* East Lansing, Michigan: Michigan State University.

4 The Evolution of Ateker 'New Model' Armies: Jie & Turkana
JOHN LAMPHEAR

One stereotypical image of Eastern Africa is that of a stalwart herdsman leaning on his spear (never his musket or rifle!), as he gazes stoically into the distance. Indeed, a number of valuable studies have convincingly demonstrated that firearms played little if any role in the military organization or tactics of many East African pastoral and semipastoral communities (Fukui & Turton, 1979). And yet, over the past couple of decades, significant numbers of those same communities have become increasingly reliant on large stores of rifles, and those weapons have made a profound impact on social, economic and military structures. This has contributed, in turn, to a tragically endemic climate of violence which has beset many parts of the region.

This chapter suggests that in some cases the process of militarization among pastoral peoples has roots going back a century. This vital era of transition, corresponding to the period when outside intruders first appeared in this region, has received relatively little scholarly attention. Specifically, this chapter will investigate the nineteenth- and early twentieth-century experience of two closely related Ateker communities of the eastern Nilotes, the Jie and the Turkana, in order to determine why each was to develop a military structure and an attitude towards outside military technology and organizational forms sharply different from the other.[1] In the process of this analysis, it is hoped that some light may be shed on broader processes of military transition that have been going on in this region for some time, and continue today.

At the beginning of the nineteenth century, many ancestral Jie were part of a rather loose 'cultural confederation' of disparate peoples living in central Karamoja of Uganda. Some, mainly

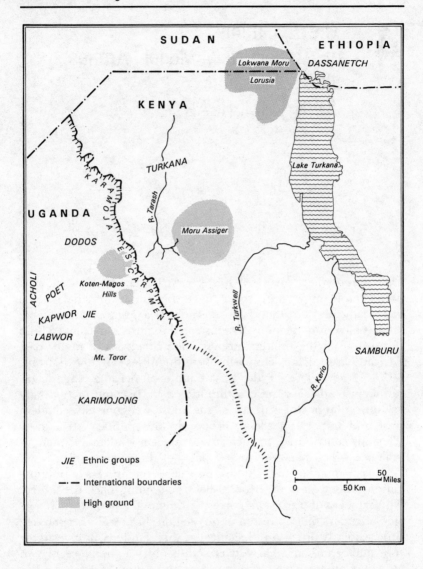

Map 4   Jie and Turkana

descended from an early Ateker group based on the Koten-Magos hill country further east, were essentially pastoralist. Others, derived from a more westerly branch of the Ateker, appropriately nicknamed *Ngikatapa*, 'bread people', subscribed to an economy featuring grain agriculture, and had experienced considerable earlier interactions with Luo-speakers. Associated with both groups, and rapidly being assimilated by them, were bands of Kuliak hunter-cultivators, remnants of several earlier non-Ateker populations. Apart from sharing a pit of sacred clay, subscribing to a common emblematic totem and engaging in various economic interactions, there was apparently little sense of community, as each group adhered to its own line of hereditary fire-makers, who served as the main source of its own separate identity (Lamphear, 1976).

Oral tradition suggests that military activity during the earlier part of the nineteenth century was limited. Only two specific clashes are recalled. In the first, a western people, the Kepwor, was decimated, partly by the raids of ancestral Jie, but even more by severe drought and famine. About a generation later, another group, the Poet, also were defeated, many being assimilated into the fledgling Jie community. Military co-operation between the disparate Jie elements, as well as ongoing internal population movements, led to closer societal integration. For the first time, a common name, 'Ngiro', which had deeply cosmological associations with 'Longiro', the legendary Ateker cradle land in Sudan, was adopted by the community as a whole. This closer association stopped short of complete political unity, however, as each Ngiro subgroup continued to maintain separate, though very similar, political, military and religious institutions (Lamphear, 1976).

In the meantime a number of other Ateker communities, including the Dodos, Karimojong, Toposa, Dongiro and Turkana, had been going through their own processes of coalescence. By the mid-nineteenth century, the Ngiro were becoming uncomfortably aware of the growing unity of the Dodos to their north and the Karimojong to the south. By then, all the Ateker groups had developed economies with important pastoral elements, and competition for resources, exacerbated by a deteriorating ecological environment and expanding population, was becoming acute, leading to steadily escalating conflicts. For a while, belts of no man's land in some areas helped to defuse tension. In the grasslands around Mt Toror in the south, treaties called for an equitable sharing of resources between Ngiro and Karimojong. Soon, however, Karimojong cattle camps began monopolizing the Toror grazing, and even thrust into some areas of permanent

65

Ngiro settlements. At the battle of Nangodiai, remembered by tradition as the largest single engagement fought up to that time, the Ngiro managed to hurl the Karimojong back from Toror. But their victory was short-lived, and the Karimojong soon regained complete domination of the Toror area. By about 1870, they were co-ordinating further attacks with the Dodos, with the avowed intention of eliminating the Ngiro altogether. Collectively outnumbering their rivals by perhaps four to one, it might well have seemed that the Karimojong and Dodos would succeed.

But despite the grim determination of raiding parties, which swept through many parts of the Ngiro country 'like a fishing net' — giving the campaign its name, *Apetai* ('everywhere') — desperate and confused fighting ended when a Karimojong contingent fell into a trap at a river ford and was wiped out. Disheartened, Karimojong and Dodos raiders fell back on their respective territories, but they carried with them much live-stock and other booty. In reflection of the annoyance they felt towards their numerically weak but tenacious neighbours, the Karimojong and Dodos began referring to the Ngiro as *Ngijie*, 'the fighting people'. Instead of resenting the nickname, intended as a scornful reference to their truculence, the Ngiro accepted the name with pride and even began calling themselves 'Jie'. Reflected in this acceptance was a stronger sense of unity and corporate identity than had ever existed before. Forced to re-adjust both settlement and grazing patterns, much of the Jie com-munity now became much more spatially compact than before. For defensive reasons many people abandoned the old system of isolated individual homesteads, for a new one in which hundreds of homesteads banded together into giant complexes surrounded by stout defensive barricades.

From the late 1870s until the 1890s, the beleaguered Jie were given a respite from the frequent raids as a terrible series of epizootics decimated herds and seriously weakened societies throughout Karamoja. By the later 1890s, however, an economic revival prompted a renewal of the attacks and, although Jie dogged resistance had just barely preserved their community in the past, their continued survival as an independent entity now looked very precarious indeed.

As the Jie ethnogenesis thus proceeded in Karamoja, that of another Ateker society, the Turkana, was taking place to the east, presenting both similarities to and differences from that of the Jie. Tradition portray the Turkana as the eastern vanguard of the Ateker, descended from clans that broke off from the old

Koten-Magos concentration to push down the rugged escarpment which now marks the Uganda–Kenya frontier. At the head-waters of the Tarash River the emigrants formed an association with Ngikatapa 'bread people', and perhaps a few far-ranging, Bantu-speaking elements. In pushing eastward to the Tarash, the ancestral Turkana had arrived at a dramatic ecological and cultural frontier. Sprawling out before them, arid plains charac-terized by scant rainfall and searing heat, dropped steadily down to the shores of Lake Turkana. Except in a few favoured locales, cultivation was impossible. This hard country was inhabited by communities radically different from any the Ateker had previously encountered. The Turkana saw these strangers as 'red people', partly because of their lighter-coloured skins and partly because they liberally smeared themselves with ochre. Their languages and many aspects of their cultures and economy were utterly unfamiliar. As strange as the people themselves were some of their livestock, exotic creatures with long necks and humps on their backs — the first camels the Ateker had encountered.

Initially, the early Turkana appear to have lived as a compact group subscribing to a common generation-set system, although they also experienced close and essentially peaceful interaction with neighbouring peoples. By the end of the eighteenth century, impelled by ecological and demographic pressures, conflict devel-oped with a group of strangers, the Siger, a loose, multicultural confederation of Cushitic-, Maa- and Southern Nilotic-speakers. These Siger represented a surviving pocket of 'old-style' pastora-list, often associated in many oral traditions with the nearly legendary 'Sirikwa', who herded a distinctive type of longhorned black cattle — probably cervicothoracic-humped Sanga cross-breeds. The Ateker and a few other East African peoples, in con-trast, appear rapidly to have been developing a 'new pastoralism' based on their early possession of hardy thoracic-humped Zebus, much more resistant to heat stress, drought and disease. Even as Turkana cattle camps, coveting their highland pastures, began to encroach on the Siger, much of the Rift Valley region was seized by the terrible *Aoyate* drought, which decimated the Siger herds and led to the rapid disintegration of their community. Many of the survivors were absorbed by the Turkana (Lamphear, 1988).

At about the same time, rivalry was also developing with another foreign population, the numerous Maa-speaking 'Kor', who lived in close pastoral association with various Cushitic-speaking peoples. All of them herded a variety of livestock, but the Cushites specialized in camels and the Kor in cattle, including some of the same hardy Zebus kept by the Ateker. Like the

67

evolving Turkana, the Kor and their allies withstood the *Aoyate* drought better than the Siger, and also absorbed many of the latter as their community collapsed. Holding most of the arid plains beyond the Tarash, the powerful Kor alliance must have seemed a serious barrier to any further Turkana advances.

And yet Turkana rapidly began pushing out from their Tarash footholds, forcing the Kor and their allies eastward to the shores of the lake, and then moving south to gain control of the vast region between the Turkwel and Kerio valleys. Other advances drove north to occupy additional areas, including highlands stretching into southern Sudan. While some traditions give the impression that this dramatic expansion was essentially a military one, in fact it certainly derived from a complex combination of factors, including vital commercial relations which kept the Turkana supplied with a constant flow of ironware and grain. In some cases large numbers of aliens apparently opted, for various reasons, to 'become Turkana' *en masse*, making the process of expansion as much the spread of a culturolinguistic system as a direct armed invasion (Lamphear, 1988).

Early Ateker military structures

It seems clear that a certain bellicosity accompanied the ethnogenesis of the Jie and Turkana communities, and certainly many superficial aspects of their cultures had begun to display a strong military ethos. Their tough, mobile life styles evolved rugged individuals, expert in the handling of weapons. Great social and psychological value was attached to a wide array of symbols reflecting military achievement. Men with outstanding martial skills might rapidly gain superior economic, and even limited political, status.

Just below the surface, however, was a much less martial environment, featuring military systems which were in many respects decidedly rudimentary. Overall, these systems were quite typical of those found throughout pre-colonial Africa. Divisions between the army and the general community, for example, were indistinct, and military affairs blended so thoroughly with political, economic and religious matters as to make them virtually inseparable. Fighting men were paradigmatic citizen militiamen, with every able-bodied man being mobilized for conflict on an *ad hoc* basis, and then reverting to 'civilian' roles of herdsmen at the cessation of hostilities (Welch, 1975; Uzoigwe, 1977; Tornay, 1979).

In the Ateker version, the generation-set system provided some basis for military organization, and its graded hierarchy gave a vital sense of 'rank' and *esprit de corps* to its members, while assigning to the congregation of senior elders the direction of military affairs. In some instances, specific age sets might even correspond to nascent military units. Ideally, for instance, by the time they were trying to protect their country against Karimojong and Dodos incursions, Jie armies were supposed to be arranged by age sets. 'The senior age set would be placed in the centre, with the others formed up to the right and left. The army would advance towards the enemy like the fingers of a hand, with each finger being one age set.'[2] In actual practice, however, ideal formations were seldom achieved and, even when they were, most raiding parties and larger forces quickly dissolved into little more than armed mobs: 'there was no special arrangement [for armies]. Everyone would go together in one big group.' Individual bravery and initiative were greatly admired and a man of outstanding courage and military skill could become a 'battle leader' to whom a small band of men — usually his age-mates — might attach themselves as a kind of 'private company'. Thus, even the largest armies were merely 'aggregations of individual heroic warriors'. Most military activity took the form of intermittent raiding rather than anything like large-scale campaigns, and typically it stemmed from a desire to capture livestock, to gain access to natural resources or, perhaps most commonly, simply to gain a military reputation and prestige (Dent, 1977; Parker, 1988).

Nor was the generation-set system a very effective mechanism for mobilizing martial activity. On the contrary, elders usually stood in opposition to the younger men's aggressive tendencies, which might lead to unwelcome expansion of conflict and even undercut the authority and pre-eminence of the older men. 'War', Paul Baxter has remarked, 'was too serious a matter to be left to the young.' The generation system, therefore, provided a vital means by which elders could exert authority over truculent juniors and impose strict limitations on warfare itself (Almagor, 1979; Baxter, 1979; Galaty, 1987). As a result, strategic and tactical goals tended to be notoriously vague. Moreover, while tradition might sometimes describe the goals of military action in terms of the 'extermination' of rival communities, it is clear that assimilation, not annihilation, was usually the rule.

Beyond this, it is apparent that many military 'victories' such as that of the Jie over the Siger were attributable at least as much to the deteriorating ecological environment as to actual force of

69

arms. With the Ateker, and for that matter apparently with virtually all other East African pastoralists and semipastoralists, an outward emphasis on martial trappings masked an elementary military system verging more on 'militarism' — the vast 'array of customs, interests, prestige, actions and thoughts associated with armies and wars and yet transcending true military purposes' — than on what Western military historians term 'the military way': an efficient 'concentration of men and materials on winning specific objectives of power' (Vagts, 1959).

Indeed, conflict was often governed by a code of military etiquette, with clashes often resembling a chivalrous tournament rather than serious warfare, as the following Turkana tradition concerning the era of their dramatic 'expansion' demonstrates:

[The Turkana age set] Tiira . . . were brave men. Wherever they went, they swept away enemies. Once, when they were at Morungole, one of them went to Moru Assiger. There he met some men of the Karimojong age set called Wapeto, who were also good fighters, and he said to them: 'You are a famous age set like Tiira. But nothing can be thrown on our shields.' The Wapeto answered: 'No, we can throw something on them.' And so 30 of the Wapeto came to fight the Tiira. They said: 'Are we enough?' The Tiira answered: 'No.' So the Wapeto returned with 70, but they were still not enough. Then they returned with 80 or 90, and they were enough. The Tiira took their army to Moruelongot and fought the Wapeto there. The mountain was named Morulongot, 'the mountain of the penis', that day, because one man was speared in that part of his body. All the Wapeto were killed, except about 12, who escaped and climbed up *Moruangikilok* ['the mountain of men', so named to honour the Wapeto survivors]. The Tiira surrounded the mountain, and then the Wapeto surrendered all their possessions. The Tiira let them go, telling them to go and greet their people, and tell them what had happened to them here in Eturkan (Turkanaland).

With the Jie, the scope of conflict certainly expanded as the pressure from their Karimojong and Dodos rivals increased in the later nineteenth century. Actions such as the battle of Nangodiai and the *Apetai* campaign may well have involved much larger numbers of fighting men and an intensity of combat rarely, if ever, experienced by other Ateker communities up to that time. But even here the highly segmentary nature of Ateker military organization, with the fundamental reliance on personal courage and independent action, is plain, as is reflected by traditional accounts of the action at Nangodiai:

The fighting was very confused, with everyone just fighting together. It was difficult even to be sure who was a friend and who was an enemy . . . the place where that battle was fought is still called *Nangodiai* [from *akingodia*, 'to mix up people in one place'].

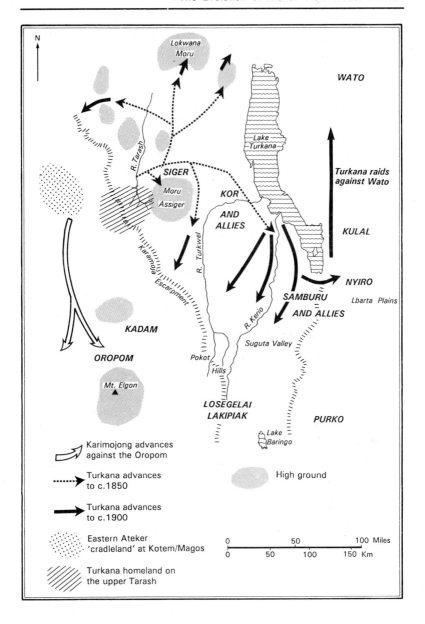

Map 5   Karimojong and Turkana expansion in the 19th century

The evolution of Jie and Turkana 'new model' armies

In the later part of the nineteenth century, however, both the Turkana and the Jie were to alter their military systems, substantially increasing their efficiency. With the Turkana, these alterations were intimately linked with the process of territorial expansion. As that expansion moved further and further afield to occupy the vast area west of Lake Turkana, their earlier sense of corporate identity had become progressively diluted. The once compact community rapidly was becoming a loose confederation of local territorial sections, distinguished by distinct differences in dialect, dress and other cultural features. This was especially true for those sections which had incorporated large numbers of Siger and other strangers. The generation-set system had provided a sense of cohesion for a while. During the earlier stages of the expansion it had been possible to convene the entire congregation of senior elders in a single location, where decisions affecting the whole community could be made. As the advances progressed, however, such concerted action became impossible and generation-set activity came to be focused on the individual local sections, leading to a progressive decline in the status of the senior elders.

Concurrently, the initial momentum of the Turkana expansion began to slow. In northern and some southern areas it had stalled along natural highland frontiers, but to the east, in the vicinity of the lake, it was caused by the more determined resistance of the Kor and their allies, who previously had been falling back before Turkana raids, incorporating Siger and other displaced people as they went. As Turkana internal integration began to decrease, that of their rivals had increased and, in the face of incessant Turkana pressure, the latter had coalesced into the Sampur (Samburu), Ariaal and Rendille communities, who now presented powerful barriers to any Turkana advances beyond the Kerio River.

This growing resistance was at least partly responsible for some fundamental changes to the generation-set system. As we have seen, the system had been a decidedly inefficient means of mobilizing young fighting men. Basic contradictions between biological and generational age caused many men to remain uninitiated until middle age or later. Because of this, the Turkana and other Ateker societies had permitted any male, regardless of initiation status, to go off on raids:

Anyone, even the uninitiated, could go and fight . . . What would uninitiated men eat if they just remained at home? Does the stomach distinguish between men?

But, although they could raid, uninitiated men did not belong to a corporate age set, whose close-knit organization, *esprit de corps* and precise rank in the generation-set hierarchy provided an important basis of Turkana military activity. As the congregation of senior elders began to lose some of its former status and generation-set activity became more locally focused, biological principles increasingly took precedence over generational ones. Even the previously fundamental alternation of 'father–son' generations was ignored, so that young men of the 'proper age' of initiation — about 20 — were initiated regardless of generational status. A more effective system for the universal mobilization of young fighting men into corporate units began to evolve. Initiation now became closely linked with raiding activity, with the inauguration of new sets tending dramatically to increase military activity, as groups of newly initiated men, anxious to prove themselves, roamed through the countryside joining raiding parties wherever they found them. The very appearance of such bands often provided, in itself, the inspiration for raids (Muller, 1989; Lamphear, 1992). These changes, however, were hardly sufficient to keep Turkana expansion from being stymied by the Sampur alliance for some time at the Kerio.

After the middle of the nineteenth century, the expansion did finally resume, but only under the leadership of a powerful diviner (*emuron*, pl. *ngimurok*) named Lokerio. Among all the other Ateker communities this office was a minor one. As an important office it was more typically found among other Nilotic-speakers, such as the Maasai and Lwo, where powerful diviners sometimes supervised age-class systems and directed raiding activity. While their offices were primarily religious, a number of East African diviners had begun to build an authority during the nineteenth century that was decidedly political, even to the extent of becoming 'emergent centralizing figures' (Munro, 1975). Some traditional accounts claim that Lokerio's line of diviners, the Meturona, had been important since the earliest settlements on the Tarash, and suggest that they had given the Turkana a sense of selfhood for some time. It is likely, though, that such tales were fostered *ex post facto* following Lokerio's rise to prominence, to claim that only he played a significant role in the process of Turkana expansion. Unquestionably, it had been the congregation of senior elders who provided the essential focus of Turkana corporate identity and leadership for the expansion.

The decline of the senior elders created something of a power vacuum in an increasingly acephalous political environment, which Lokerio sought to fill. Through various religious ceremonies, Lokerio gradually gained great influence over the altered age system and even assumed decidedly executive functions, providing tactical direction and strategic co-ordination to raiding activity. Using an efficient system of messengers working in relays from one section to another, Lokerio now mustered larger armies than had been assembled in the past. The misgivings about the escalation of conflict which had been a powerful constraint on the congregation of senior elders did not apply to Lokerio the diviner. On the contrary, he began to reap a rich reward of captured livestock, which victorious armies paid to him as his fee for blessing and directing them. Military activity also became more sustained than before, with raids pushing ahead virtually without interruption. Relentless forays surged across the Kerio. The Sampur and their allies gave way before the Turkana, who pushed right around the southern tip of the lake and up its eastern shore, capturing great numbers of livestock, especially camels. According to a widely known tradition, Lokerio's mystical powers were the chief ingredient in the Turkana success:

Lokerio . . . commanded the lake to make a dry path through the water so the Turkana could go over and capture camels from those people on the other side of the lake. So the Turkana drove those camels back along the path, and then Lokerio commanded the water to close behind them.

On another level, this tradition can be seen to convey, via the popular motif of the magical crossing of waters, the idiom of societal transcendence, in this instance a kind of *rite de passage* by which the Turkana now assumed a new collective identity focused on Lokerio. In the process, Lokerio had transformed his office into a new form of diviner altogether, the 'Diviners of God' (*Ngimurok aakuj*) or 'Great Diviners', whose authority extended throughout every Turkana section.

At this point, the same series of epizootics which had beset the Jie and the other societies of Karamoja from the late 1870s to the 1890s also decimated the communities neighbouring the Turkana, though not the Turkana themselves. In fact, of all the pastoral societies of the eastern Lake Turkana basin, only the Turkana escaped the full ravages of these disasters. Neighbouring peoples, terribly weakened, were driven back from a few more areas on the periphery of the country already controlled by the Turkana. By the late 1890s, the Turkana had gained access to virtually all the territory that would ever be regarded as *Eturkan* (Turkanaland).

In the meantime, Lokerio had died, to be succeeded by one of his sons, Merimug. Obviously impressed by the authority

Lokerio had accrued to his office of Great Diviner, several other contenders now presented themselves as rivals to Merimug. The most successful of them, Lokorijam, a man of the Katekok clan, rapidly built a reputation in parts of western Eturkan, where he took over the blessing and direction of armies. By the late 1890s, after the sudden death of Merimug, Lokorijam had gained a full ascendancy and was exerting a leadership for the Turkana almost equalling Lokerio's.

But the powerful sense of unity derived from Lokerio had been seriously eroded as Merimug and Lokorijam struggled for power, and it was even further diminished when a bitter succession dispute broke out after Lokorijam's death in about 1903. By that time, many of the frontiers of Eturkan, while still fluid and ill defined, were showing signs of a marked 'stabilization'. In some areas, close interactions between the Turkana and neighbouring peoples blurred the still rather fragile ethnic identities. Accentuating those notoriously transitory group distinctions typical of East African pastoral societies, such interactions were rapidly evolving new bicultural and bilingual communities in some areas. Even along actively contested frontiers, such as that with the Sampur to the south of the lake, conflict mainly took the form of 'reciprocal raiding', a military balance where intermarriage and other peaceful contacts were becoming common (Lamphear, 1992).

As the Turkana thus appeared rapidly to be disintegrating into a loose 'cultural confederation' or, even more likely, a whole collection of such confederations at the turn of the twentieth century, the Jie by that time were on the verge of being overwhelmed and forcibly assimilated by their powerful Karimojong and Dodos neighours. As the terrible effects of the epizootics finally began to ebb in the late 1890s, there had been a major resurgence of hostilities. At the very end of the century, the Jie barely managed to repulse a serious Dodos incursion at the battle of Tiira.

Unlike the other Ateker societies, where tactical leadership was entirely wielded by individual battle leaders, there existed in the Jie military system an important potential refinement in command structure: the office of hereditary war leader (*ekapalon kaajore*). Theoretically regarded as overall commander of all military forces, in practice the war leader's actual authority had always been minimal. Strategic planning, such as it was, was exercised by the congregation of senior elders, religious preparations were the province of fire-makers and diviners, and tactical

75

leadership was monopolized by the battle leaders in command of their largely autonomous private companies. The hereditary leader, therefore, was little more than a figure-head whose overall control was distinctly minimal: '[Before about 1902] Jie armies had no special leaders, except for those brave men who encouraged others by their example [the battle leaders].'

Present at the battle of Tiira had been Loriang, the new hereditary war leader recognized by most Jie divisions, who had just succeeded to the office after the death of his half-brother. The battle had taught him a valuable lesson in military organization and tactics. He had been dismayed at how slowly fragmentary bands of reinforcements had trickled in from various parts of Najie (Jieland). Clearly the military organization based on age sets and the small 'private companies' of individual battle leaders was dangerously inadequate to effect a rapid and large-scale mobilization. Soon after the battle, therefore, Loriang began designing an entirely new organization based on most of the territorial divisions, which, since the defeats of the 1860s and 1870s, had been jammed together in a rather compact area. Intuitively understanding the importance of 'interior lines', Loriang suggested that contingents be formed from the kinsmen and neighbours of each division to ensure a much quicker mobilization of large forces to combat the attacks of the Dodos and Karimojong.

Ironically, however, the first test of Loriang's reorganization was not against either of these enemies, but against the Acholi, the agricultural western neighbours of the Jie, with whom previously good relations had deteriorated during the great disasters. By 1902, several Acholi kingdoms were acquiring muzzle-loading muskets from long-distance traders and, armed with this new technology, they launched a massive army of at least 2000 men against the Jie. The Jie of the Chaichaon area against whom the attack was focused managed to hold back the Acholi through sheer courage and bravado until, with amazing speed and efficiency, Loriang's new territorial division 'battalions' arrived, one after another, to shore up a fragile defensive line. The Acholi army, with some of their muskets malfunctioning because of wet powder, lost all semblance of order and fled. Drawing all of his battalions into a unified force, Loriang then led a methodical, well-coordinated pursuit which turned a successful defence into a stunning victory. The Jie, outnumbered at least four to one and armed entirely with traditional weapons, had utterly crushed the largest army they had ever faced (Lamphear & Webster, 1971).

With this great victory accomplished, Loriang pressed ahead

with further military reforms. He devised an offensive formation for his new territorial division 'battalions' in which each had its own place in a battle line, anchored on the flanks by the two divisions which had seen the most conflict with the Karimojong and Dodos in the past. The old organization based on the generation-set system was not entirely abandoned, however, and Loriang's plans called for each battalion to be internally arranged by age sets, at least in offensive actions. This organization, as it subsequently functioned in combat situations, was described by elders who in their youth were part of it:

The Jie army was really arranged by territorial divisions. Each division was arranged as its own small army within the big army. But age sets were also important. That is, the younger men were in the front of each battalion because they could move well and run quickly. The older men who could not run so quickly, but who had fought many times, came behind. Sometimes the plan would be for the young men to attack the enemy and then suddenly break off and rush away, as though they were beaten. The enemy would chase them. Then the older men, who had concealed themselves to the rear, would jump up from their hiding places and ambush the enemy, who would be surrounded and defeated.

Loriang also took steps to reduce the authority of the individual battle leaders and thereby centralize the command structure:

Loriang forbade small groups of warriors to go on raids of their own, as they had done in the past. He made all the warriors of every territorial division come together to one place to form one army which he himself led. Before his time, armies had been small and were never united, and they were always defeated.

Other innovations included the establishment of a system of messengers to streamline the mobilization of the battalions, and the creation of a crack bodyguard of the best fighting men. Many of these men were the same battle leaders whose independent authority Loriang had reduced, and their incorporation into the bodyguard seems to have soothed the ill-feeling some may have harboured. He also instituted a rather complex chain of command. Each battalion had its own commander, personally selected by Loriang, who was responsible both for its mobilization and for leading it in battle. Subordinate to the commanders, and chosen by them, were a number of junior officers. Loriang himself, armed only with a sacred stick, commanded operations from the rear of the battle line, surrounded by his bodyguard, which functioned as a tactical reserve. Another innovation was the creation of a 'home guard' force, recruited mainly from junior age sets, but also probably including uninitiated adult men and elders, to guard Najie and the cattle camps while the main army was on campaign. In addition, he incorporated large numbers of teenaged boys into the army to serve as porters and drovers, and to gain valuable military experience. But perhaps Loriang's greatest contribution was to bring several western territorial divisions, known collectively as the Rengen, whose military forces had always functioned separately from the rest of the Jie, effectively under his command, thus signalling the fullest degree of Jie integration yet achieved. With the incorporation of the Renge, Loriang was able to mobilize a force of perhaps 500 fighting men, by far the largest army the Jie/'Ngiro' had ever fielded.

In addition to these tactical and organizational changes, Loriang also introduced an entirely new strategic outlook. While the battle of Chaichaon had proved that Loriang's new organization could offer effective protection to the settled parts of Najie, outlying settlements and the far-ranging cattle camps remained vulnerable to attacks and raids. To Loriang the answer to this problem was obvious: his battalions would go on the offensive and vigorously carry the war for the first time to the countries of his enemies. In this, the Jie apparently resembled other spatially restricted pastoral communities, who frequently tended to adopt offensive strategies to keep hostilities as far from their frontiers as possible (Almagor, 1979).

Employing the offensive version of the new tactical organization to perfection, Loriang's army won a rapid series of victories against the Karimojong and Dodos. All the grazing lands around Toror were regained, and the Karimojong were forced to abandon many of their northern settled areas. Vast numbers of livestock and other booty were captured, and the brilliant success of Loriang's forces, together with his outstanding diplomatic skills, rapidly began to attract allies. The Labwor, Luo-speaking neighbours and friends of the Jie, sent contingents to join Loriang, as did the very same Acholi kingdoms which had earlier attacked Chaichaon. Perhaps another 250 men were thus added to their Jie forces, many of them musketeers, with a few riflemen. Having so handily defeated the Acholi musketeers at Chaichaon with traditional weapons, the Jie themselves had been little impressed by the military potential of firearms. Although Loriang now permitted the inclusion of Acholi and Labwor musketeers in his army — more to swell his numbers than to augment his fire-power, it might be argued — he discouraged the use of firearms by his own men, and very few Jie employed them, despite the fact that ivory traders, who now roamed through Karamoja, sometimes brought such weapons as trade items. Nevertheless, the allied musketeers did play a role in battles against the Karimojong in 1909 and 1910, presenting rolling volleys to cover the Jie attacks and retiring behind the protection of the shields of Jie spearmen to reload.

This marked the pinnacle of Loriang's military career. While the Jie community was desperately in need of an able, charismatic leader, and while the office of hereditary war leader provided the avenue for Loriang's rise, his individual military genius, as reflected by his innovations, is clear. Tradition credits him with the very survival of the Jie community as an independent entity. Other traditions — Jie, Karimojong and Dodos alike — suggest a certain deterioration of the unity of enemy societies in the face of incessant Jie offensives, and show that their own military systems remained old-style, fragmentary ones. It is also clear that Loriang's authority began to impinge somewhat on that of the hereditary fire-makers and the congregation of senior elders. The former, who were enjoined by custom not to play any important role in warfare, continued to provide foci of religious and political homogeneity for their respective major divisions, but in some ways they were now overshadowed by Loriang, whose military leadership transcended major divisions to embrace the Jie community as a whole.[3] Similarly, Loriang progressively assumed the main direction of strategic policies, which formerly had been the exclusive concern of the elders.

Nevertheless, both institutions continued to be important and influential even at the height of Loriang's power. Indeed, it is important to emphasize that all of Loriang's innovations were accomplished only by first gaining the active support of the congregation of senior elders. Although under Loriang's dynamic leadership the office of hereditary war leader was accorded some real authority, it still remained distinctly subordinate to that of the elders:

After he became the war leader, Loriang would give presents of beer or even oxen to the very old men — those who walked with sticks. He did this to get their permission to do the things he wanted to do. No war leader before Loriang ever did these things, and no war leader before him ever led all the Jie in one army, as Loriang did.

It was at this dramatic point that the vanguard of the British colonial administration suddenly appeared in Karamoja. Although marked by the bullying and intimidation, and in the case of the Karimojong by a grim demonstration of 'gunpowder diplomacy', typical of the imperial advance, the British quickly began playing a role similar to that of an intermediary society in a pre-colonial setting. In the main, their early relations with the Jie were marked by peaceful diplomacy. Quite probably, the military expansion of the Jie had gone about as far as was possible, or desirable, by the time of the British arrival, in any case, and, from a logistical perspective, Loriang's campaigns were already becoming overextended. The Jie therefore accepted the conditions of the *pax britannica*, by which they were assigned an administrative unit dubbed 'Jie County', which included all the territory — some of it never traditionally part of Najie — effectively under their control by the end of Loriang's offensives. As was so often true under the colonial order, an ever stronger sense of 'Jie-ness' was now created by the imposition of rigid boundaries and the invention of a hierarchy of government chiefs (Davidson, 1989).

With the death of Loriang shortly after, the congregation of senior leaders re-emerged as an important focus of Jie identity and unity and, in the face of strict prohibitions against raiding, the office of hereditary war leader progressively lost much of its pre-eminence. There was a strong revival of military activity in the 1950s and 1960s, however, when Atom, Loriang's grandson, used the office once again to assemble large, well-organized armies with some firearms, for huge raids on the Karimojong. Such activity was curtailed again after independence, as the vigorous presence of Ugandan army contingents precluded the marshalling of large forces. By the 1970s, a military system focused on small-scale raids undertaken by individual battle leaders and their 'private companies', and under the close direction of the senior elders, had resumed.

The experience of the Turkana in the early twentieth century was in many respects dissimilar to that of the Jie. Even as Lokorijam was usurping the office of Great Diviner, as noted above, groups of strangers — Swahili, Ethiopians and Europeans — had begun appearing tentatively in some parts of Eturkan. From the start there were a few clashes with Ethiopian and British expeditions, but most Turkana remained untouched by them. By the turn of the twentieth century, however, Lokorijam, who had built an ascendancy similar to Lokerio's, was becoming concerned by reports of British conquests in other parts of East Africa. Similar to diviners in other societies, Lokorijam sought to disguise the identity of his family and warned his sons not to engage in the direction of military action, by now the hallmark of the Great Diviners. In a dramatic ceremony just before his death, Lokorijam put forward one of his retainers, Kokoi Loolel, an aspiring minor diviner of the Pucho clan, as 'the head of the spear', a surrogate to insulate his family from the British onslaught. Presented with this opportunity to monopolize raiding activity, Kokoi rapidly proved himself a very capable leader, and quickly built up a loyal following. One of Lokorijam's descendants, an illegitimate son named Koltieng, became so envious that he ignored his father's instructions and started organizing raids of his own. The two men now entered into a determined competition to gain universal acceptance as Diviner of God and, as each gained his own clientele, their rivalry led to further deterioration of Turkana corporate identity.

In the meantime, the military forces of the British East Africa Company had established themselves in southern sections of Eturkan. In these areas the Turkana were prohibited from raiding, and a series of harsh 'punitive expeditions' were launched to force compliance. By about 1912, the British had come to regard the competing diviners as the greatest impediments to the extension of their control, both because they continued to direct raids and because they sought to bring religious retribution against those Turkana who were assisting the colonial administration. Koltieng and another of Lokorijam's sons were relentlessly pursued and imprisoned. With the elimination of his major competitors, Kokoi, staying beyond the imperial reach, was left as the unrivalled claimant of the office of Diviner of God. As he won this ascendancy, Kokoi established great influence over the leading Turkana war leaders, who exercised actual tactical command over the fighting men. None of these men had the hereditary status or even the nominally universal authority that Loriang's family was accorded by the Jie, but several of them had built wide regional reputations, and one, a man named Ebei, was increasingly attracting recruits for his raids from virtually every part of the country.

During the early stages of the British conquest, however, the Turkana hardly displayed a very unified reaction. Some elements actively assisted the imperialists, but most sections remained defiant, relying on their mobility to stay outside the grasp of imperial authority, though seldom exhibiting any real co-ordination in their responses. In an arrangement all too typical of colonial arbitrariness, the northern sections of Eturkan had been assigned to the Uganda Protectorate, which, unlike British East Africa in the south, had been slow to establish control. As a result, the vanguard of the steadily advancing Ethiopian empire had made considerable headway there. After an initial phase of bad relations, the Ethiopians established a loose, informal presence that amounted more to an alliance than imperial domination.

Increasingly, therefore, the north provided a haven for dissident southern Turkana. Even Kokoi and Ebei took refuge there about 1913, and a flood of embittered southerners arrived there two years later, after an especially large and brutal British expedition had ravaged the south. The Ethiopian alliance now came to dominate Turkana military affairs, as gun dealers began supplying considerable numbers of rifles, and officers promised the direct support of Ethiopian troops to contain the British advance. For a while, Kokoi's potential role was eclipsed and his office failed to provide the same source of military leadership it had done under Lokerio or Lokorijam. Although now accepted as Diviner of God by a majority of Turkana, he began to devote himself essentially to non-military activities, such as healing and employing mystical injunctions against the British and their levies.

By mid-1917, however, it had become plain that the Ethiopian alliance was not protecting the Turkana very effectively, and the defeat of an Ethiopian contingent by a much smaller British force seriously eroded Turkana confidence. Ultimately, they decided they must fall back on their own resources and, as they had done in the past, turned to the Diviner of God to assert this leadership over martial affairs. While the circumstances were extraordinary ones, and the stress of military escalation unparalleled, the time was ripe for Kokoi to perform a function for his people similar to that provided by his illustrious predecessors. Together with several of his most powerful war leaders, headed by the charismatic Ebei, who became his 'field commander', Kokoi now undertook a sweeping remodelling of the Turkana army. Kokoi's resumption of the direction of military affairs almost immediately encouraged huge numbers of fighting men to assemble. British reports and Turkana tradition alike indicate massive forces of 4000 or 5000 forming by the end of 1917.

While these armies were tremendously larger than those of the past, the methods used to raise them were essentially traditional ones. Having identified some rival community as a raiding target in a dream, Kokoi's messengers would move throughout the country spreading the word. Ebei, who was usually given overall tactical command of the armies, would then commence a formal recruiting tour to gather fighting men. Once assembled, the army would begin moving towards its goal, usually a southern enemy, to be joined by other contingents *en route*. As much as possible, commissariat matters were also handled in time-honoured ways. Wealthy elders would be asked to supply oxen for meat along the route of the army, with the understanding they would be compensated after the victorious army's return. Sometimes an army would drive a small herd of livestock with it, slaughtering the animals as needed once friendly settlements were left behind, and individual men carried various rations with them as well.

The huge size of the Turkana armies of 1917 greatly exacerbated logistical problems. It was simply impossible for several thousand hungry men moving together as a corporate group to subsist off the limited resources of the Turkana deserts for any considerable length of time. The solution — to which armies who live off the land often have to resort — was to divide the army into smaller units and keep some distance between them, so as not to put too great a strain on any one area. Unencumbered by supply trains or extraneous equipment, and conditioned to moving long distances in the blazing heat of Eturkan, Turkana armies were astoundingly mobile. Ebei's veterans asserted that they commonly marched up to 65 miles a day, taking a short rest in the evening, and even continuing to advance throughout the night whenever there was sufficient moonlight.

There were also important changes in strategy and organization. Strategically, there was a new emphasis on far-ranging offensive actions, designed to drive crippling attacks deep into the territories of those communities allied with the British, and to lure small parties of imperial troops out from defences into the open. Organizationally, a body of men known as 'Ruru' now assumed a vital role in this new model army. Originally the name of one age set of Kokoi's forces, the name rapidly came to be applied to a significant part of the army: 'The Ruru were not just an age set; they were that large group of people from many areas who were the army.' Most of Ebei's lieutenants were said to have been Ruru, and some sections of the Ruru were known by the names of their commanders: 'Nathura was a war leader of the Ruru, and so part of them were known as *Ngikanathura* [those of Nathura, or Nathura's men] to honour him.'

The Ruru were always the quickest to respond when an army was being formed, and most Turkana who had acquired firearms — various patterns of breech-loading rifles — were in their ranks. They maintained a very close association with Ebei, who frequently brought them together for meat feasts, and would use such occasions to discuss the current military situation and to drill them in tactics and the handling of weapons, apparently in a conscious attempt to make more effective use of the new military technology being supplied by the Ethiopian traders. By 1917, therefore, the name 'Ruru' had come to designate a hard core of inveterate, well-trained and well-armed opponents to British rule, upon whom Ebei and Kokoi could always depend when forming a military expedition. Indeed, they were rapidly becoming a semipermanent military force.

In pre-colonial Turkana and Ateker societies, the generation-set apparatus worked against the formation of such a force. In times of conflict, the elders staunchly opposed any escalation of hostilities which might result in young fighting men forming themselves into something approaching a professional military class, and thereby asserting a degree of independence from gerontocratic authority. With the alteration of the age-class system and the ascendancy of the diviners, the Turkana were much less bound by such constraints, and age sets now began to take on aspects of military units. None the less, the nature of 'reciprocal raiding' which underlay traditional warfare still worked against undue escalation. But the British were not traditional enemies. Their concept of warfare and methods of fighting were much closer to 'total war' than anything the Turkana had experienced. As the escalation of hostilities against so relentless a foe continued, neither the elders nor any other element of Turkana society could effectively counter this trend. Instead, Kokoi and Ebei sought to exploit it as best they could.

Many of the Ruru, their families wiped out and livestock confiscated by British expeditions, found themselves in desperate circumstances, forcibly uprooted from the traditional Turkana mode of life. In the past, such individuals had taken refuge with Kebootok cultivators, Bochoros fishermen or some neighbouring society. Now, in the altered circumstances of the burgeoning colonial era, membership in the Ruru offered an alternative 'safety valve'; many rallied to Ebei and Koki and acquired firearms.

In the latter part of 1917 and on into 1918, the huge new model armies struck hard at the 'pacified' societies of British allies to the south and west. After one campaign, part of an army mainly composed of Ruru riflemen did not disperse and return to their homes, but remained in the field for some months methodically carrying out a series of additional forays on their own account. For armies to continue operations so long was virtually unheard of among the Turkana or other East African pastoralists, and was symptomatic of the degree to which the Ruru were becoming a professional standing force. In several clashes with colonial troops, the Ruru exhibited a discipline and persistence British officers found remarkable. 'Anyone who has come into contact with Turkana riflemen takes them very seriously indeed; they are brave men, skilled in battle and stand modern rifle fire well' (Rayne, 1918).

To meet the Turkana threat, British authorities finally assembled in mid-1918 one of the largest and best equipped expeditions ever to be sent against an East African society. In several engagements British officers were again impressed by the disciplined tenacity of the Ruru, comparing their effectiveness to that of regular troops. In one battle, the Ruru even held an entrenched defensive line and fought an almost continuous action for nearly 24 hours against an advancing British column — hardly the traditional 'hit-and-run' tactics of East African pastoralists (Lamphear, 1992).

But, despite such heroic resistance, the Turkana suffered heavy human casualties and debilitating livestock losses during the expedition, and in other actions for several years thereafter. One after another, most northern Turkana sections were forced to surrender. A last pocket of inveterate resistance, including the Ruru, many of the war leaders and Kokoi himself, sheltered in the northern mountains for a few years. The Ruru, however, by now a bona fide military élite, increasingly began acting in a bullying, high-handed manner, challenging the authority of the elders and even of Kokoi. As British confiscations reduced the supplies of firearms and made it nearly impossible for the last pocket of Turkana resisters to secure replacement weapons and ammunition, the Dassanetch, their powerful northern neighbours across the southwestern frontier of Ethiopia, had steadily been gaining in fire-power and military strength. Friction between the two peoples escalated into war in 1924, with disastrous results for the Turkana. In a battle in which both sides used large numbers of rifles, the Ruru were nearly obliterated and most of the leading war leaders, including Ebei, were killed. In the aftermath, the few remaining Turkana dissidents were forced to accept British protection. Among them was Kokoi, whose authority had dwindled badly. He died a tragic death awaiting trial in a British prison.

Fearing a similar fate, no other claimants to the office of Great Diviner dared emerge during the colonial period, and the senior elders, while still revered, were unable to regain the authority they once had. As with the Jie, the creation of a Turkana administrative district and a system of government chiefs, reinforced by a strict 'closed district' status, helped to maintain an ongoing sense of Turkana unity, albeit very artificially.

In the absence of any countervailing traditional authority, the 'Moroko', a semipermanent force of men well armed with rifles who stayed in highland areas beyond the reach of the administration, became the ultimate heirs of the Ruru military tradition. After independence, a descendant of Lokorijam began directing some of their raids until his arrest by the government. As they acquired even larger stocks of rifles in the 1970s and later, the

Moroko began functioning as a self-appointed 'defence force' along the Ugandan and Sudanese frontiers, extracting tribute from their own people for proffered 'protection' and acting in a brutally overbearing manner, ignoring the orders of government chiefs and the traditional authority of the elders and diviners alike.

Conclusion

While the foregoing narrative shows that military activity often played an important role in the creation and maintenance of Jie and Turkana identities, their initial ethnogenesis apparently entailed little actual military conflict. It was other factors which helped foster a basic sense of political, religious and economic integrity, discernibly stronger at first for the Turkana than the 'Ngiro'. It was from such basic integrity that each group began to build a 'notion of power' it could test in relationships with other communities, and in many instances warfare progressively became the most useful formula for gauging such relationships (Blainey, 1973). As conflicts increased during the early nineteenth century, both the Jie and the Turkana found existing Ateker military structures inadequate to cope with greater demands. In particular, those structures had two major deficiencies, both related to the age-class system. In the first place, the system did not provide an effective basis for military organization or mobilization and, in the second, the congregation of senior elders tended to stand in firm opposition to military escalation, placing strict limits on the scope and conduct of warfare. Therefore, as each community steadily developed a stronger sense of unique identity, it sought to reform the earlier structures in its own distinct way.

While brilliant and far-ranging, Loriang's military changes emanated essentially from traditional structures. Possibly they were linked to broad military adaptations being made by societies in many parts of East Africa during the nineteenth century which owed little, if anything, to outside influences. Because of cosmological constraints derived in part from their perception of themselves as 'the centre' of their universe, the emerging Jie community was consistently resistant to radical changes, and tended to cling to venerable political and religious forms. Thus, fundamental perceptions concerning the status and role of the army remained basically constant despite Loriang's innovations. Except, perhaps, for the creation of his personal bodyguard, there was little in Loriang's adaptations that fostered élitism. Fighting men continued to be thoroughly integrated into the wider society and in harmony with its interests.

Likewise, Jie conservatism at least partly underlay their reluctance to adopt firearms. As with other societies who continued to favour traditional weapons over imported Western technology, the decisive Jie victory at Chaichaon left them with a poor assessment of muzzle-loading weapons. There was simply no incentive to adapt the grimly effective system forged through Loriang's brilliant innovations to the alien weaponry. While Loriang managed to increase the authority of his office of hereditary war leader to effect a certain centralization of the Jie military system and a closer community-wide integration, the senior elders withstood the potential threat posed by his emergent authority to maintain ultimate control over the political apparatus. Vital to this process was the Jie decision to avoid armed conflict with the forces of British imperialism, and their ability to manipulate the *pax britannica* to reduce the exterior military pressures of their traditional rivals (Guy, 1971; Low, 1975; Lamphear, 1989).

Another factor at work here was the type of outside technology potentially available to the Jie during their process of military transition. While various observers have reached sharply different views concerning the impact of Western military forms on traditional African armies, it does seem clear that muzzle-loading muskets and rifles of the sort to which the Jie mainly had access were in most cases particularly ill suited to basic African concepts of war. Military historians such as Geoffrey Parker (1988) and William McNeill (1982) have wryly observed that, while violence was arguably the chief export of Europe before the surge of imperialism in the late nineteenth century, it had been impossible to export the military system which underlay that violence. African military structures, featuring individual heroism, informal tactics and militia-like organizations, were patently unable to imitate rigid European armies, which were typically composed of brutally disciplined, conscripted and mercenary musketeers. Alien technology, where it was borrowed at all, tended merely to be grafted loosely on to traditional structures, and then almost exclusively by the more centralized African states. With a few exceptions, such weaponry was simply not compatible at all with the more acephalous systems of pastoral peoples.

In contrast to the Jie, the early Turkana community was born from a process of determined expansion across dramatic ecological and cultural frontiers. As large numbers of non-Ateker strangers were incorporated, many of their economic and political forms were adopted by the burgeoning society. It is quite likely, for instance, that the changes to the Turkana age system were inspired by Maa-speaking assimilates, resulting in a more effective mobilization of young fighting men. In addition the new age organization apparently helped break down ethnic distinctions between 'original' Turkana and those more recently absorbed, providing an internal integration rather similar to that derived by Nguni-speaking peoples from their age-regiment system. All of this combined to produce a community which regarded itself more as 'an expansion' than as 'the centre', and which was therefore freed from the same sorts of cosmological constraints that bound the Jie to traditional forms.

But the integrative aspects of the new age system were not enough to offset the simultaneous dilution of Turkana corporate unity inherent in the very process of territorial expansion itself. As local territorial units assumed a greater importance and the status of senior elders declined, the Turkana lost a vital index of their group identity. Such decentralization in turn helped pave the way for the emergence of the Diviners of God (again possibly inspired by Maa-speaking strangers), who began to perform an even stronger centralizing function.

Their emergence was intimately linked to military matters. To fill the power vacuum caused by the decline of the elders, the diviners adopted a strategy focused on gaining control over the new age system. By establishing religious authority over observances vital to the preparation of armies for conflict, they also effectively exploited the 'militarized economic acquisitiveness' basic to the process of raiding itself. As they established co-ordination over the age system, the diviners rapidly created a new military efficiency, approaching in some respects a Zulu-like model of nascent age regiments at the disposal of emergent centralizing figures. As the working alliance between diviners and age sets increased, so too did their propensity to become 'instruments of primordial nationalism'. In particular, the office of diviner now provided a familiar point of reference to assist the smooth assimilation of Maa- and Cushitic-speaking strangers. Indeed, it is clear that by the time of Lokerio, allegiance to his diviner provided the essential basis for classification as a 'Turkana'.

Ironically, this new unity and centralization proved transitory as Turkana expansion and concomitant military activity began to abate. The steady evolution of bicultural communities along many of the fluid frontiers greatly diluted the sense of community bestowed by the ascendant Great Diviners, while the succession disputes between claimants to the office produced serious internal dissension. During the early stages of the colonial conquest, internal cohesion diminished even further. While relatively few Turkana actually allied themselves with the imperialists, the various sections developed their own uncoordinated strategies to deal with the intruders.

The latter stages of Turkana resistance, in contrast, witnessed profound changes in the military system resulting in a powerful, though temporary, revival of centralized authority and group solidarity. With the deterioration of the Ethiopian alliance, Turkana sections which previously had sought accommodation with the British now joined with those who remained defiant, and rallied to Kokoi Loolel as he and the war leader Ebei began their military innovations. By 1917, Kokoi was mobilizing huge armies for his far-ranging, carefully co-ordinated attacks on 'pacified' neighbouring societies and even against British forces. A significant aspect of these new model armies was the development of the Ruru corps of riflemen, who steadily began to emulate something of Western military technology and methods.

By now, a military technology strikingly different from the earlier muzzle-loading weapons was beginning to reach even the remotest sections of East Africa. The new breech-loaders, utilizing metallic-cased smokeless powder cartridges, constituted a bona fide military revolution. Not only did they represent a tremendous technological refinement, but they were in many respects more immediately compatible, socially and culturally, with African modes of warfare. Here were weapons that no longer required the same rigidly disciplined, compactly co-ordinated masses of men to be effective. Indeed, the European forces themselves, who first employed these new weapons, in their own internal conflicts and in the late nineteenth century wars of colonial expansion, were quickly forced to make dramatic changes to their existing military structures. Especially the colonial armies, responding to tactical and logistical conditions, began to adopt smaller fighting units, a more individualized and open style of combat, and a greatly enhanced mobility. Here, then, was a technology and a system which seemed, at least on the surface, much more in line with African ways of warfare.

A second circumstance also helped pave the way for revolutionary changes in the Turkana and many other African military systems. Typically, it was only after a serious deterioration of traditional military structures, especially when confronted by aggressive imperialist pressure, that firearms became effective additions to African armies. Likewise, expansive African raiding societies usually had to be forced to adopt an unfamiliar defensive tactical mode, before beginning to make significant use of guns. Thus, in the aftermath of the brutal British expedition of 1918, the Turkana found many of their fundamental military, social and economic institutions in shambles. Even Kokoi's massive new armies had shown themselves unable to withstand imperial fire-power, and his aggressive offensive strategy was effectively reversed. It was at this point that the role of the Ruru 'corps' took on a new urgency, and they came to bear a remarkable resemblance to strikingly new and different types of military units which appeared in many parts of Africa in similar circumstances. In almost all cases, these new units were to make a profound impact on their parent societies by facilitating dramatic escalations of hostilities, the emergence of centralizing and often monocratic authority and, in the short run, more effective opposition to imperial conquest. To an extent rarely, if ever, encountered in traditional Africa, such new forces, or at least important segments of them, also began to reflect aspects of the professional, standing armies of the West. Those men who acquired rifles rapidly came to constitute a military élite of 'professional specialists', again sharply dissimilar to traditional fighting men, as their new weaponry gave them a fire-power equal to vastly greater numbers of conventionally armed men.

In a majority of African cases, the final incentive for such changes stemmed from a sometimes quite desperate need to defend old and revered ways of life from the relentless assaults of imperialism. Ironically, however, the emergence of the new military structures usually had a different, even quite opposite, effect, of which the Turkana experience was typical. While the new armies might initially support the traditional centralizing authorities of their societies, in most instances they themselves eventually emerged as the dominant political force, especially as indigenous institutions continued to deteriorate in the face of colonial pressure. As they gained their inordinate power, these military élites increasingly violated social norms, even to the extent of extracting tribute and raiding their own people, creating a serious dissonance between themselves and their wider communities. As their social integration became increasingly fragile and tentative, they finally moved beyond the limits of the old order altogether.

Notes

1 'Ateker' replaces the term 'Central Paranilotes' that I used in some earlier writings. Other Ateker communities are the Karimojong, Dodos, Nyangatom, Toposa, Jiye and Iteso. The Turkana, numbering well over 200,000, are the largest Ateker group, while the Jie, for whom it is difficult to establish even an approximate population, are much smaller.

2 All traditional accounts cited were obtained through interview with members of the groups concerned.

3 It should be noted that Loriang's new 'battalion' organization based on local residential units may well have reinforced old notions of the relative autonomy of territorial divisions, and to an extent may actually have worked against the fostering of a broader 'national' identity.

References

Almagor, U. (1979) Raiders and elders: a confrontation of generations among the Dassanetch. In K. Fukui & D. Turton (eds), *Warfare among East African Herders*. Osaka: Senri Ethnological Foundation, National Museum of Ethnology.

Baxter, P. (1979) Boran age-sets and warfare. In K. Fukui & D. Turton. (eds), *Warfare among East African Herders*. Osaka: Senri Ethnological Foundation, National Museum of Ethnology.

Blainey, G. (1973) *The Causes of War*. New York: Free Press.

Davidson, B. (1989) *Modern Africa*. London: Longman.

Dent Ocaya-Lakidi (1977) Manhood, warriorhood and sex in Eastern Africa. In A. Mazrui (ed.), *The Warrior Tradition in Modern Africa*. Leiden: E.J. Brill.

Fukui, K. & Turton, D. (eds) (1979) *Warfare among East African Herders*. Osaka: Senri Ethnological Foundation, National Museum of Ethnology.

Galaty, J.D. (1987) Form and intention in East African strategies of dominance. In D. McGuinness (ed.), *Dominance, Aggression and War*. New York: Paragon House Publishers.

Guy, J. (1971) A note on firearms in the Zulu kingdom. *Journal of African History*, **12** (4).

Lamphear, J. (1976) *The Traditional History of the Jie of Uganda*. Oxford: Clarendon Press.

—— (1988) The People of the Grey Bull: the origin and expansion of the Turkana. *Journal of African History*, **29**.

—— (1989) Historical dimensions of dual organization: the generation-class system of the Jie and the Turkana. In D. Maybury-Lewis & U. Almagor (eds), *The Attraction of Opposites*. Ann Arbor, Michigan: University of Michigan Press.

—— (1992) *The Scattering Time: Turkana Responses to Colonial Rule*. Oxford University Press.

Lamphear, J. & Webster, J.B. (1971) The Jie–Acholi war. *Uganda Journal*, **35** (1).

Low, D.A. (1975) Warbands and ground-level imperialism in Uganda, 1870–1900. *Historical Studies*, **16**, 65.

McNeil, W.H. (1982) *The Pursuit of Power: Technology, Armed Force and Society since AD 1000*. Chicago University Press.

Muller, H. (1989) *Changing Generations: Dynamics of Generation and Age-Sets in Southeastern Sudan (Toposa) and Northeastern Kenya (Turkana).* Saarbrucken: Breitenbach Publishers.

Munro, F.J. (1975) *Colonial Rule in Kenya.* Oxford University Press.

Parker, G. (1988) *The Military Revolution.* Cambridge: Cambridge University Press.

Rayne, H. (1918) Turkana (Part II). *Journal of the Africa Society*, **18**.

Tornay, S. (1979) Armed conflict in the lower Omo valley, 1970–1976: an analysis from within Nyangatom society. In K. Fukui & D. Turton (eds), *Warfare among East African Herders.* Osaka: Senri Ethnological Foundation, National Museum of Ethnology.

Uzoigwe, G. (1977) The warrior and the state in precolonial Africa. In A. Mazrui (ed.), *The Warrior Tradition in Modern Africa.* Leiden: E.J. Brill.

Vagts, A. (1959) *A History of Militarism.* New York: Meridian Books.

Welch, C.E. (1975) Continuity and discontinuity in African military organization. *Journal of Modern African Studies*, **13** (2).

CAUGHT IN THE MIDDLE

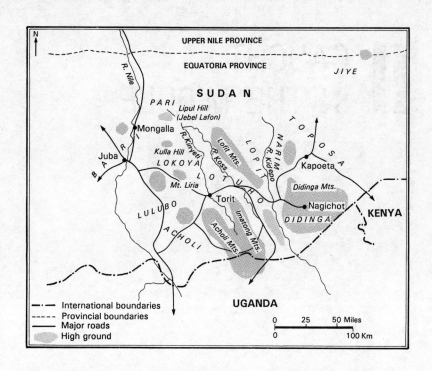

Map 6   Equatoria Province, Southern Sudan

5 Civil War & Regional Conflicts: The Pari & their Neighbours in South-eastern Sudan
EISEI KURIMOTO

The study of warfare is a recent interest in social anthropology, dating from the 1980s. It developed as a distinctive genre mainly in the United States, where a theoretical debate also arose concerning the causes of war (Ferguson, 1984; Haas, 1990; Ferguson & Whitehead, 1992). However, most of the work done falls within the established framework of anthropological study which focuses on 'tribal warfare' in the light of tradition and history. Studies of war in a contemporary setting, where marginal peoples struggle against the oppressive authority of a predatory state or against the menace of an external power, variously labelled as ethnic conflict, civil war or liberation struggles, are still rare. One instructive exception is Lan (1985).[1] It is an irony and a weakness of modern anthropology that it has failed to make this subject its concern, even though it is the reality in which a great number of the people in the Third World whom anthropologists study are trapped in.

Sudan is a country which has enjoyed only a brief period of peace since independence in 1956. In 1955, southern Sudanese soldiers at the Tori garrison mutinied and defected, an incident that began a process of political conflict that eventually developed into a full-scale war between north and south. The first civil war ended in 1972, and a southern regional government was established as the fruit of 17 years of struggle (Mohamed Omer Beshir, 1975). Dissatisfaction with partial autonomy and resentment of continued northern domination led to a second civil war, which began in 1983 with the establishment of the Sudan People's Liberation Army (SPLA) and its political wing, the Sudan People's Liberation Movement (SPLM) (Mawut, 1986; Johnson, 1988).

The current civil war, now completing its first decade, has deeply affected the whole Sudanese people, and those who live in eastern Equatoria province of southern Sudan, where I was engaged in research, are no exception. Since the end of 1984, when the SPLA began operating in this area, they have experienced many changes and disasters. Thousands of men joined the SPLA and became guerrilla fighters. On the other hand, many others were armed as government militia to fight against the SPLA. Tens of thousands of people were displaced and fled to Juba, the regional capital, and other towns, or to refugee camps in Ethiopia and Uganda.

How are we to analyse the present conflict in this area? Is it merely a new expression of old ethnic conflicts under the name of 'war of liberation'? Or should we see it as a struggle against oppression? What are the motives of the people who take part in this struggle? How is the civil war experienced by their communities? To what extent can we view the conflict in the context of indigenous social structures and values? In this chapter I shall try to answer these questions in the case of the Pari of eastern Equatoria among whom I conducted field research intermittently between 1978 and 1985.[2]

The Pari were heavily involved in the second Sudanese civil war. Out of a community of about 11,000 people, more than 2500 men joined the SPLA and became very active in its military operations. They played a significant role in the liberation of eastern Equatoria by the SPLA, and carried out attacks against neighbouring peoples such as the Lopit, Lotuho and Toposa. The Pari are rather exceptional in Equatoria, it should be noted, where many people had been reluctant to join the SPLA because it is thought to be dominated by the Dinka, the largest ethnic group in the south. It is important to note also that the military activities of the Pari were not always under the control of the SPLA. The armed Pari men operated as a semiautonomous unit, in whose operations not only SPLA-trained men but outsiders also joined. The autonomy of Pari behaviour in the midst of the civil war is one of the main themes of this article.

I shall try to describe the involvement of the Pari in warfare, and to account for the factors, both internal and external, underlying the active military role played by them. The chapter covers the period of the second civil war until 1990. More recent politico-military developments in the area, especially after the split of the SPLM/SPLA in August 1991, are outside its scope. Information for the period after July 1986, when I had to leave Juba in haste because of the approaching war, were obtained in two ways. One was through correspondence with a couple of Pari men in Juba and Torit. The other was through conversations with several Pari men and SPLA officers whom I met in Kenya and Ethiopia between 1986 and 1991. While conducting field research on the Anywaa (Anuak) in Ethiopia, I met a number of Pari refugees and SPLA officers, some of whom were well informed about the situation of the Pari at home.

The Pari and their neighbours

The Pari are a Lwo-speaking people (western Nilotes), who live at the foot of the Lipul hill (Jebel Lafon), a solitary mount in the savannah plain (Kurimoto, 1984, 1986a, 1986b, 1988). Since the Anglo-Egyptian period, their homeland has been called Lafon. Their neighbours are the Lopit in the Lopit mountains to the south-east, the Lotuho in the plain to the south, and the Lokoya around the Liria hill to the south-west. These three groups are generally called Lotuho-speakers (eastern Nilotes). The Bari (eastern Nilotes) live to the west along the Nile. Far to the east live the Toposa (eastern Nilotes). The most important mode of food production among these peoples, except the Toposa, is agriculture, with sorghum being the main crop, although pastoralism, fishing, hunting and gathering are also practised. Pastoralism is more important among the Toposa than among any of the others. It should be noted that the Bari and Lotuho also had a great number of cattle until the end of the last century.

The entire Pari community consists of six villages, which surround the Lipul hill like a chain. The rain chief or king is from the largest village, and his power is exercised over all villages, except one which is semi-independent. Age sets are formed on a village basis. They are organized into three age grades: youngsters (*awope*), the middle-aged or rulers (*mojomiji*), and elders (*cidonge*). The initiation ceremony of the new *mojomiji* is collectively performed by the Pari as a whole. The term *mojomiji* is the corrupted form of its Lotuho counterpart, *monyomiji*. *Mojomiji* of each village are responsible for the affairs of their own village. But, when a problem concerns the whole Pari, such as interethnic raids, war or severe drought, *mojomiji* of the six villages get together.

The *mojomiji* are a very strong corporate group. Generally speaking, their job is to maintain the welfare and order of society. The group is endowed with the right to punish a wrongdoer. When they have reached a conclusion that a person is the cause of drought, for example, they may kill him even though he may

97

be the rain chief himself. Some aspects of the judicial function of *mojomiji* have been preserved under the administrative structure of the Sudanese state. Another important function is to wage war and organize counter-attacks after an enemy raid.

The peoples of south-eastern Sudan were exposed to the outside world only after the 1840s, when navigation on the White Nile commenced (Holt & Daly, 1979: 67–70), though a trade link with the Oromo of western Ethiopia, in which the Pari presumably acted as middlemen seems to have existed earlier (Grüb, 1992: 42; Simonse, 1992: 44–5). Afterwards armed groups came from the north, such as slave-traders, soldiers deployed by the Egyptian rulers of northern Sudan, and later the forces of the Mahdiya. But the peoples of this region were never administered by any of these intruders, though they were often raided and looted by them. The Pari themselves were once attacked by Mahdist forces in 1897, but managed to repulse them.[3]

When Britain 'reconquered' Sudan, this region was included in the colonial administration. Initially, relations between the indigenous peoples and the colonial government were not friendly or peaceful. It took two decades for the Pari and their neighbours to be finally incorporated into the Anglo-Egyptian rule. There was considerable armed resistance by the people, against whom 'punitive patrols' were dispatched. In 1912, the Pari were attacked by government troops because they did not supply porters and food (Simonse, 1992: 131–2). Even after this 'punishment', it took another few years until the Pari finally became obedient to the colonial administrators.[4] Other peoples, such as the Lokoya and Lotuho, continued their armed resistance until 1918, when they were finally defeated and brought under control (Collins, 1971: 223–227; Simonse, 1992: 132–4).

Gaala is a Pari word which connotes all foreigners of lighter skin, both Arabs and Europeans, as well as residents of towns. Government is also called *gaala*, although *hakuma*, an Arabic word, is also used. The implication in the use of this term is that for the Pari successive rulers of the Sudan are just foreigners and their governments are also alien. To the Pari people all outsiders are enemies to a certain degree. Before the establishment of '*Pax Britannica*' under the colonial administration of Anglo-Egyptian Sudan, they used to fight against the Lopit, the Lotuho (especially the Loronyo village) and the Toposa. The Toposa and Lotuho are considered old foes whose military power and bravery are recognized, though the Pari love to boast of their own superiority. The Lopit are considered cowards who are not able to wage a war. With the Lokoya, on the other hand, the Pari have enjoyed friendly relations. It is significant to note that many age-set names of the two peoples are common, and succession by the new ruling age grade of the two societies takes place almost at the same time. The Lokoya see the Pari age system as a model to be copied.[5]

Of course, general hostility does not imply that there are no socio-economic relations between the Pari and their neighbours. On the contrary, the Pari trade sorghum and dried fish with them for goats, sheep, grain, pots and iron tools. During a time of hunger, this trade becomes more active. In order to survive when they are stricken by famine, the Pari migrate to villages of neighbouring people where food is available. Many of the Pari have 'bond friends' among the Lopit, Lotuho and Lokoya and even the Acholi, who live to the south of Lotuholand, at whose homes they can stay as guests. They also visit when there is no hunger.

Pari and the SPLA

During the latter half of 1984, small groups of SPLA guerrillas started moving secretly across the eastern part of eastern Equatoria. They presumably came from the Boma plateau on the Ethiopian border, where the SPLA had established a base. At that time, Pari people already knew the new civil war had started, but very few people knew even the name of SPLA. The organization known to them was the Anya-nya II. This was another movement whose goal is the secession of the south from Sudan, and which had started an armed struggle before the formation of the SPLM/ SPLA. In fact, these two movements had clashed and the Anya-nya II was defeated. Some of its forces were absorbed into the SPLA, while others were reorganized by the government as a militia still bearing the name Anya-nya II, to combat the SPLA. Though the SPLA began radio broadcasting in English and Arabic in October 1984, its message had not reached the Pari as few of them owned radios and most of them do not understand either English or Arabic. As a result, the Pari confused the Any-nya II with the SPLA. Even at this early stage, however, some young Pari men who lived in Juba came to know about the SPLA. They left Juba and walked a long distance to Gambela inside Ethiopia to find the guerrillas, and became the first Pari to join the SPLA. Most of them were secondary school graduates.

An SPLA battalion named Jandiya, more than 1000 strong, arrived at Lafon in January 1985. It had come a long way on foot from Gambela, and this was the first appearance of a sizeable SPLA unit in Equatoria. Many of its members, including the

99

commander, Major Arok Thon Arok, were Dinka. There were also Shilluk, Nuer, Murle, Anuak and some Equatorians among them. Relations between the Pari and the SPLA battalion were peaceful. When they first came, the guerrillas explained they had no bad intentions, and asked the *mojomiji* to supply food. They were given sorghum, cattle, goats and sheep. All trained oxen at the Lafon Rural Development Centre run by the Norwegian Church Aid (NCA) were taken and slaughtered by the SPLA. It was said that when they wanted more things such as sorghum beer and cocks, the SPLA fighters bought them with cash. They were well disciplined. The battalion stayed at Lipul hill for a week. On hearing that the Sudanese army was approaching, they moved southwards. Several hundred Pari young men went with them. They had joined out of their own free will, and not because of forced recruitment by the SPLA.

After the battalion had left, traders' shops, the police station and the Norwegian Rural Development Centre were looted and destroyed by the local people. All these were owned by outsiders, those called *gaala* by the Pari. My own small grass-thatched hut was demolished as well. However, the Lafon primary school and the dispensary built by the NCA were not damaged. I was shocked to see the ruins when I returned to the village in May 1985. Shops built strongly with stones and cement were so thoroughly demolished that it was hard to see where buildings had stood before. Such wanton destruction seemed to me unreasonable, and I thought at first that it was done in a fit of 'collective madness'. A Pari explained his people believed the coming of the SPLA would result in a situation of 'no government', as had been the case during the first civil war, and they destroyed all the things belonging to the government. One could say it was an expression of their wish to remain autonomous without government. However, the fact that 200 bags of sorghum stored by the co-operative association were seized and distributed by the *mojomiji* of the six villages might mean that the looting was controlled by the *mojomiji* and may not have been an uncontrolled mob action.

In the middle of February 1985, a unit of the Sudanese army came to Lafon in 15 vehicles. On its arrival, the Pari fled to the bush, fearing it had come to burn the village and kill them in retaliation for supporting the SPLA. Then, a delegation of *mojomiji* was sent, and the army commander explained they had come to attack SPLA forces now approaching the village. Unconvinced, many Pari remained in the bush for several days. The day following the army's arrival, news reached the Pari that the Jandiya battalion had arrived at a place about 15 kilometres from the hill. Since it had left Lafon a month earlier, it had trekked through Lotuholand and Acholiland while fighting against the army. It was now on its way back to the upper Nile by way of Lafon, having run short of ammunition and failed to set up a base in Equatoria. A delegation of *mojomiji* was secretly sent to ask the guerrillas not to come to the village, for if they fought with the army there, it would be a disaster for the people. The SPLA commander agreed, and the next day the battalion passed outside the village on its way north. The army did not attempt to stop them, and only opened fire after the guerrillas had passed. The Pari saw this as a sign of the soldiers' cowardice.

Afterwards the army arrested several Pari men, including a former government chief and the headmaster of Lafon primary school on the grounds that they were SPLA collaborators. Soldiers looted property from many homesteads. Most of the looters were said to be from the north, while some were Lotuho. Thus, the Pari saw this plunder in the traditional context of Afro-Arab and Pari–Lotuho enmity. The behaviour of the SPLA and the national army showed a great contrast, and there is no doubt that the Pari had more sympathy for the SPLA after these incidents. The SPLA battalion took along several hundred young recruits, and they were to become the first sizeable Pari contingent in the guerrilla army.

The Pari remained under army control until early 1986, when another SPLA battalion, named Tinglli, arrived in Equatoria. It had about 600 men, 400 of them being Pari who had joined the previous year. At the end of April 1986, about 70 Pari men from this battalion deserted and returned to Lafon. They made a surprise attack against the army unit stationed there, and forced it to flee to Torit. Soon, a force of the Sudanese army with tanks was sent from Torit to recapture Lafon. Many Lotuho men from Loronyo village — traditional enemy of the Pari — followed the convoy. The Pari understood that they were coming to plunder. By that time more SPLA fighters, most of them Pari, had arrived at Lafon. They ambushed the army convoy before it arrived and destroyed it. In this way the Pari were liberated, and they have been under SPLA rule since then. The people were happy with the 'coming home' of their young men.

The Pari were the first ethnic group in Equatoria to come under SPLA control. They have had very little trouble with the SPLA, unlike other groups in the area, which suffered looting and harassment by the rebels. There are several reasons for this. Firstly, the first Pari encounter with the SPLA was a peaceful one. Secondly the Pari were liberated by their own people.

101

Thirdly, it seems they had enough food to feed the guerrillas, and the *mojomiji* were strong enough to maintain friendly relations with the SPLA. Subsequently, more Pari men joined the rebel movement — up to 2500 of them, that is nearly all the young men of this ethnic group.

One case illustrates the autonomy of the *mojomiji* in their relations with the SPLA. Two Sudanese army soldiers who were stranded in Lafon after liberation were protected by the *mojomiji* and later escorted to a goverment-controlled area, instead of being handed over to the SPLA. One of them was the former commander of the garrison at Lafon. He was a Lokoya, a group traditionally on good terms with the Pari, and, while he was the commander, his conduct had been friendly. The other was a Baqqara Arab from the north, who used to walk around the village drinking and eating with people and was well liked by them.

War and ethnic conflict: 1986-90

In 1986, small units of the SPLA became active in eastern Equatoria. Convoys guarded by the Sudanese army were ambushed, and cases of plunder and harassment of villages were also reported. Most of these incidents were said to be the work of the Pari. This made the situation of the Pari community in Juba and Torit towns very sensitive. Anti-SPLA feeling was strong in Equatoria at the time, and it was being said: 'It is the Pari and Dinka who spoiled Sudan.' In May 1986, many Dinka civilians were massacred by a mob in Juba. In June, a Pari trader who came to Juba on a visit was killed by the army, and another was killed in Torit by Lotuho men after he had been questioned by the army. Two Pari boys on their way to their village from Juba were killed at Liria, a Lokoya village. For the Pari people now, travelling became increasingly difficult and risky, because not only the army and militias threatened them, but all their neighbours turned hostile as well.

In 1987, another large group of Pari from the SPLA, about 500 men, returned home. They had been recruited in 1986 from Lafon, and formed the bulk of the Sonke battalion. It is significant to note that their coming to Lafon was not ordered by the SPLA command. When they were supplied with weapons and ammunition, the Pari simply deserted. This was also true of the men from the Tinglli battalion who had gone back to liberate Lafon earlier. This does not mean the Pari had turned against the SPLA. They still regarded themselves as members of the movement and, in fact, in 1988 they were grouped by the SPLA into the so-called 'Lafon Task-force'.

After the liberation of Lafon, the Pari–SPLA became very active in attacks against government garrisons and neighbouring peoples. Three types of actions can be distinguished. One is a revenge attack organized by the *mojomiji* against hostile neighbours like the Lopit, Lotuho and Toposa, in which SPLA members as well as other Pari took part. It should be noted that many Pari men were given guns by the SPLA to protect themselves. Another type is an attack by a small group of Pari SPLA members, usually less than 100 men, against military posts. Most of these were carried out on their own initiative and without orders from the SPLA higher command. The last type of operation was conducted by the Lafon Task-force under orders from the SPLA command.

There were two incidents of the first type. In May 1986, the *mojomiji* waged war against the Lotuho of Loronyo village, in retaliation for the time when the Lotuho followed the army as it came to recapture Lafon, with the intention of looting the Pari. Part of Loronyo was burned and cattle were taken. The other incident occurred in February 1990. At that time there was hunger in the land, and Pari women were visiting Lopit villages in search of food. Several Pari women were killed, allegedly by Lopit men. The *mojomiji* immediately took action. They went and burned down three Lopit villages. In both cases, the Lotuho and Lopit did not retaliate.

A similar incident occurred at the end of 1990. Sixty Toposa militiamen came through Lafon from Juba on their way back to Toposaland. They had been trained by the government and were presumably sent to operate in Kapoeta, an area controlled by the SPLA. They asked the Pari for food. The *mojomiji* did not react until a leader of the Pari SPLA incited them to attack the Toposa militia because they might harm the Pari in the future. Indeed, the Toposa has raided Pari cattle camps four times between 1982 and 1985, and the Tinglli and Sonke battalions of the SPLA had clashed with them when they passed through Toposaland. The *mojomiji* assaulted them, killing 35 Toposa. The rest managed to escape.

There are many instances of the second type of Pari military action. In 1986, nine Pari SPLA men captured the Lainya post on the Juba–Yei road for two days, and in 1987 the same group seized Tamania Talatin, a market-place on the Uganda–Zaïre–Sudan border, for a day. In 1988, hundreds of them attacked military posts at Magwe, Palataka and Obou in Acholiland and liberated them. Another group went to Gumbo on the outskirts of Juba town, on the right bank of the Nile, to attack the radio station. Yet another group captured the post at the junction of the Juba–Torit and Juba–Nimule roads for some days. All these assaults were launched without orders from the SPLA command. Two battles with Toposa men can be put in the same category. When Pari men of the Tinglli batallion passed a Toposa village on their way home from Gambela in 1986, they asked for some cattle to eat and the Toposa complied. However, while the Pari were eating, they were attacked by Toposa men and a Pari was killed. The Pari then attacked the village. In 1987, when Pari men of the Sonke battalion were on the same journey, they stopped at Rwoto, a Toposa village, and also asked for cattle to eat. This time they were refused. The Pari became angry and assaulted the village. In both incidents there was serious fighting and many people died on both sides.

In 1988, the Lafon Task-force carried out two operations under orders of the SPLA commander of Equatoria. The Task-force had been formed that year in order to bring the Pari SPLA in Lafon under control. The Pari attacked Liria, but were repulsed by the army and Lokoya militia. They also attacked the post at Khor Inglis bridge between Liria and Torit, this time successfully. By early 1989, the SPLA had captured all the posts and towns on the eastern bank of the Nile, and had brought the entire region, except Juba, under its control. Independent Pari military activity was much reduced afterwards.

The Pari in regional politics

In 1984, a dozen years after the signing of the Addis Ababa Agreement, the position of the Pari in the southern regional government and the armed services (army, police, prison, wild-life), which provided most of the job opportunities available to educated southerners, was insignificant. Only a few people occupied higher positions. When we compare the Pari with other ethnic groups in the region, the difference becomes clear. The following Pari had senior posts. Dr Beneditto Nyikalo, who had a Ph.D. in architecture, was a director in the regional Ministry of Housing. Valente Upuri, a former Catholic priest, was a secretary in the regional assembly, and later became assistant director in the regional Ministry of Information and Culture. Augustino Ulwar was a colonel in the prison service, and Sebit Ukodi was a police captain. Dr Nyikalo was a member of the

Equatoria regional assembly from northern Torit constituency (including the Pari, the Lopit and part of the Lotuho) in 1986 and was a spokesman for the Pari in the political arena in Juba. It is significant that there were no Pari commissioned officers in the national army.

In order to understand the situation of the Pari we have to note two interrelated factors: their educational status, and their position during the first civil war (1955–72). This is because these two factors influenced power-sharing among southerners in the period following the implementation of the Addis Ababa Agreement. During the first civil war, the Pari remained relatively untouched, while most Lotuho villages were burned down by the Sudanese army and many people fled to Uganda. The Pari were attacked only once by the army and lost cattle, but their villages were not burned. Not many Pari joined the Anya-nya, although they were an important source of food for the guerrillas.

In 1971, the Pari rain chief and the *mojomiji* led 3000 of their men to the Anya-nya base in Acholiland and offered to join the rebels, but the offer was rejected. Some Pari felt this was because Joseph Lagu, the Anya-nya leader, and other Lotuho officers feared the Pari would dominate the movement. Be that as it may, the Pari felt they were ignored by a movement with which they sympathized. As a result of the Addis Ababa Agreement, many Anya-nya soldiers and officers were absorbed in the armed services and promoted, but there were no Pari among them. Two Pari who were senior Anya-nya officers did not benefit from this process, and this became a source of resentment at the results of the Addis Ababa Agreement.

A primary school was opened in 1939 at Lafon by Catholic missionaries, the Verona fathers. The church itself had been there since the end of the 1920s, and some boys had been educated at the Okaru mission school. These were the first educated Pari. The primary school was closed in 1964 when all missionaries were expelled from southern Sudan by the Abbud regime. After that, many boys were taken to Uganda to be baptized and educated. As a result most of the educated Pari between the ages of 30 and the early 40s had primary and intermediate education in Uganda. Very few were educated in Khartoum during the first civil war.

After 1972, local education was resumed by the regional government. By 1985 more than 100 Pari youths had completed intermediate and senior high school. There were very few girls among them. At that time only one Pari had a higher degree, and another two were studying at universities in Juba and Gezira. We may add those who became Catholic priests to the list of Pari intellectuals. Four Pari had become priests earlier, but two of them had abandoned this profession.[6] In the 1980s, it was very difficult for young men who had completed intermediate and senior high school to find a job or to continue their studies in higher institutions. Most of them were forced to return to their villages, and the rest stayed in the towns, still hoping for employment. Later, almost all of them joined the SPLA and played a leading role in its military operations. Many Pari who were employed in the regional administration and the Norwegian Church Aid also joined the SPLA. They also had few prospects for the future, and this may have been one of the reasons they joined the SPLA.

Between 1981 and 1983, the 'redivision' of the south into three regions became a major controversial issue. Many Equatorians who resented 'Dinka domination' of the regional government supported the division, but others were opposed because they were of the opinion that division would weaken the position of the south in relation to the central government in Khartoum. In 1983, Nimeiri proclaimed the division against the will of the majority of the people in the south. Only in Equatoria did public opinion support him. In the regional assembly, only the sole Pari member, Dr Nyikalo, and the Toposa members supported unity. This Pari–Toposa concurrence was short-lived. When a Toposa former member of the dissolved regional assembly was appointed minister in the new regional government of Equatoria, Toposa politicians became supporters of the new scheme. As a result, the position of the Pari in regional politics became isolated. Dr Nyikalo himself was made director of an aviation agency that existed in name only.

Pari age organization and the SPLA

In October 1988, the new *mojomiji* ruling age grade succeeded. The succession ceremony is called 'seizing the village' or 'taking out the head'. The new *mojomiji*, named Madan, took over from the old one, Anywaa. A *mojomiji* is called after the name of the most senior age set of the grade. The old *mojomiji* consisted of four age sets: Anywaa, Akeo, Maridi and Adeo. The new one consisted initially of two age sets, Madan and Morumaafi. The next two age sets, Bolish and Lidit, were to join the new *mojomiji* some years later, and they may have done so by now. Some 10 years after the succession, these last two age sets will be joined by two other junior age sets, Dringa and Teteu, and Madan and Morumaafi will retire into the elders' grade.

Anywaa succeeded their predecessors, Kilang, in 1977. By 1988 the age span of *mojomiji* was between 40 and 55 years. During the later years of their rule, their administration was considered weak and there was growing antagonism between the *mojomiji* and the youth. A couple of disasters fell on the Pari during this time, responsibility for which was laid on the inefficient rule of the *mojomiji*. First, the Pari were stricken by drought and hunger. From 1982 until 1986 there were continuous 'rain conflicts', in which three persons were ostracized and four were killed by the *mojomiji*. Three others ran away from the village after being threatened with death (Kurimoto, 1986b). Though Anywaa did all these things in order to restore the proper order of rainfall and thus to secure enough food, some youngsters told me the *mojomiji* had been deliberately preventing rain in order to retain power, since the succession ceremony cannot be performed in times of poor harvest.

Four Toposa raids between 1982 and 1985 were another disaster. Lots of cattle were lost and many Pari were killed. This kind of raid had not been experienced by the Pari for the last 50 years. To the great disappointment of the people, the *mojomiji* could neither recover the lost cattle from the Toposa nor wreak vengeance upon them. Neither did efforts by the police and regional government to mediate have any result.

It is a striking fact that, out of more than 2500 Pari who joined the SPLA, only about 10 were from the old *mojomiji*. Almost all were in the youngster age grade when they joined the SPLA. This is certainly not only due to age. In my opinion, antagonism between the age grades causing resentment and dissatisfaction on the part of the youngsters is a major factor explaining their mass enrolment in the SPLA. This point has been recently made by Simon Simonse, who argues that such antagonism plays an important role in regional politics.

Inter-generational rivalry continues to play a role in contemporary local politics. The radicalism that is characteristic for a generation that has recently risen to power may to some extent have been responsible for the acts of sabotage against the local representatives of the new government of the independent Sudan in 1954 and 1955 [*sic*]. It may also have been a base for recruitment for the rebel movement from the Lotuho in the late 1950s. During the second wave of fighting, around 1965, the Lulubo and Lokoya men enrolling in the Anya-nya on the whole belonged to age-sets which had not yet reached *monyomiji*-hood.

In the election campaigns for the Regional Assemblies in Juba, young candidates generally appealed to the old-time generational antagonism by presenting themselves as protagonists of a new generational style of rule. Support for the Sudan People's Liberation Army in the mid-1980s in some places on the east bank had a decidedly generational character. The support offered to the rebel army in Lafon mostly came from the younger age-sets that were particularly dissatisfied with the rule of *Anyua* which was blamed for the persistent drought. (1992: 177)

The Pari case seems to be typical. Military activities by the Pari SPLA were carried out particularly between 1985 and 1989, a period before and immediately after the succession ceremony of new *mojomiji*.

All the leaders of the Pari SPLA belong to the new generation, the Madan, Morumaafi, Bolish and Lidit age sets. For example, the leader of the group that captured Lainya and Tamania Talatin in 1987 was a Lidit. The leader of those who attacked the radio station at Gumbo was also a Lidit. The former commander of the Lafon Task-force was a Madan, and the present one is a Lidit. These leaders have completed senior secondary school, and were given the rank of first or second lieutenant in the SPLA.

In 1985, it was said that a new *mojomiji* was about to take over. They were already mature enough. But Madan had to wait three more years before they succeeded. During that period there was antagonism between the two age grades, but in the hierarchy of the age system the youngsters had no means to directly challenge and expel the *mojomiji*. In a meeting where the *mojomiji* discuss village affairs, the youngsters have no say, while elders may advise, support or accuse the *mojomiji*. They may not succeed unless the *mojomiji* agree to hand over power. What they can do is to demonstrate their power and strength so that the *mojomiji* will recognize they are strong enough to take over. In this context, joining the SPLA and obtaining weapons provided a chance for the younger men to show their power, something they did really well.

Pari male ethos is based on what Mazrui called the 'warrior tradition' (1975, 1977) though I am aware this concept should be applied carefully, as Southall (1977) advised. This tradition is cultivated and reproduced through the age organization. I am of the opinion that the military adventurism of young Pari in the SPLA is a modern version of the warrior tradition. The tradition itself may be modern, in the sense that it may have emerged or been reinforced in the turmoil caused by invaders in the region since the late nineteenth century. Pari boys start to test their physical strength in running, wrestling and hunting games. When they become teenagers, they start to hunt and to practise stick fights. An age set is the group for these activities. Pari hunting with members of their age set is not only a means to obtain meat, but is also an occasion to prove their bravery and manhood, as is the stick fight. On these occasions they hunt with spears, not rifles, and only four kinds of large animals — lions, leopards, elephants and buffaloes — are hunted. When they kill many animals, they carry as much meat as they can, leaving the rest in the bush. No one is called from home to take it. They take much pride in killing many animals. Each age set has its own songs to boast of its hunting achievements and its members' bravery. Each man is proud of the numbers of big game he has killed, something well known to his age mates. In fact, they say 'to go and count animals', meaning to go hunting.

A stick fight between age sets may be triggered by slight provocation. After a quarrel and a skirmish, they announce the fight, and the following morning gather at the dancing ground of the village. Many men and women, the young and the old, come to watch the fight, so the fighting skill, bravery or cowardice of each participant becomes known to the people. Neither the type of hunting described above nor stick fights are indulged in by the *mojomiji*. We might say that the military activities of the Pari in the SPLA are in a sense an extension of the warrior tradition cultivated in the age organization.

Conclusion

Eager to gain power and status both in the region and in their own society, Pari young men were frustrated in two ways. First, on account of Pari's marginal position in regional politics, they had little opportunity for advancement. Secondly, they felt oppressed by the *mojomiji*, who were unwilling to hand over power. These two factors must be considered part of the motivation for the mass enrolment of the Pari in the SPLA and the active military role played by them.

When we compare the Pari with other groups, the point may become clearer. For instance, the Lotuho had many men in the Sudanese armed forces, including some high-ranking officers. They also had highly educated people, who occupied senior posts in the regional government. Consequently, they were relatively reluctant to join the SPLA. The same thing can be said for the Bari, Lokoya and Acholi. On the other hand, peoples like the Lopit, Toposa and Narim, who were more marginalized than the Pari in the regional power structure and who had even less education, also had little enrolment in the SPLA. The Pari, whose position in the region is located in the middle of these two extremes, joined the SPLA in large numbers.

It seems true that the military conflict since 1984 has exacerbated existing 'tribal' or 'ethnic' hostility: Pari versus Lotuho, Pari versus Toposa, Dinka versus Mandari, and so on. However, we should not view these conflicts in a simple 'tribal' context. Although Pari–SPLA military activities were semiautonomous and based on their own ethnic ideology, they should be put in a wider regional and national context. In reality, it is impossible to assess the extent to which an ongoing conflict is motivated by ethnic ideology and group concerns on the one hand, and by regional and national concerns on the other. This is especially true in a situation where both the SPLA and the Sudanese government seek to manipulate 'traditional' ethnic antagonism for their respective advantage.

What is not clear is to what extent Pari men have been affected by the experiences related above. There was some effort to promote political and ideological indoctrination in the SPLA ranks, though this was not comparable with the effort made by other movements in the region, especially the Eritreans and Tigray. Hundreds of Pari men travelled to other parts of Sudan and even Ethiopia and met with different peoples. All these are bound to have an effect on the Pari, but what it will be only time will tell. For the time being, the new *mojomiji* appear to have satisfied their desire for power. They had become the rulers of Lafon, and had established military superiority over their neighbours. How long this situation will last in the turmoil of the Sudanese civil war is another question that must remain unanswered at present.

Notes

1 For Africa, David Lan's pioneering work *Guns and Rain* (1985) gives a moving account of how peasants perceived their involvement in the liberation struggle in Zimbabwe. On the current civil war in the Sudan, Akira Okazaki's paper (1992) describes how the Gamk responded with ritual to the 'power' of the SPLA. Carmack (1988), Manz (1988) and Wilson (1991) are relevant studies of war in Latin America.

2 Time spent in Pari amounted to 10 months, while about 14 months were spent in Torit and Juba towns.

3 Sudan Intelligence Report, nos 118, 134, Intel. 6/4/15 (1904, 1905), National Records Office, Khartoum. Uganda Protectorate Intelligence Report, no. 23, Appendix D (1904), Uganda Archives, Entebbe.

4 Sudan Intelligence Report, no. 212, Appendix, Intel. 6/7/23 (1912). National Records Office, Khartoum.

5 This kind of resonance in age organizations among neighbouring ethnic groups should be seen in a wider regional context (Kurimoto, 1992; Simonse, 1992).

6 One of the remaining priests is in Khartoum, and the other became the Bishop of Torit while the SPLA was in control of the town.

References

Carmack, R.M. (ed.) (1988) *Harvest of Violence*. Oklahoma University Press.

Collins, R.O. (1971) *Land Beyond the Rivers: the Southern Sudan, 1898–1918*. New Haven, Connecticut: Yale University Press.

Ferguson, R.B. (ed.) (1984) *Warfare, Culture, and Environment*. New York: Academic Press.

Ferguson, R. & Whitehead, N.L. (eds) (1992) *War in the Tribal Zone: Expanding States and Indigenous Warfare*. Santa Fe, New Mexico: School of American Research Press.

Grüb, A. (1992) *The Lotuho of the Southern Sudan: an Ethnological Monograph*. Stuttgart: Franz Steiner Verlag.

Haas, J. (ed.) (1990) *The Anthropology of War*. Cambridge: Cambridge University Press.

Holt, P.M. & Daly, M.W. (1979) *The History of the Sudan: From the Coming of Islam to the Present Day*. London: Weidenfeld & Nicolson.

Johnson, D. (1988) *The Southern Sudan*. London: Minority Rights Group Report no. 78.

Kurimoto, E. (1984) Agriculture in the multiple subsistence economy of the Pari. In K. Sakamoto (ed.), *Agriculture and Land Utilization in the Eastern Zaire and the Southern Sudan*. Kyoto: Kyoto University.

—— (1986a) Traditional fishery among the Nilotic Pari of the southern Sudan. In K. Sakamoto (ed.), *Comparative Study of the Agricultural Production in the Upper Nile Area and the Great Lakes Area*. Kyoto: Kyoto University.

—— (1986b) The rain and disputes: a case study of the Nilotic Pari. *Bulletin of the National Museum of Ethnology* (Osaka) **11** (1) (Japanese).

—— (1988) On the concept of *jwok* among the Nilotic Pari: folk cognition of ultra-human forces. *Japanese Journal of Ethnology*, **52** (4) (Japanese).

—— (1992) Area, age organization and inter-ethnic system. *Minpaku Tsushin*, **58**, (Japanese).

Lan, D. (1985) *Guns and Rain: Guerrillas and Spirit Mediums in Zimbabwe*. London: James Currey.

Manz, B. (1988) *Refugees of a Hidden War: the Aftermath of Counter-insurgency in Guatemala*. New York: State of New York University Press.

Mawut, L.L. (1986) *The Southern Sudan: Why Back to Arms*. Khartoum: St George Printing Press.

Mazrui, A.A. (1975) The resurrection of the warrior tradition in African political culture. *Journal of Modern African Studies*, **13** (1).

—— (1977) Introduction. In A.A. Marzui (ed.), *The Warrior Tradition In Modern Africa*. Leiden: E.J. Brill.

Mohamed Omer Beshir (1975) *The Southern Sudan: From Conflict to Peace*. Khartoum: The Khartoum Bookshop.

Okazaki, A. (1992) A Gamk anti-'Dingi' Ritual: the imagination of power among a 'Pre-Nilotic' people. *Journal of Religion in Africa*, **22** (1).

Simonse, S. (1992) *Kings of Disaster: Dualism, Centralism and the Scapegoat King in the Southeastern Sudan*. Leiden: E.J. Brill.

Southall, A. (1977) The bankruptcy of the warrior tradition. In A.A. Mazrui (ed.), *The Warrior Tradition in Modern Africa*. Leiden: E.J. Brill.

Wilson, R. (1991) Machine guns and mountain spirits: the cultural effects of state repression among the Q'eqchi' of Guatemala. *Critique of Anthropology*, **11** (1).

6 Ethnicity & Tribalism on the Sudan-Uganda Border

TIM ALLEN

In this chapter I draw upon fieldwork undertaken in Sudan during 1983–4 and in Uganda between 1987 and 1991, to focus on some aspects of the fraught relationship between the Acholi and the Madi. I begin by discussing labels which have been used to analyse this conflict, and propose a return to the old terms 'tribe' and 'tribalism', not in a crude generalized manner, but as particular manifestations of ethnicity and ethnic conflict. I then go on to comment on some of the ways in which Acholi and Madi 'tribal' identities are formulated, and on the nature of hostility between these two groups. I stress that the Acholi and Madi are opposed as hostile 'tribes', but not as individuals or lineages. In other words, to be opposed as 'tribes' is something specific, and has to be understood in its own terms.

Remarks are made in this essay about the introduction of these 'tribal' categories under colonial rule, and their political manipulation since independence. I also briefly review debates about 'tribalism' as a problem affecting African governments. But my main interest is more localized. I examine 'tribalism' in the village-level cultural context, and consider other expressions of ethnicity. I suggest that Acholi and Madi perceptions of 'tribal' conflict are imbued, on the one hand, with ideas about moral space set against the incursions of amoral 'outside' forces in daily life and, on the other hand, with the impact of state formation and Christian-influenced historiography on conceptions of tradition.

Labelling factions

A basic problem confronted in discussing conflict anywhere, and particularly in Africa, is the labelling of ostensibly opposed factions. It is an issue confronted by the actors themselves in the conflict, because they need to be able to state who they are and who their enemies are, something which may not be at all obvious. In a different way, it is an issue confronted by social analysts, because they want to avoid a straightforward acceptance of the actors' perceptions of what they are doing, and also want an objective interpretation of ideologies and events. The tendency is for analysts to employ the least pejorative of the actors' terms for each other (Tamils, Catholics, northerners, Arabs, Oromo, Hindus, etc.), and to combine these labels with more general forms of categorization which allow for comparison to be made with similar situations in other parts of the world. Nowadays the terms 'ethnic group' and 'ethnic conflict' are commonly employed as general categories, partly in order to avoid expressions that were used in the past but have now become controversial. These terms, however, are not ideal, and it is worth noting their limitations.

While 'ethnic group' and 'ethnic conflict' appear to be innocuous terms, they are open to the same criticism as other labels, such as 'tribe' and 'tribalism', because they are normally applied to other people. For instance, if black people in Britain protest violently in the street, it is an ethnic riot, but the confrontation in northern Ireland is not usually referred to as an 'ethnic conflict'. Moreover, 'ethnic group' and 'ethnic conflict' are terms lacking specificity. 'Ethnic conflict' is employed for a wide range of situations, from clashes between Zulus and African National Congress supporters in South Africa's townships, to playground squabbles between white and black children in London's schools.

If the expression 'ethnic groups' is to be used for analytical purposes, it should be applied broadly and not ethnocentrically. 'Ethnic conflict' has to be viewed as the interplay between multiple, fragmented and overlapping identities, which take on social meaning in some contexts but not in others. But, if ethnicity is applied so broadly, it refers to phenomena which are not immediately comparable. It is not my intention to set aside ethnicity as a concept. Provided we do not forget that the terms 'ethnic group' and 'ethnic conflict' do not encapsulate objective realities, but rather act as labels that point to a range of interrelated things, then they may be very useful because they direct attention to the manner in which antagonists manufacture, or manipulate, particular kinds of shared values.

Looking thoughtfully at ethnicity should mitigate against the use of narrowly materialist or economistic explanations of why human beings group together to fight others. Ethnicity is not a deterministic explanation for conflicts between groups, any more than 'class' or 'nationalism' is, but it does raise crucial questions about how collective fears and hatreds emerge and act as catalysts in the reification of specific cultural qualities, the elaboration of tradition, the definition of moral spheres and the articulation of social boundaries.

It is these questions that are reflected upon in the following pages. But, before turning to them, it is necessary to make a few more comments about labels, this time in relation to the local terms employed in this particular case. In East Africa, ethnic labels current since colonial rule include those with a racial aspect — white, black, Asian — and those which purport to reflect the traditional social organization of the African population. It is the latter form of classification which most concerns us here. As in much of the continent, this layer of ethnic classification is associated with the supposedly pre-colonial names of 'tribes'. However, as noted above, there is now considerable ambivalence about the use of the term 'tribe'. It has been argued that it is highly misleading, because it reinforces stereotypical ideas of how Africans behave. There are millions of Dinka. Can they be a single tribe? Discussing populations in 'tribal' terms may also be unhelpful if it implies discrete groups living as socio-cultural islands. Empirical research has revealed that this is not how things actually are.

Many analysts try to side-step these problems. They keep the names of 'tribes' but classify them as something else. Hence there are references to the Acholi 'people', Acholi 'identity' and even Acholi 'nationality'. Arguments can be put forward for all of these expressions, but the problem of suggesting static, primordial entities remains. Another way in which analysts try to move away from the old 'tribal' classification is to combine them with linguistic or regional categorizations. These may also be derived from colonial precedents, but are thought to be less politically suspect since they seem to relate to more readily verifiable things, that is, language and geography.

Thus the Shilluk, the Anuak, the Acholi and the Langi may be classified as Lwo, because they all speak Lwo languages, a subgroup of the Western Nilotic language family. A classification of this kind appears logical, and in Uganda a Lwo political alliance was actually forged between Acholi and Langi soldiers in 1980, and they did act for a while as a relatively cohesive ethnic entity. Yet, 'traditionally', the Langi and Acholi are hostile to each other, and the alliance was always uneasy. It fell apart violently in 1985. Moreover, Sudanese Lwo-speakers and Ugandan Lwo-speakers are separated by people speaking other languages, and have little direct contact with one another. By and large, it seems that, although language may be important in the formation of ethnic identities, just as often it is not. This is partly due to the remarkable extent of multilingualism in the region, which makes languages a less divisive factor than might be supposed, and makes it difficult to make a clear correlation between common language and ethnic solidarity.

Regional modes of classification are even more problematic. In writing on Sudan, for example, the Shilluk may be grouped with the Dinka and the Nuer and called 'Nilotes' or 'Nilotics', distinguishing them from the 'Equatorian' peoples to the south, even though many 'Equatorian' people actually speak Nilotic languages. In writings on Uganda, the opposite may be the case, and the same people who are called 'Equatorians' in Sudan are termed 'Nilotics', even if, like the Madi, they speak a Sudanic language.

It is doubtless partly because of the fluidity and confusion in regional/linguistic classifications that most analysts still rely on the ethnic terminology used in colonial times, even if they eschew the word 'tribe' itself. In countries like Sudan and Uganda, which have undergone so many years of upheaval, these local identities appear to be among the very few constants, no matter how multiple, fragmented and overlapping they may be for those who adopt them. Regional or linguistic groupings have to be examined in relation to their 'tribal' components and, in spite of the best efforts of some political economists to explain away or deny the significance of 'tribes', it remains impossible to interpret the appalling events of the past 30 years without recourse to them. Furthermore, in spite of their limitations as analytical devices, these old labels have the advantage of being categories used by actors themselves. People living in southern Sudan and Uganda know what 'tribe' they belong to, at least at any given point in time. There is a shared understanding of what a tribe is or ought to be, and groups which sense that they are not adequately recognized as 'tribes' may aspire to this goal.

Of course, there are dangers in linking our interpretation too closely with the categories used by the people we are trying to understand, but, even if we do not want to accept the views of the actors, we should respect them. It may be true that 50 years ago the notion of 'tribe' was an ethnic categorization imposed upon subject African populations by colonial administrations and colonial social science. But it has become an indigenous term for something which can be of immense importance. We have to ask in what context does 'tribe' have meaning, and why?

Border 'tribes' at independence

Let me begin when ethnic issues in Africa seemed clearer than they do today. Although some anthropologists had already raised problems with official 'tribal' classifications, and had demonstrated that 'tribal' identity could be negotiable, this had not made much impact on the perceptions of the outgoing colonial government. In the *Atlas of Uganda* (Uganda Government Mapping Office, 1962), published in the year of Uganda's independence, there is a splendid map of the country called 'Tribal and ethnic groups' (a section of this map is reproduced in black and white on p. 117, Map 7). The original map is dotted with multi-coloured pie charts, slices of which represent percentages of each county's population according to 'tribal' affiliation. We discover that all the 80,355 Ugandan Madi lived in Madi County of West Nile District (now Arua District) and the two counties of Madi District (now Moyo District). Meanwhile, the 284,929 Ugandan Acholi lived in the six counties of Acholi District (now divided into Kitgum and Gulu Districts).

If a similar approach had been taken to presenting 'tribes' across the border in Sudan, there would have been about 20,000 Sudanese Madi living in Madi County of Sudan, and about the same number of Acholi in Sudan's Acholi County. However, in the early 1960s many of these Sudanese nationals were in fact living in Uganda. Some had migrated south since the 1950s in search of work, and others had followed as refugees when Sudan's first civil war spread to their home areas. Doubtless they were not included in the ethnic diagrams of the atlas for the sake of clarity. But the atlas also makes another, presumably deliberate, simplification. It locates all the ethnic groups in their home areas, ignoring the fact that large numbers of northern Ugandans had also migrated south in search of employment in the factories of Kampala and Jinja or in the plantations of Buganda, or to join the armed forces.

An official version of this map would be untenable today for political reasons. But pages from the 1962 atlas can still be

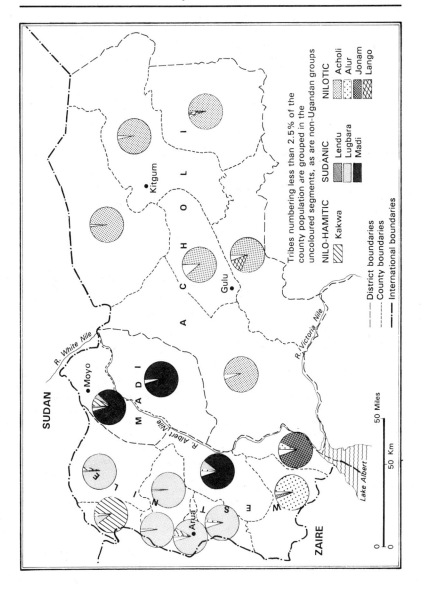

Map 7   Tribal groups of north-west Uganda, a black and white section of the original.
Source: 'Tribal and ethnic groups', Atlas of Uganda, Uganda Government Mapping Office, 1962.

117

purchased from the government mapping office in Entebbe, and this particular map is always selling out. Moreover, the tendency to conceptualize tribes in terms of districts is often barely disguised. The old ethnic names of districts have been replaced with the names of the largest towns. Madi District has become Moyo District because its largest town is called Moyo, but everyone knows that Moyo District is where the Madi come from, just as Gulu District is where the Acholi come from, so tribal populations are simply interpolated from the recent census figures. This is what happened with the 1980 figures, and it will happen again with the 1991 figures if they are ever made public.

The colours chosen to indicate the Acholi and Madi on the 1962 atlas map are contrasted. The Madi are a rich purple and the Acholi are a light orange, highlighting the fact that they belong to different language families. The Madi, like their western neighbours the Lugbara, were classified as 'Sudanic', and the Acholi, like the Alur and the Jonam, were 'Nilotic'. These linguistic groupings were a source of some bemusement to colonial administrators in the last years of colonial rule, since they seemed to bear little relation to 'tribal' behaviour. In 1956, the district commissioner at Moyo made the following observations:

Even educated Madi will admit that they must be fundamentally the same people as the Lugbara, their neighbours to the West, and it is not easy to decide why the Madi now feel such a strong sense of difference and, indeed, some antagonism. One gets the impression that the Madi entertain feelings of greater friendliness towards their South-Eastern neighbours, the Acholi. Superficial reasons of relatively recent date may be: Madi children are said to be much brighter academically than the Lubgara and even half a century ago the Lugbara are described as being more savage and wild than the Madi; whereas the Madi are largely Catholic the majority of the Lugbara on the border are Muslim; despite, or perhaps because of their lack of success in school the Lugbara seem to make better traders than the Madi and most of the African trade in the sub-district is in the hands of the Lugbara Muslims. (Annual Report for Madi Sub-District, 1956, Entebbe Archives)

The same report goes on to remark that 'quite a lot' of Madi spoke Acholi as well as their mother tongue, but most would deny any facility in Lugbara. Like many such reports, this shows very little knowledge about the history of the border region. The 'tribes' are thought of as discrete groups which have existed for a long time, each with its own special 'tribal' characteristics. The commissioner seems completely unaware of the extent to which these identities emerged as a consequence of the Turco-Egyptian and European invasions of the late nineteenth century, and the policy of establishing indirect rule through 'tribal' chiefs in the early decades of the Uganda Protectorate, a policy that was continued across the border in Sudan almost to the eve of independence. Nevertheless, the district commissioner has probably given an accurate representation of the African attitudes he encountered during the mid-1950s. He is not just imposing his own views, and is actually surprised at what he has discovered precisely because it has not borne out his expectations.

I shall return to the issue of Lugbara–Madi antagonism below. At this point, let us accept this rigidly 'tribalized' perception of the African population. In summary, in the late colonial period the Acholi, the Madi and the Lugbara appeared to map-makers and government officers to be separate groups, each with their own history and traditions. For various reasons that were not altogether clear, at least to the district commissioner in Moyo in 1956, the Madi and Lugbara disliked each other, while the Madi and Acholi enjoyed an amicable relationship. Within a decade, however, this situation was reversed. What went wrong?

The conflict between the Acholi and the Madi

Inevitably, tales of what went wrong vary greatly according to who is asked. So I will first tell the story from an Acholi point of view, and then I will tell it again from a Madi point of view. Both accounts are obviously partial and, of course, not all Acholi and Madi would agree with the views I ascribe to them. However, these are arguments which are commonly expressed, and in the present context what people believe happened is at least as significant as what actually occurred.

An Acholi version

In the years following independence, Gulu continued to develop as the major commercial centre of northern Uganda. Many Madi came to live there, some to work in the administrative offices and others to operate as traders in the large market. Madi also migrated to the Acholi area in order to open farms, because in places the land there is more fertile than in Madiland, and the population density is quite low. They were welcomed by the local people and lived in peace, often marrying from the vicinity, and bringing up their children to speak Acholi as a first language. Things changed suddenly when Idi Amin seized power in 1971. Amin feared the Acholi because generally they had supported the government of Milton Obote, and because there were so many

119

Acholi in the army. He had the Acholi soldiers rounded up and murdered and, during his reign of terror, hundreds of civilians were also killed. The Madi supported Amin. They joined the army and participated in the atrocities. Those living in Gulu even started to kill their Acholi neighbours.

A few Ugandan Acholi took refuge in Sudan, and Sudanese Acholi living in Uganda quickly returned home following the Addis Ababa settlement of 1972. Things were not too bad in Sudan until 1979, when Amin fell from power, but, in the following years, those Sudanese Madi who had remained in Uganda also returned home and began to play an important role in southern Sudanese politics. Madi started to take important jobs in Sudan's Acholi County, and began to farm there. To make matters worse, over 30,000 Ugandan Madi refugees were settled in refugee camps in or near Acholi County. The Acholi remembered what had happened in Gulu, and were very concerned about their presence. Why could they not all be settled in Sudan's Madi County? Why should they be given Acholi land? But nothing was done. Many of the Ugandan Madi could speak good English, so they were able to get support from international aid agencies as well as from politicians in Juba. They helped Sudanese Madi to become influential in the southern Sudanese regional government, and secured the benefits of many development projects which ought to have assisted the local Acholi.

Meanwhile, in Uganda the return to power of Milton Obote following the 1980 elections gave the Acholi an opportunity to re-establish themselves. But in West Nile and Moyo Districts, the soldiers of Amin continued to wage war against the democratically elected government, and made it difficult to administer the country. Hundreds of Acholi soldiers were killed by the rebels. Eventually, Obote's government became unable to operate, so the Acholi soldiers decided to replace him with an experienced Acholi officer, Tito Okello. He tried to bring peace to the country, but the rebel groups used the cease-fire to reorganize themselves, and eventually Museveni came to power in January 1986. Since then, the Acholi have suffered at the hands of the National Resistance Army, while the Madi who had been in Amin's government and army have now returned to positions of power.

A Madi version

Although the Acholi soldiers in the Ugandan army following independence were sometimes aggressive to Madi civilians, the relationship between the Acholi and Madi was generally good. In fact, there were some prominent Madi in Obote's government. Things only became bad after the fall of Amin. The Madi had not really supported Amin. They did not like the fact that he was a Muslim, and that he tried to make people convert to Islam. Amin himself was a Kakwa from West Nile's Koboko County, and the Kakwa, together with the Nubians and the Sudanese, were the primary beneficiaries of the regime. Some Nubians who had been born in Moyo District used their government connections to establish large farms, evicting hundreds of poor Madi farmers.

Nevertheless, following the Tanzanian invasion and the rigged elections of 1980, the soldiers of Obote decided to take revenge on all the people of north-west Uganda, including the innocent Madi. They began killing people in large numbers, and Obote went so far as to claim that he would clear the whole area and turn it into a game reserve. The Madi had no choice but to flee into Sudan. Most of them were settled in refugee camps, some to the east of the Nile in or close to Acholi County, and the rest to the west. Life in exile was difficult, but people worked hard and managed to establish a reasonable standard of living. At least they generally had enough land to cultivate.

Unfortunately, the security situation in this part of Sudan suddenly deteriorated in 1985, when the Sudan People's Liberation Army began to operate in the area. To make matters worse, in the following year hundreds of Ugandan Acholi soldiers crossed the border after Museveni took over in Kampala. Some of them, together with some of the Sudanese Acholi, collaborated with the Sudanese People's Liberation Army in attacking the Madi refugee camps, killing several people. The Ugandan Madi living to the east of the Nile had no choice but to flee back to Uganda, and in the following years they have been followed by those settled on the west bank, as well as virtually the whole Sudanese Madi population (who are now settled in refugee camps in Moyo District). In Uganda, the Madi had to struggle again to rebuild their communities, but it has not been easy. There have been repeated attacks in East Moyo County by the various Acholi rebel armies operating in Gulu District, including the Holy Spirit Forces of the female medium, Alice Lakwena. For much of the time, the road from Moyo District to Kampala is insecure, greatly limiting trade, and preventing the integration of the area into the national economy. Things will not improve until the Acholi finally stop fighting, but they are a warlike people and will have to be crushed.

Explaining the conflict

These local explanations of the Acholi–Madi conflict treat the two groups as discrete 'tribal' categories. It is therefore not surprising that many of those who do research in Sudan and Uganda use these categories to explain what has been going on. 'Tribalism' is seen as the basic problem. The colonial encounter, state formation, technological change and commoditization have presumably left the basic structure of African societies intact. Although much criticized, this remains a popular perspective, regularly adopted in Western media coverage of conflict in Africa. It also has its academic adherents. At one time, anthropologists and political scientists were prone to argue that knowledge of 'tribal' life was fundamental for the study of African government at the state level. This view informs a significant portion of works published by the East African Institute of Social Research (Fallers, 1964). More recently, Goran Hyden's influential thesis proposing that African counties are crippled by an 'economy of affection' is also founded on the premise that primordial sentiment of a 'tribal' nature dominates political life (Hyden, 1980, 1983).

However, many analysts have taken issue with this kind of explanation, arguing that ethnic conflict, far from being the reason for upheaval, is one of its symptoms. They maintain that 'tribal' categories were in many instances actually created in the course of setting up colonial rule, and were reinforced by attempts to keep administration costs to a minimum through the use of what were thought to be indigenous power structures. These structures were later cynically manipulated by unscrupulous politicians following independence (Young, 1976: 216–73). There is certainly merit in this type of interpretation. Under British rule, the Acholi and the Madi were imbued with 'tribal' characteristics. The Acholi were encouraged to think of themselves as a 'warrior race', while the Madi were regarded as peace-loving intellectuals who sometimes drank too much. Yet both the Acholi and the Madi 'tribes' were in fact colonial creations.

The term 'Madi' is probably derived from the vernacular for 'man' (*ma'di*, a word common to several Sudanic languages, including Lugbara). It seems to have been used as an ethnic label by successive invaders — Arabs, Turco-Egyptians, Belgians, British — who established outposts close to the Nile from the 1860s onwards. It was used very vaguely, sometimes to refer to people living in present-day Moyo District, sometimes to groups living to the east and sometimes to groups to the north. It really became systematized as a 'tribal' identity during the 1920s, when

the borders of Madi Sub-District were established. The antagonism between the Madi and Lugbara 'tribes', noted by the
district commissioner at Moyo in 1956, was a consequence of
this policy. Following the First World War, deliberate attempts
were made to stop the people of what became Madi Sub-District
from moving about. It was considered that they had been corrupted by Arab influence, and might infect neighbouring groups
with diseases which they were thought to carry, notably sleeping
sickness. A 'tribal' boundary was established, which, as the district commissioner of West Nile reported in 1919, was 'more
definitely drawn by the removal of many Lugwari [Lugara] from
close proximity to Luferri [Lefori, which marks the present border
between Moyo and Arua Districts]' (DC, West Nile, to PCNP,
3.2.19, Entebbe Archives).

For most of the rest of the colonial era, Madi Sub-District continued to form part of West Nile District, but was administered
separately. However, the Sudanic dialects spoken there were not
officially registered as a language in the way that the Sudanic
dialects of West Nile were recognized as the Lugbara language. In
fact, the subdistrict was administered in English rather than a vernacular tongue for much of the colonial period, and the commis-
sioners posted to the subdistrict were supposed to do their
language exams in the official Lugbara or Acholi tongues. The
Madi did not get their own translation of the Bible until 1979, and
lacked the benefits of full district status until independence.

An attempt seems to have been made to assert a separate Madi
identity by refusing to speak Lugbara, which the population certainly understood, and using fluency in English as one of their
ethnic characteristics. Indeed, Madi 'tribal' identity was established under British rule in juxtaposition to a Lugbara 'tribal'
identity. As the administrative reasons for distinguishing between
the two became less significant, chiefs and other local government
representatives among the Madi needed to assert their cultural
difference from their Sudanic-speaking neighbours in order to
protect their own positions. Once the 'tribal' borders were established and access to services was structured through 'tribal'
channels, there was inevitably a tendency for people to rely on
the new collective grouping in situations involving governmental
authority. From the Madi point of view, the Acholi were less
threatening, because they were recognized as a different 'tribal'
group. The relationship between the Madi and Acholi as 'tribes'
was consequently more friendly, and the relative economic afflu-
ence of Acholi District in northern Uganda during the later
colonial period — the provincial headquarters was at Gulu —

made it the natural centre of employment for Madi unable or unwilling to travel to the south of the country.

Various suggestions have been made about the origin of the word 'Acholi'. Crazzolara suggested it may be derived from *Collo*, the nineteenth-century Arab name for the linguistically related Shilluk of Sudan. The fact that the Acholi, and neighbouring groups now classified as belonging to different tribes, were often called Shullis during the early colonial period would seem to support this view. Crazzolara also notes that his Acholi informants linked their 'tribal' name to the word *col*, meaning black (Crazzolara, 1938: viii). On the other hand, Girling suggests 'Acholi' may be a simplification of the vernacular sentence *an lacoo-li*, meaning 'I am a man' (Girling, 1960: 1). Girling maintains that the name only began to be used in the 1920s, superseding other labels, like Shulli and Gangi (a word derived from the vernacular for home, *gang*). However, there is in fact an early use of 'Acholi' in a report by a British officer in 1899, who, enigmatically and wrongly, explains that 'Acholi' is the plural of 'choli' (Martyr report, FO Correspondence, August 1899, Entebbe Archives). In any case, there is no doubt that Okot p'Bitek is largely correct when he tells us that:

At the turn of the century Acoliland was divided into thirty politically independent units. But these have not been called 'tribes' . . . It was the new political unit set up by the British colonial administration which was labelled Acoli District, which became known as the Acholi 'tribe'. (p'Bitek, 1970: 12)

Since independence, the divisions between the Acholi and Madi 'tribal' groupings have been reinforced by the policies of successive governments led by Obote, Okello and Amin. Like other 'national' figures, their support was linked to ethnic factions, and little attempt was made to promote a Ugandan national consciousness. Thus, ethnic conflict between the Acholi and the Madi can be understood as the inevitable consequence of the way the colonial and post-colonial governments worked. It may seem inevitable that, in both Sudan and Uganda, when the colonial grid which defined and separated 'tribal' groups was removed there would be a scramble for power at the centre with political factions split along 'tribal' lines. Does this explanation suffice? Showing that 'tribal' identities are the product of historical processes is surely helpful. It does not make them go away. People kill each other because of them. It is no use maintaining that they should not do so because their mutual antagonism is not really traditional behaviour. As far as they are concerned, it is. Or, rather, it is in some circumstances while in other circumstances

125

it is irrelevant; and this is where things become very complicated.

Attempts have been made to break the polarization in explanations of 'tribalism'. Michael Twaddle, for example, has reconsidered his earlier views and aptly remarked:

the basic trouble with previous discussions (or dismissals) of tribalism as a factor in African politics is that it has been viewed too often as an 'either/or' matter: either it is largely primordial sentiment or it is basically ideological manipulation by unscrupulous politicians. It is rarely seen as both, still more infrequently as primordial sentiment and ideological manipulation in political interaction. (Twaddle, 1983: 159)

But Twaddle directs us into difficult waters, where not many writers have been prepared to go. We are invited to abandon the conventional use of colonial ethnic labels as building-blocks of analysis. We have to discuss the Madi and the Acholi 'tribes' as they are defined, implicitly or explicitly, by particular political factions, at a particular time and in particular situations. Or we have to use the 'tribal' terms as labels which a variety of people, in different ways and over several generations, have adopted as a means of conceptualizing themselves as a group. It is not possible to write about the history of the Madi and the Acholi. We have to write about the idea of the Madi and the idea of the Acholi in history. We have to think of other ways of referring to populations, so that we have categories with which to interrogate the content of all collective identities, including 'tribal' ones.

The implications of such an approach are far-reaching, and it is hard to see how an analysis of Uganda or Sudan as a whole could be attempted on this basis without it becoming hopelessly confusing. Some things have to be held constant in order to be able to discuss other things. But the approach becomes more feasible when the populations focused on are smaller. Below I attempt an assessment of some aspects of Acholi and Madi 'tribal' identity in their specific cultural context. First, I discuss other forms of local level ethnicity, and then I comment on the currency of the 'tribe' as an ideal model of social organization.

Ethnicity and moral space

Something that surprised me in the course of my fieldwork was the fact that relationships at a personal, family or village level between Acholi and Madi were often close, despite the openly acknowledged antipathy between these two groups. In Laropi, the Madi village in Uganda where I lived, the population had recently fled back from Sudan when their refugee camps were attacked by Acholi and the Sudanese People's Liberation Army. After I had been there for some time, I was taken to see the rain shrine. Small pots, containing white, conical stones, were arranged around brick-sized rocks. It looked identical to shrines I had seen in Acholiland. I asked the rain-maker what had happened to the shrine when he fled to Sudan. He explained that he had left it where it was, and the Acholi soldiers had not touched it, although they destroyed all the homes near by. I expressed surprise at this, for it seemed odd that the stones had not been stolen. 'Ah well,' he replied, 'it is because we are really the same people.'

On the day that a government minister visited Laropi, local people were invited to express their views about the National Resistance Movement government led by Museveni. The old subchief, who had served for more than 20 years and who bore the scars of torture at the hands of Obote's Langi and Acholi soldiers, did not speak, but the elected local Resistance Committee chairman did, and so did the commander of the army detachment. Of the two, it was the soldier who received the warmest applause. He was well liked, easily the most popular commander to have been posted to the village during my stay. He happened to be an Acholi. In addition, it became apparent to me that there had been considerable shifting of identities between the two 'tribes'. The Madi family I lived with had not only resided for years in the Acholi area before fleeing to Sudan, but one sister was married to an Acholi, and they had at one time thought of themselves as Acholi. Elsewhere, I have described how in the Sudanese Acholi District a new kind of farm work group forged clan-like relations between non-kin, and facilitated the incorporation of neighbouring Madi in such a manner that they could claim to be, and were accepted as being, Acholi (Allen, 1987: 78).

In fact, although Madi is a Sudanic tongue and Acholi is Nilotic, numerous Madi can speak Acholi and many western Acholi speak Madi, and there is evidence that such fluency has been common for a long time. When I researched the oral history of the Sudanese Acholi area, I found that several lineages, including chiefly lineages, traced their descent to Madi clans, and, when I examined in more detail the so-called tribal wars of the pre-colonial era, it became apparent that the opposing sides were made up of combinations of clans which are now thought of as belonging to different ethnicities. It seems there was never a war between the Acholi and the Madi, but confrontations between allied patrilineages. This was also the case with the Lamogi revolts against the British in 1912. The rebels comprised a mixture of multilingual groups, whose descendants are now thought of as being either Acholi or Madi. Most striking of all, considering the differences between the two languages, certain significant words are the same, including *kaka*, a term usually translated as 'clan', 'lineage' or 'relative'. It is worth examining the resonance of *kaka* in some detail.

Acholi and Madi villages are ideally made up of a number of patrilocal lineages, each having its own shrine at which patrilineal ghosts should periodically be fed in ceremonies performed by male elders. A man uses the term *kaka* for his immediate lineage and his clan — a combination of lineages recognizing an eponymous ancestor — as well as for other groups with which he cannot intermarry because of matrilineal relationships. This is also true of a woman until marriage, when her position becomes ambiguous. She effectively becomes part of her husband's *kaka* through her children and the exchange of bridewealth, but retains ties to her father's lineage, and may return to live with her brothers in later life. Her children's position may also be ambiguous if no bridewealth is exchanged, or only part of it is exchanged before her death. Neighbouring clans are affinally linked, and form loosely organized polities, recognizing a single chiefly lineage. Occasionally, the term *kaka* can also be used to indicate this larger group.

Looked at from another angle, *kaka* refers not so much to the genealogical closeness of a relationship, but its quality: what can be expected of it and what demands it can legitimately make. From what can be ascertained of life in this part of Africa before the invasions of the nineteenth century, there seems to have been considerable population movement, either on an individual basis, due to trade in items like the ceremonial iron hoes widely used in bridewealth exchanges, or in patrilineal groups, as a consequence of localized drought, crop failure, war, epidemics and lineage fission. Contacts were maintained over relatively long distances, and there are several groups now divided between Acholiland and Madiland which share a clan name, recognize a common eponymous ancestor and are supposed not to intermarry.

During the colonial period and afterwards, administrative measures which concentrated the population near roads, the introduction of markets, cash cropping and labour migration, often forced people to move away from land associated with ancestors and to settle among strangers. This, among other factors, caused tremendous social pressures and undermined the authority of male elders. Accusations of sorcery and poisoning were frequent. But ways had to be found to get along, and principles of moral interpersonal relations had to be established. In both my fieldwork locations, I witnessed *kaka*, in effect, being created. I have mentioned how in Acholiland farm work groups became clan substitutes in certain respects. Similarly, in the Madi area lying at the foothills of the Metu Mountains, the people belong to a mixture of clans. They have chosen not to return to their ancestral homes higher up, where farm land is scarce. While they continue to attend funerals with their clan relatives several miles away, they now no longer marry among themselves. They have become *kaka*, and think of themselves as such in relation to other groups in their parish of residence.

On an individual basis, it is in fact possible to find a *kaka* relationship based on ancestry with a large number of people, if the need arises. Usually matrilineal descent is traced back three or four generations, and a relationship traced back beyond this is not considered a barrier to marriage. However, in other circumstances such a relationship is useful. Thus, whenever I would take someone with me on a trip to another part of the Madi area, the first thing he or she would do on arrival would be to discuss genealogical histories, and after a few minutes would almost invariably turn to me in surprise and say: 'I thought these people were strangers, but now I find we are *kaka*.' This was also done in any business enterprise that involved trust, because by defining the relationship it was implicitly agreed which elders ought to act as arbitrators in the event of disagreement.

Kaka is one of a number of concepts associated with what can be depended upon, with what is 'inside'. These concepts are contrasted with what is 'outside', from the forest or bush, unpredictable, dangerous and amoral. Put in this way, as a dichotomy between 'outside' and 'inside', the point I am making may seem rather crude, a conjuring up of the much discussed binary opposition between nature and culture and, by extension, between female and male (MacCormack & Strathern, 1980). But this metaphor was a potent one for the people among whom I lived. It imbued subtly, sometimes not so subtly, ritual, dancing, language and conversation, much as it has been shown to do among the Madi's western neighbours, the Lugbara (Middleton, 1960: 248–50, 1969: 176, 1985; Casale, 1982: 395; Barnes-Dean, 1986: 339). A few diverse examples will give an impression of this. They are drawn from my fieldwork in Laropi.

Madi dances

All 'traditional' Madi dances require a circle to be formed by the participants, which represents the edge of the forest, or the 'outside' (*angwe*). The most popular dance is the *mure*, which involves singing songs, often in praise of a dead patrilineal ancestor, to a fast rhythm beaten on drums or scratched on chains of beads. The women dominate the singing, while the men call out *cira*, a word linked to the crowing of cocks. These are praises, usually of their ancestors' bravery or their sexual capacity:

My father was tough and married many beautiful girls. My mother cared for me properly, that is why I am big and strong.

The women respond with ululation, and call out praises of their husbands:

My husband is hard-working and we have plenty of food. No other woman should attempt marriage with my great lover.

At the same time, men will perform *toi*, a kind of salutation. One man pretends to attack another in the middle of the ring with mock spears. They make short stabbing thrusts at each other. After a few moments they stop, and suddenly rush towards the edge of the circle, often breaking through it to the edge of the compound, and pretend to hurl their spears at the 'forest'. They return to the centre and repeat the action two or three times, accompanied by a handful of ululating women, who encourage them with praises. The men call out *laza*, exclamations which assert triumph over the things of the 'outside':

Oh my father was very brave and killed many enemies. Oh my father was a great hunter of big animals. Oh my people are dominant, they are rich and have many cattle.

The place of burial

The Madi, like the Acholi, take pains to ensure that a dead relative is buried at home, in the compound within a couple of paces of the deceased's house. However, there are exceptions. Ritual chiefs, notably rain-makers (*opi ei dri*), were buried out in the forest, at a special grove (*rudu*), where not even their closest relatives are supposed to go. The prospect of burial away from home is something awesome, and reinforces the idea that a rain-maker has metaphysical capacities. The father of the two brothers in whose home I lived had been buried at the *rudu*, because he was the heir of the last ritual chief, though not a rain-maker himself, despite his expressed desire to be buried at home. One of his sons told me that one day he hoped to collect his father's remains, bring them home and build a concrete tomb in his honour. The fear of burial in the outside, away from where descendants live, affects some people more than others. But it is quite widespread. I heard of cases where people risked their lives to bring a dying relative home at the time when Obote's forces were active in the area.

Women

People fear the forest because there are things there that are *onzi*. *Onzi* is difficult to translate into English. The Madi dictionary renders it as 'bad', 'evil', 'wicked', 'ugly'. (Bilbao & Moizi, 1984: 171) That is part of it. Certainly the government soldiers who pillaged and looted were *onzi* in this sense. *Onzi* additionally encompasses ideas of mystical power and danger. Any spiritual force may be thought of as *onzi*; so may some women, by women as well as men. *Onzi* relates to things that are not as they should be according to the ideal patrilineally regulated social order. It is something most definitely of the 'outside', even when it is located within the home (Allen, 1991a, b, 1992).

The connection between *onzi* and femaleness underlines the ambiguous status of women as wives. Although a *kaka* identity may be traced through the mother's line as well as the father's, patrilocal lineages ideally acquire stability by the effective arbitration of disputes by male elders, who are responsible for patrilineal ancestor shrines and have the power to invoke patrilineal ghosts to maintain moral order. A new wife is a potentially dangerous outsider. She may be a sorcerer/poisoner. She is unpredictable, her loyalties are unclear, she is a threat to her husband's sisters living at home and to other wives and their children. She does not automatically become *kaka*. The term *a'ja* refers to the primary cause of troubles in the home, which is 'envy' brought from the 'outside' by wives.

As she becomes older, a woman should become 'like a man', because her position has become clear due to the transfer of sufficient bridewealth to her father and the bearing of children to her husband's patrilineage. Alternatively she may become 'like a man' because she returns to live with her brothers. Similarly, a man may become 'like a woman' if he lives with his in-laws, or if he becomes a client away from his ancestral home. Significantly, when the descendants of a client are incorporated as *kaka*, they may be referred to as 'women', *izonzi*, if they remain mistrusted. *Izonzi* is a compound word made up of the word for woman, *izi*, and *onzi*.

Forces of the forest

The idea that women have access to forces outside the ideal, patrilineally regulated moral world means, on the one hand, that they are most likely to be accused of poisoning/sorcery and, on the other, that they are most likely to be sought as diviners and healers when abnormal things are happening. It is widely believed that the ghosts of those killed locally during the fighting in the 1980s may possess the living, and this was thought to happen very frequently. Virtually every family in Laropi had a member who became possessed by wild spirits. Unlike ancestral ghosts, still venerated from time to time at ancestral shrines, wild spirits are not *kaka*. With few exceptions, they are ghosts with whom the possessed person has no kinship tie. They may, for example, be Acholi soldiers, abandoned children or Muslim traders. Not surprisingly, given their relationship with the 'outside', most of those possessed are women.

Interestingly, the female healers who have emerged to deal with this problem are often referred to as *ajwaka*, the Acholi word for diviner or spirit medium, and the ghosts themselves are called *jokjok*, a term derived from the Acholi term *jok* (pl. *jogi*). Moreover, the spirit medium herself and the possessed women will regularly talk in Acholi instead of Madi when entranced. In this way a clear association is made between the present forces of the forest, which are viewed as playing a significant and frightening role in daily life, and the Acholi tongue, the language of many of Obote's soldiers.

It is plain to see from these four examples that what is thought to be 'inside' is continuously changing. Women shift between patrilineages, patrilineages divide due to competition between elders, individuals or families move for any number of reasons and establish new homes as kin with non-kin elsewhere and, in practice, who is *kaka* and who is not depends upon the nature of the discourse: who is speaking to whom and why. *Kaka* is a notion linked to the delineation of spheres of moral interaction. The 'tribal' categories of Acholi and Madi may, on occasion, be imbued with moral meaning along the same lines, in mutual juxtaposition, or with respect to another category of a similar sort. But in day-to-day terms, 'being Acholi' or 'being Madi' is irrelevant at village-level social intercourse — at least until soldiers start killing people. What matters is to know who is to be relied upon in affliction, and who could be the cause of that affliction due to 'envy' and 'sorcery/poisoning'.

There is much here that is similar to the situation among Cushitic-speaking pastoralists in northern Kenya described by Schlee (1985). He points out that ethnic differences between these peoples have been regarded as stable over time, making it surprising to find that members of mutually hostile ethnic groups regard each other as 'clan brothers'. He argues that:

> The model of segmentary lineage systems developed by British social anthropologists may lead to wrong predictions about patterns of co-operation and solidarity in these societies. For pastoral partnerships, economic asylum in times of starvation and general hospitality can run along cross-ethnic clan lines. . . . A clan is not simply a sub-unit of a 'tribe', because it can be represented in more than one 'tribe' and the hierarchy between superordinate units and sub-units becomes arbitrary. Clans are not necessarily smaller than ethnic groups, because the total numerical strength of a clan is the sum of its representations in different ethnic groups. (Schlee, 1985: 19)

Schlee concludes that this diachronic aspect of identity has been misleadingly neglected, because 'tribal' ethnic categories are used as a privileged grid of classification. He suggests that it might be more productive to start with 'a radical application of the "network" concept than from established social units' (Schlee, 1985: 33).

Among the sedentary Acholi and Madi farmers, cross-ethnic relations of this kind are even more striking because the languages of the two 'tribes' are grammatically so different. I have concentrated on the Acholi–Madi relationship because it is one of conflict and because I happen to know most about it, but cross-'tribal' relationships are equally complex between the Madi and the Bari and between the Madi and the Lugbara, who are linguistically related. What I am suggesting is that for people thought of as Madi and Acholi, and their neighbours, non-'tribal' ethnic identity validates daily social intercourse by drawing upon a flexible resource of shared values. These values are not necessarily arranged as a logical explanation of what happens, but like an archive may constitute a lasting base of past reference and future validation. In this way, ideas like *kaka* give social significance to group boundaries which may cut across politicized 'tribal' identities, and only rarely, but tragically, coincide with them. As Wendy James has argued in her study of the Uduk, such notions, may at times rest dormant but on occasion be drawn upon for the formation of new discourse. The elements of this cultural archive, revealed as much in the repertoire of habitual ritual action as in language, constitute the foundations of a moral world. (James, 1988: 6)

Formulation of tribal history

Non-'tribal' identities have thus survived in this part of Africa, in spite of the 'tribal' antagonisms which have played a prominent part in the upheavals since independence. However, this is not the whole story. It is not possible to maintain the argument that 'tribal' values are just something introduced and manipulated at the national level, and that they acquire meaning at village level either in direct reaction to the activities of pillaging soldiers, or by imbuing the idea of 'tribe' with notions of morality derived from a cultural archive. The promotion of 'tribes' by state authority, both colonial and post-colonial, has had an effect on local attitudes. Although there may be a multiplicity of overlapping local identities, when there is serious ethnic conflict it tends to be perceived and explained in 'tribal' terms, as shown above.

Furthermore, an assertion of 'tribal' cohesiveness may now be viewed as something 'progressive', in much the same way as formal education, cash cropping, speaking English, going to the health centre and reading the Bible. In this final section of the chapter, I remark on one aspect of this local incorporation of 'tribal' identity, that is, the formulation of 'tribal' history. Comparing Acholi and Madi 'tribal' identities, it is clear that the former is more potent than the latter. It is usually Madi who become Acholi, and it has to be admitted that, despite Acholi accusations of Madi killing their Acholi neighbours in Gulu following Amin's coup, it is usually Acholi who have done the attacking. The sort of collective 'tribal' ideology promoted by Alice Lakwena's Holy Spirit Movement is unlikely to occur in Madiland, even though spirit mediums may be just as influential at village level there as they are in Acholiland. In the course of my fieldwork, I collected oral testimonies about the past, but it was far more difficult to find good informants among the Madi than among the Acholi. Even senior members of Madi chiefly lineages could not trace patrilineal ancestry back more than five or six generations, and few had detailed stories to tell about migrations. In response to my questions people would say: 'We do not know where we came from, but it was probably from Sudan. We do not think about those things much any more. Only a few old people worry about them.' Yet even the very old were not very helpful. They could tell me about events that happened in their youth, and perhaps events that occurred during their parents' lives, but rarely more.

On a couple of occasions I was referred to an old man who lived in one of the mountain villages as the only real expert. I eventually sought him out and made an appointment to interview him. When I arrived for the interview with my tape recorder, I found him surrounded by a crowd of expectant, and rather drunk, younger men. He was prepared with a 'history of Madi', written in the Madi language in an exercise book, and he proceeded to read this out. He began with a list of the chiefs of the Pamugo chiefdom, but several names were repeated, and the first of them was said to have come from Buganda and was probably one of the Baganda sent to train chiefs in the early days of colonial rule. This list was followed by another of 'whites', which began with an Italian missionary, and ended with the first African district commissioner. This in turn was followed by a date chart, which started in 1908 and ended in 1968. It was all very interesting, but it was not quite what I had in mind.

It seemed to me that the Madi were a people lacking 'tradition' and 'history'. It was something that worried some educated 'community leaders', and at a big meeting in Moyo town in 1989 there was much discussion about what could be done about it. It was pointed out that the Madi, unlike the Acholi, were not yet a 'proper tribe' and, as a first step, their language should be systematized. There followed a heated but inconclusive debate on which dialect was the pure Madi.

It all made a striking contrast with my experiences in Acholiland. In 1988, I made a trip from Moyo to Gulu, stopping on the way at the border village of Attiak. This place was classified as Acholi during colonial times. On arrival, a middle-aged man came up to me and introduced himself as the chief. I asked if he was the *jago* (government subchief) or the *rwot* (traditional chief). He replied that he was the seventeenth *rwot*, and that he could tell me the names of all his predecessors. He knew I had just come from the Madi area, and in this manner proclaimed his Acholiness. The Acholi fascination with the past has much to do with specific developments set under way during the colonial period. In particular, the existence of an Acholi Bible from an early date and the systematization of the Acholi dialects into a standard language meant it was possible to print school-books in the vernacular. Various grammars and dictionaries of the Acholi language were published, and from the 1930s there has been a

135

relatively constant trickle of vernacular publications, including an Acholi-language magazine. Many of these publications were of a religious nature, but several were ostensibly secular and included several works on Acholi history.

I write 'ostensibly' because the first history book in the Acholi language, and certainly the most influential, was Fr. Pelligrini's *Lok pa Acoli Macon*. This little book was published in Verona in 1949 and reprinted in Gulu several times. A total of 51,000 copies have been produced. In the 1950s and 1960s, it was read by students throughout the area, and hundreds of copies remain in circulation. It ranges from myths, which Pelligrini links to stories in the Bible, to oral history, plus Catholic and British imperial folklore. We are told how the Acholi ancestors entered the land of Bunyoro and ruled the Bantu people; how various clans eventually settled in the land of Acholi; what happened when the British came; and how the Catholic missions were established. In relevant places, the genealogies of major chiefly lineages are listed.

At the time *Lok pa Acoli Macon* was published, there were already several Acholi historians collecting clan histories. Some of their work appeared in English in the *Uganda Journal*, or in Acholi in the *Acholi Magazine*. Two of the most active were leading Protestants, Reuben Anywar and Nikodemo Latigo. They probably thought of themselves to some extent as being in competition with Pelligrini and his colleague Fr. Crazzolara, but were doubtless also responding to the earlier vernacular publications on Baganda history. Anywar's *Acoli kiKer Megi* was published some years after his death in 1956. In addition, according to Girling, by the late 1940s it was common to find men with exercise-books in which they had written accounts of their clan taken from the lips of their grandfathers. Girling linked this interest in clan histories directly with the formation of a 'new Acholi consciousness'. I would add that this 'new Acholi consciousness' had by then already fed back into English-language Acholi studies, including, to some extent, Girling's own work (1960).

The most obvious example of this feedback is Fr. Crazzolara's massive *The Lwoo*, published in three volumes between 1951 and 1953. Parts of the book are more or less straightforward presentations of testimonies the author collected, mainly in the 1930s and 1940s. But other sections link these testimonies to a conjectured general history of Lwo migrations from Sudan to Uganda and on into Kenya, in order to explain why there are pockets of Lwo-speakers dispersed in the upper Nile basin, surrounded by non-Lwo speakers. Inevitably, he falls into the trap of reading some form of discrete Lwo identity into the past, and sometimes does the same with an Acholi identity. Like Pelligrini, he also argues that the migrations of Lwo groups explains the emergence of the interlacustrine kingdoms, because the Lwo brought from Sudan the institution of monarchy. In this manner, individual clan histories are woven into a grand story which is resonant with the wandering of the 'chosen people' in the wilderness in search of the 'Promised land'.

Crazzolara's book had a considerable impact on African historical writing, not so much because it was widely read itself, but because Bethwell Ogot drew upon it in his seminal *History of the Southern Luo* (1967). Ogot incorporated parts of Crazzolara's conjectured early history of the Lwo into his thesis and, somewhat arbitrarily allowed 27 years per generation in order to work out a chronology of migrations dating back to the turn of the fifteenth century. His method and conclusions proved an inspiration for the History of Uganda Project, based at Makerere University in Kampala, under the direction of J.B. Webster, between 1969 and 1972. Webster and his students concentrated their attention on what they called the 'Central Lwo', a group comprised of the Lwo-speaking groups in Uganda — Acholi, Alur, Palwo, etc. — and published their findings in *The Central Lwo During the Aconya* (Onyango-ku-Odongo & Webster, 1976). Using a method similar to Ogot's, the editors of this volume maintain that, beginning with 1600, it is possible to date with confidence events mentioned in oral texts, and in certain instances it is possible to push the chronology even further back. They even discuss events which, they suggest, occurred before the year 1000.

This literature, which has been widely available in Uganda, has had a considerable impact on the way people think about their ethnic identity. Madi often complained to me that they had no history because it had not been written down, and some suggested I do it. In contrast, Acholi take a corresponding pride in the fact that they have a recognized past. Elsewhere I have discussed how Alice Lakwena's Holy Spirit Movement drew upon ideas expressed by Pellegrini, as well as in the Bible, to build up an Acholi 'tribal' following (Allen, 1991b). Acholi traditions have become reified, significantly influencing the way 'tribal' identity is conceived.

Conclusion

This chapter has comprised a series of linked reflections about Acholi and Madi 'tribalism'. I have argued that, although these particular 'tribes' were colonial inventions, it is not possible to ignore them. 'Tribal' identities have taken on local social meanings, and the specific nature of these meanings needs to be carefully examined.

Although 'tribes' may be discussed by some analysts, and by those caught up in certain kinds of disputes, as discrete, socio-political entities, in fact the idea of a 'tribe' is continually being negotiated. Among the Acholi and the Madi, 'tribal' identity draws on other notions of ethnicity, such as *kaka*. These other notions may be imbued with local ideas about moral space. They do not necessarily coincide with tribal boundaries but, when they do, 'tribal' antagonisms are fierce.

Most of the time 'tribal' identity seems to be something rather abstract and remote from the concerns of daily life. Often there are close relationships between individuals and lineages cutting across 'tribal' boundaries, and sometimes people may emphasize non-tribal notions of ethnicity and actually shift from one 'tribe' to another.

Nevertheless, local conceptions of tradition have been influenced by colonial policies, formal education and missionary activity as well as the deliberate politicization of tribes at the national level in the post-colonial period. While Madis and Acholis have retained multiple and overlapping ethnicities, 'tribal' identity is commonly perceived as the correct and even 'progressive' way of defining populations in relation to the government.

For some groups, this way of asserting collectivity is more locally resonant than it is for others. Acholi 'tribal' identity seems to have a greater dynamism than Madi 'tribal' identity. This can be linked to the promotion of a standardized Acholi language, and to elaboration of the oral histories of patrilineages into an Acholi past which is full of implicit biblical imagery.

References

Allen, T. (1987) Kwete and Kweri: Acholi farm work groups in southern Sudan. *Manchester Papers on Development*, **3** (1): 60–92.

—— (1991a) The quest for therapy in Moyo District. In H.B. Hansen & M. Twaddle (eds), *Changing Uganda*. London: James Currey.

—— (1991b) Understanding Alice: Uganda's Holy Spirit Movement in context. *Africa*, **61** (3): 370–99.

—— (1992) Upheaval, affliction and health: a Ugandan case study. In H. Bernstein, B. Crow & H. Johnson (eds), *Rural Households: Crises and Responses*. Oxford: Oxford University Press.

Anywar, R.S. (1956) *Acoli kiKer Megi*. Nairobi: East African Literature Bureau.

Barnes-Dean, V.L. (1986) Lugbara illness beliefs and social change. *Africa*, **56** (3).

Bernstein, H., Crow, B. & Johnson, H. (eds) (1992) *Rural Households: Crises and Responses*. Oxford: Oxford University Press.

Bilbao, O. & Moizi, L. (1984) *Ma'di-English Dictionary*. Limone: Casa Comboni.

Casale, M. (1982) Women, power, and change in Lugbara (Uganda) cosmology: a re-interpretation. *Anthropos*, **77**.

Crazzolara, J.P. (1938) *A Study of the Acooli Language*. London: Oxford University Press.

—— (1951-3) *The Lwoo*. Verona: Missionari Comboniani.

Fallers, L.A. (1964) (ed.) *The King's Men*. London: Oxford University Press.

Girling, F. (1960) *The Acholi of Uganda*. London: HMSO.

Hyden, G. (1980) *Beyond Ujamaa in Tanzania*. London: Heinemann.

—— (1983) *No Shortcuts to Progress*. London: Heinemann.

James, W. (1988) *The Listening Ebony: Moral Knowledge, Religion, and Power Among the Uduk of Sudan*. Oxford: Clarendon Press.

MacCormack, C. & Strathern, M. (eds) (1980) *Nature, Culture and Gender*. Cambridge: Cambridge University Press.

Middleton, J. (1960) *Lugbara Religion*. London: Oxford University Press.

—— (ed.) (1969) *Magic, Witchcraft and Curing*. New York: The Natural History Press.

—— (1985) The dance among the Lugbara of Uganda. In P. Spencer (ed.), *Society and Dance*. Cambridge: Cambridge University Press.

Ogot, B. (1967) *History of the Southern Luo*. Nairobi: East African Publishing House.

Onyango-ku-Odongo, J. & Webster, J. (eds) (1976) *The Central Lwo during the Aconya*. Nairobi: East African Literature Bureau.

p'Bitek, O. (1970) *African Religions in Western Scholarship*. Nairobi: East African Literature Bureau.

Pellegrini, V. (1949) *Lok pa Acoli Macon*. Kitgum: Catholic Mission.

Schlee, G. (1985) Interethnic clan identities among Cushitic-speaking pastoralists. *Africa*, **55** (1).

Twaddle, M. (1983) Ethnic politics and support for political parties in Uganda. In P. Lyon & J. Manor (eds), *Transfer and Transformation: Political Institutions in the New Commonwealth*. Leicester: Leicester University Press.

Uganda Government Mapping Office (1962) *Atlas of Uganda*. Entebbe, Uganda: Uganda Government Mapping Office.

Young, C. (1976) *The Politics of Cultural Pluralism*. Madison, Wisconsin: University of Wisconsin.

Archival sources

Annual Report for Madi Sub-District, 1956, Entebbe Archives.

DC, West Nile, to PCNP, 3.2.19, Entebbe Archives.

Martyr, report, FO Correspondence, August 1899, Entebbe Archives.

7 War & 'Ethnic Visibility': The Uduk of the Sudan-Ethiopia Border
WENDY JAMES

The population known today as 'the Uduk' were not politically visible as a distinct ethnic group, to themselves or to others, before the present century. During it, however, the processes rendering them visible have accelerated, especially in the civil wars that followed the independence of Sudan. As a direct consequence of the sharpening of their ethnic image in a contested zone of the war frontier, they have become more exposed and vulnerable than before.

Even in the 1960s, when the first civil war was under way, 'the Uduk' had a low profile politically, especially after the missionaries left in 1964, and few distinguished them from the rest of the Ethiopian border peoples. At that time there were 10,000 or so people who spoke the 'Uduk' language as a mother tongue, referring to themselves as 'kwanim pa, but using this self-category in a variety of modes, sometimes including in it some non-Uduk-speakers (James, 1979, 1988). They were labelled in different ways by their immediate neighbours, communities speaking one or more of the vernacular tongues of the Sudan–Ethiopian border, such as Bertha, Jum Jum, Meban, Koma, Kwama and Ganza. All these peoples tended to be lumped together under various names by 'outsiders' to the border region. Speakers of various Nilotic tongues called them *Cai*, and Arab settlers labelled most of them *Burun*. Some of these groups have also been called collectively *Shangalla* and *Yambo* by Amharic- and Oromo-speakers.

All share the peculiar geopolitical situation of being marginal to the processes of state formation in the adjoining regions of the Nile basin and the Ethiopian highlands. On the Nile basin side, the frontiers of state influence, trade, the Arabic language and

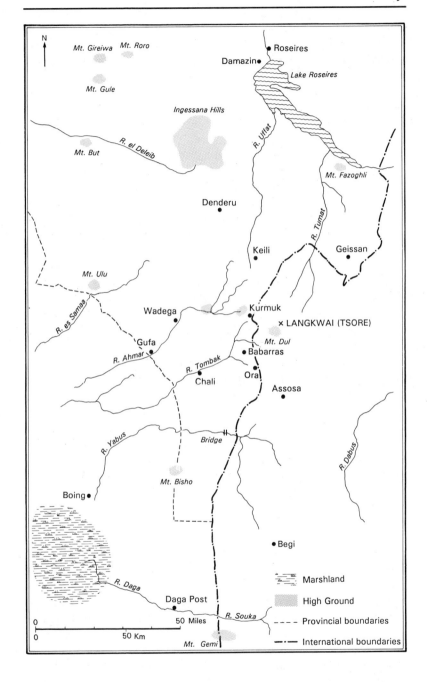

Map 8   The southern Blue Nile

Islam have been fairly stable in the foothills of the upper Blue Nile for two or three centuries. This doubly pivotal position with respect to internal and international definitions of cultural space has always had threatening implications for the local peoples. Their situation has deepened into tragedy with the advent of twentieth-century forms of power and weaponry, and the recent collapse of any semblance of stable government in the region.

Three main factors have contributed to the modern emergence of a distinctive 'ethnic' group known fairly widely today as 'Uduk'. First, we must take account of the peace-making and protective policies of the Anglo-Egyptian Sudan administration following the early twentieth-century settlement of the turbulent border region. Second, we should note the establishment of a station of the Sudan Interior Mission (SIM) in 1938, which acted as a social and cultural focus for speakers of Uduk and also for some of their neighbours, and helped to draw political attention to them nationally. The mission's presence seemed to identify them as a 'southern' group in this sensitive frontier zone, where they were administered as a part of the northern Blue Nile Province from 1953. Third, we have to acknowledge that the north-ward spread of the Sudanese civil war since 1983 led to deepening patterns of suspicion, hostility and conflict right across the transitional zone between the north and south of the country. This gave great impetus to ethnic stereotyping of relatively neutral rural communities in this zone as 'southerners' in a cultural, racial or religious sense and therefore as likely to be rebel supporters. This was the situation in which the 'Uduk' began to be identified as such and, more often than not, to suffer for it.

The historical political tradition of the Uduk has never been of the heroic variety. Their narratives of the past do not record great confrontations with encroaching neighbours, or victories and moral triumph over weakness or evil. Rather, like the Tonga of Zambia described by Elizabeth Colson (1971), they wryly remember prudent retreat and careful acquiescence as a means to survival. Powerful intruders, challengers and rulers have on the whole been recognized for what they were, and life was reconstructed defensively around them, when plain escape or evasion was not possible. Mutual agreements of protection and adoption, and the succour of refugees run through their remembered history. These themes are still relevant to the current situation, in which the conflicts in Sudan have been compounded by those in Ethiopia.

The Uduk-speaking communities are now widely scattered. Some people are in Khartoum and the towns of the Blue Nile, some are stranded in various refugee or returnee centres, and others are dispersed on both sides of the international frontier. What was until 1987 a fairly cohesive rural population is now broken up and dispersed, and their homeland in the Kurmuk district of the Blue Nile Province is deserted. A visitor has described to me how the bush and forest has crept back over the villages where people lived and the fields they had once cleared. Their past existence is no longer visible on the ground. And yet indigenous claims to leadership of the Uduk and for their rights as a group are heard today. This is a very recent development, generated partly by the thriving activities of church groups in the diaspora and their wider mission support network. These voices have found a response in today's context of international aid and relief programmes. Outside recognition of the Uduk as a distinct group among the world's needy is a strange kind of compensation for having been identified as a target population in a war over which they have no control. As the civil war progressed from 1983 onwards, the Uduk were increasingly identified in national discourse as southerners — in a distinctly racial sense — and therefore as SPLA sympathizers. This identification ignored a much more complex reality.

To set the scene for an account of the recent heightened marking of the Uduk as an ethnic group, it is worth recapitulating briefly some of the key points about their past (see Map 8, p. 141).

Early to mid-nineteenth century

From the early to the mid-nineteenth century there was a trickle of migration by Uduk-speaking communities northwards from the hills overlooking the Daga valley to the Yabus, Tombak and Ahmar valleys. This was in part a response to the eastward expansion of the Nuer, which affected the whole population of the upper Sobat and Ethiopian foothills.

Mid- to late nineteenth century

Raiding ensued, first from the heartland of Turco-Egyptian Sudan, and then from the Arabic/Bertha-speaking chiefdoms of the upper Blue Nile, such as Bela Shangul. The raiding intensified, especially after the incorporation of these chiefdoms into the new empire of Menelik II. Patterns of suspicion and hostility were established at this time between neighbouring groups who found themselves on different sides — for example, the Uduk and the Bertha — and patterns of division between different Uduk communities were opened up, according to whether they collaborated with the Bertha chiefdoms or not.

Turn of the present century

The whole of the area formerly settled by Uduk was empty for several years. Some had fled for protection to chiefs on the fringe of the region controlled by the Mahdist government of Sudan, others had voluntarily or involuntarily been attached to the chiefs of the Ethiopian border area, and yet others had sought refuge in the hills south of the Yabus River.

Early twentieth-century administration

In 1904, a military patrol of the Anglo-Egyptian government pacified the new line of the border, and all dislocated populations were recalled to settle in their former home areas. By the 1920s, an ethnically distinctive 'Uduk' population was recognized by the government. In 1938, the Uduk and Koma areas were detached from the Fung Province in northern Sudan, and became part of the Upper Nile Province in the south, to be administered from Renk on the White Nile. This transfer brought the Uduk under the general principles of the colonial government's 'southern' policy, and the Sudan Interior Mission was given permission to start work at Chali.

Post-war development and incorporation in 'the North'

In spite of considerable disruption by military activity on the Ethiopian border during the first years of the Second World War, the mission had a certain degree of success in the educational field by the time the Uduk and Koma areas were transferred back to the north in 1953, as part of the Kurmuk District in the Blue Nile Province. Political tension was already rising in the country, and the presence of 'southern-style' education and the Christian religion in this northern province became a conspicuous anomaly in the eyes of some northern Sudanese.

Independence (1956) and the beginnings of the first Sudanese civil war

Tensions gradually began to affect the Uduk. There had been a few weapons in private hands, but the Uduk population was disarmed by the government shortly after independence. The missionaries were deported in 1964, but there was something of a religious revival in the following period. The first civil war did not directly reach this area. After the Addis Ababa Agreement of 1972, however, it was designated one of those localities which should have the opportunity of a referendum to decide on its future inclusion in the north or the south. Though some appeals were made from Chali, no referendum was held, and those who requested it were harassed. With peace, the area saw some prosperity, and Chali acquired new commercial enterprises.

However, being part of a northern province, the Chali district did not benefit from the development projects administered throughout the southern region of the Sudan from 1972 to 1983. Rather, the area was neglected, and northern political and religious dominance in the market centres of the district was intensified. An army garrison was established in Chali in the late 1970s, and also a *mahad*, an Islamic school for students drawn mainly from other parts of the Blue Nile. These were followed by a mosque in 1983. The church community continued to thrive, however, recruiting widely from the outlying villages, and when the civil war resumed, in 1983, there was a feeling of confrontation and danger in Chali.

War comes to the Blue Nile

My account of the events which affected the Uduk after the outbreak of the current war, greatly increasing their conspicuousness and vulnerability, is based on evidence I was able to gather in Sudan, Ethiopia and Kenya during 1988–9. Most of the details come from conversations with displaced people known personally to me, and what follows is offered as a partial analysis based on the experience of some individuals. The quotations translated verbatim, illustrate ways in which the 'ethnic visibility' of the Uduk, as I have called it, was growing rapidly. The image was generated and sustained by the circumstances of the conflict, not only in the eyes of the government forces and their sympathizers — and no doubt the rebel Sudan People's Liberation

Army (SPLA) forces and their sympathizers as well — but in the self-perception of the people themselves.

From mid-1983 to late 1985

Incidents of harassment of the local Omda (government-appointed chief) and church leaders increased, as reports were heard of SPLA advances northward in the adjoining regions of the upper Nile. Security forces from the Chali garrison began to arrest, interrogate, torture and kill local civilians suspected of sympathizing with the SPLA from mid-1984, after the guerrilla attack on the town of Boing to the south. People drinking beer around Chali were seized and beaten because of the new Islamic laws decreed in September 1983. After the overthrow of Nimeiri in April 1985, because of the continuing drought throughout Sudan, international relief agencies began to channel food supplies to the southern Blue Nile region and elsewhere in the country. Suspicion and hostility intensified because some of the supplies were allocated by international agencies to the church leadership in Chali. These supplies had to continue their southward journey another 30 miles or so from Kurmuk, into what was seen as guerrilla country in the southern swamps. After preliminary skirmishes close to the provincial boundary in 1984, the SPLA established its presence in the Blue Nile at the end of 1985, when they appeared in the border hills south of Kurmuk and began to set up a base just inside Ethiopia.

Text 1
(S.R., a young labour migrant, normally resident in Khartoum, who described a brief visit back to Chali and his home village of Beni Mayu in 1984)

I went home in April 1984 [from Khartoum]. I stayed in Chali one day, I went to Beni Mayu, I stayed there three days, and then people attacked Boing [i.e. the SPLA attacked the garrison town of Boing just beyond the provincial border of Blue Nile, in the Upper Nile Province]. When Boing was attacked, I came back to Chali and found everything had changed. It was quite different, I saw it for myself. The army, the soldiers in Chali there, seized people, seized and tied them, there were very many, left them, beat them, and some people died. I got up and went to Chali and the army asked me, where has this fellow come from? From the north? The local officer said: 'You should not wander about. If you wander about, you will be arrested.' Truly. Even if you came out on the road from the church, you would be arrested. [A pastor] said: 'Don't go to the market. For if you go to the market, you will be arrested.'
  I took heed. The day I had come [from Beni Mayu to Chali], I returned

straight back to Kurmuk. The people arrested us. They asked where we had come from. I said I was from Chali. They said: 'Where are you going?' I said I had come from home, and was going back [north]. We didn't know what they would do. We went on, we were four . . . I was going to Khartoum. Some fellows were coming from the agricultural schemes, and they arrested them. Chaps from Yabus. Seized and tied, not tied in an ordinary way, tied very horribly. The people asked them, were they armed? They were tied up, and the people asked if they had guns. Some of them had guns, and they said, bring the guns for us to see. They found them, and some soldiers said, these are not the guns of the guerrillas, these are their own guns. Others said, they should be killed . . .

Then they seized and tied up [gives the names of two young men from Chali], that year, they were tied in an unnatural way. Many fled to the bush, but were captured on their return home. People from that point started saying that their people were being killed. They went and found some chaps in the Yabus, seven or five. They said they were guerrillas, and killed some. They were going to kill them all, but one fell from the shot, and rolled over, rolled down from a hill. He alone survived, and people didn't know, they gathered together and said, our brothers have all been killed. This happened in 1985. After that people were not able to stay in peace. Things went bad. The army would seize you. If you appeared for a couple of days, they would seize you and say you were a rebel . . . People fled to the bush.

Early 1986 to mid-1987

The year 1986 was marked by the following main developments which sharpened the tensions in the southern Blue Nile:

1 An elected assembly was returned in Khartoum in April. The preliminary campaigning had led to the growth of the Muslim Brotherhood movement in Kurmuk, and a National Islamic Front representative was elected for this constituency. The new MP began to take active steps to improve security (as he saw it) and to control aid distribution in the region.

2 This year also saw the arming of the Rufa'a Arabs as a government militia. They began to carry weapons openly, as they migrated northwards with their animals through the region in the early rains (May–June) and southwards again at the beginning of the dry season (December onwards).

3 From early 1986, SPLA units began to move through the outlying settlements of the southern Blue Nile region, avoiding main routes as they travelled between camps in Ethiopia and the White Nile. Sometimes they would sit and talk with villagers, and partly because of the harassment from security forces already experienced by the people, a steady trickle of youths was recruited into the guerrilla army.

4 International aid organizations, including some with church

147

links, stepped up their activities in 1986, adding to the political and religious tensions in the southern Blue Nile and worsening the difficulties faced by the church leadership in Chali. Some of these organizations, including World Vision, were later expelled from Sudan.

5 The harvest of 1986 was a good one and, as a result, by the end of the year there was a high demand for agricultural labour from merchant entrepreneurs who had established mechanized rain-fed cultivation in the central part of the Blue Nile. These schemes had extended quite recently south of Jebel Gule; for example, to the area of Jebel But. A few years previously, the pattern had been for individual young men to take the initiative and go off to market centres like Mazmum in search of seasonal labour, but by late 1986 merchants were sending trucks down to small settlements like Chali to sign up and transport labourers to their schemes.

The choices for able-bodied young men had thus become very stark in the course of 1986. Many continued to join the Sudanese armed forces, a trend set in the previous two dry years, when the Nimeiri regime encouraged regional recruitment. Some rallied around the church leadership when it was drawn into controversies over aid, and a few even found employment with the aid agencies. Others sought regular wage labour, and many had the option towards the end of the year of leaving the immediate district to work in agricultural schemes further to the north. Standing against these straightforward opportunities through the year was the option of joining the guerrillas. By early 1986, the security forces knew that some Uduk had joined the SPLA and were trying to round up suspects. They arrested 14 people from Gindi in the early rains of 1986, took them to Ora and tortured them. The first guerrilla recruits from among the Uduk came from the outlying settlements like Gindi, and only later did young men brought up in the long-established Christian community of Chali itself consider joining the movement.

It was during the late rains of 1986 that the Blue Nile saw its first engagement of the war. Information was passed to the garrison in Chali by a 'loyal' chief that some SPLA guerrillas were camped in the nearby village of Beni Mayu. Troops were despatched, and there were exchanges of fire, leaving some dead on both sides. After this, the chiefs of that locality were called to Chali but refused to come, and so the people of that area were prevented from entering Chali for normal purposes like buying food. The church leaders in Chali were summoned by the military to various meetings. Verbal threats were made by the officers but the church elders and the Omda were anxious to demonstrate their continuing loyalty to the government, and even passed on a list of names of SPLA recruits.

In late November, an SPLA party came from Ethiopia into Sudan through Babarras, and after an encounter with troops from Deim Mansour sent a message to Chali saying that they planned an attack, and that the Christians should leave for the bush. This they did, many spending Christmas there. The message was also taken (by a Bertha) to the Chali garrison, and many of the Chali Bertha also left, including traders. Just after Christmas, word arrived that a large SPLA group had come northwards from their training centre at Bilpam (near Jokau), arriving in the Blue Nile Province at the Yabus settlement of Belatoma. The majority were said to be Uduk, under Dinka and Nuba leadership, trained as members of the Arrow Battalion (Arabic: *katiba al nishab*). This unit was later to be incorporated into the New Funj Forces of the SPLA. The name 'New Funj' evokes for all Sudanese the past glories and political power of the black population of this region (James, 1977).

The Chali garrison heard that 'the Uduk were coming home' (standard rhetoric for SPLA-trained recruits from a given area returning to liberate their villages) and called for reinforcements from garrisons to the north. Before these could arrive, the SPLA party was attacked by soldiers from Yabus Bridge, but seem to have come through this quite well. After a short time they moved north-east, apparently intending to reach an SPLA base inside Ethiopia and obtain more ammunition. However, their approach was reported by nomad Arabs of the Rufaa to the Chali garrison. The newly arrived reinforcements were able to surround the SPLA column, inflict damage and disperse it.

Many of the Uduk boys who took part in this advance, having been away from home for six or more months, were able to return quietly to their homes under cover of darkness and see their relatives overnight; some stayed longer. They warned their families that the SPLA would return. Unfortunately, the garrison came to learn of these visits, and after three days began arrests and general reprisals against the civilian population. It was no longer possible for anyone, including the church leadership, to convince the garrison that they were not involved with the SPLA. The whole population was now seen as rebels and punished accordingly.

The account offered next is by an elder of the Chali church, who arrived in Khartoum in February 1987 and, because of subsequent events, became stranded there. His story shows how

149

the presence of the SPLA in Blue Nile Province had become identified with the Uduk as a group, particularly with the church, and how as a result 'the government then came down upon the Uduk people'

Text 2
(G.S., a middle aged man from Chali)

The day that the Uduk guerrillas [*ucim bwasho, ucim pa*, literally 'the boys in the bush, the Uduk boys'] appeared, in Belatoma, was the 23rd [December 1986]. In the morning. Then when the army [from Yabus Bridge] heard that the SPLA ['*kwanim bwasho*, or 'people in the bush'] had arrived, they came out to find the boys and fight with them. They came at half-past three. They met them and fought. They fought for just 15 minutes, a quarter of an hour. That day they fought was a Friday. They fought there, and in the late afternoon, on the same day, they [SPLA] set off in the evening on the road towards Chali. They slept on the road.

In the morning they arrived at a place called Pa Wotha, at Nyile. And very soon people heard the news: 'The SPLA has come'. Then people [soldiers from the Chali garrison] set off to search for them coming on the road from Belatoma, but they didn't find them. They missed them on the road. The boys had already arrived at Nyile, while the army was down there in Belatoma. After the boys had reached there, a message was sent to all the government stations, at Kurmuk, Geissan, and all the places where there were soldiers. They gathered together, and met up with the boys at three o'clock, at Babarras. And the fighting went on for three hours. They fought from three to six o'clock in the evening. When the fighting was over, by nightfall, all the Uduk boys came back to see their people. Some had wives, some had children, some stayed with their father's people. They all came to see their own people, then they returned back to their base. Having found their families, however, some stayed, even a fortnight, among the people. And this was not known. People looked after them, as sons of the home. When their stay was over, they went off again.

And after this, after three days, the army sought me out, and arrested me. They arrested me on, which day was it? Anyway, after three days. They arrested me at six in the evening. They put me in the prison, and asked me lots of questions. I told them that I didn't know anything. And they wanted me to tell them things, but I didn't tell them anything. I told them I didn't know these people. And they kept me in prison for one day, from Tuesday to Wednesday. And the people of the church gathered to pray to God [*Arumgimis*, the mission-coined term] for me. They prayed to God, and God heard their prayers, and the people freed me in the afternoon, at four o'clock. The whole church gathered, and spent a lot of time praying for me. The [officers] wanted to call others for questioning, but I said that anything they had to ask, they could ask me, and they heard what I said and didn't call anyone else. They finished what they wanted to say, with me.

For when the boys had all come home after the fighting, a few remained here and there. Just a few remained among their people, here and there. So then the government came down upon the Uduk people, harassing them. Arresting them, tying them, beating them, and many suffered great pain, at that time they were seized.

150

By early January 1987, the scene was set for outright war and the rest of that year saw battles and devastation in the southern Blue Nile. The 'Uduk SPLA' [*sic*] continued to make themselves felt in the district, and the Chali garrison started major retaliation by setting fire to the small outlying church in Gindi at the end of January. The Chali church leaders lodged a complaint with the police. The Chali church itself was surrounded one day by soldiers who threatened to kill everyone if any SPLA members were being sheltered. Some of the church leaders managed to leave for a meeting in Khartoum in February, promising to return. Various delays and the eventual disaster of late March meant they never did. They had to settle in the capital, some melting into the urban population and others remaining visible as a church group from the Blue Nile. There were a few skirmishes around Chali, including encounters between the SPLA and the Rufa'a, the latter now acting not merely in self-defence but as a militia in concert with the security forces. This period culminated in the systematic burning of all the villages in the Uduk area by the security forces, with the assistance of the Rufa'a, at the end of March.

The account of G.S. continues:

And on the day that we [elders of the church] were about to set out for Khartoum, on February the 18th or 19th, the boys came again and fought at Khor el Bodi. And on that day when they fought at Khor el Bodi, and we were about to leave, the army came again and surrounded us in the settlement. Surrounded the church village, with the Chali Uduk all inside. They surrounded us because they thought that we were hiding guerrillas among us. They wanted to kill all the Chali people. When we woke up in the morning, we found just soldiers there in the settlement of the Uduk, from the mission road, from the Beni Mayu road near the river there. They said that if they found just one guerrilla there, they would kill all the Chali people, all the Chali Uduk people. But they didn't find anyone.

We then heard [later, when they had reached Khartoum], from home, that things were very bad there. We heard what had happened to the people of Beni Mayu, Bonya [Bellila], and Gindi, and Borfa, all of them, and Gwami. As for Chali itself, nothing had happened there yet. The army had gone to Daga, to do a *natafa* [Arabic: 'search and destroy']. They threatened the people of Gindi first, saying: 'We are going [on an expedition], but when we come back you are not going to live. We are going to kill you all.' And these words caused fear among the people. People thought they would not survive this. The soldiers left. When they came back from Daga, they burned the people's houses. They burned all the food supplies in the houses. And some people were killed in their houses; blind people, or old people. Burned with fire by the army. They burned houses with people inside. They died. They died in the fire which burned up like that. For example, one from Beni Mayu, he was elder of the church, called Bije, called Thomas, he was burned inside the church, and he died. And his wife also. She was blind. She was called Ramka. The hut was burned with her inside, and she died. And again in Gindi, there are some people, some

151

women who were killed with fire, when the huts were burned. Some were blind.

And soon after this, when the Chali people heard of these things, the boys in the bush came on that day, and they escorted people away. From Gindi, from Beni Mayu, from Bellila. Earlier, the Arabs [Rufa'a] had killed people in Bellila. They shot them with guns. Many people died. They say many children died of thirst in the bush. It is not very clear what happened everywhere. One small village may not exist any more. A certain small village, called Pan Gayo, we think may have been wiped out completely by the Arabs. The people are missing. We don't know to be sure, but we have heard this. We still do not know exactly what happened, whether the people were finished, but we have heard that many small children perished in the bush.

And as for the people of Chali itself, they just heard about these awful things, that there were no people left [in the outlying villages], and they realized that they were left alone among themselves. The boys came back, to try and evacuate them, but the church people would not be led away. They planned to stay put. Then the army started to fire on the church, so the people went off and slept in the grass. The people then realized that death had appeared among them, and it was not good to stay. So then the church people decided that they should follow the others of their own accord; they were not escorted. They wanted to go all together, taking women and children. A few remained, they are there, up to now [mid-1988].

Many people died at this time. It is not possible to give exact information, and it should be remembered that the accounts quoted here were given in Khartoum about a year and a half after the events described. The outline of what happened is nevertheless corroborated from many sources, first- and second-hand. In the outlying settlements, the soldiers would first shoot at a village, scattering the people, and then set fire to the houses and grain stores, even to spare wooden beds kept outside. Some people, especially the old and blind, were said to have been caught in their houses, and one church elder was said to have been burned alive in his small church at Beni Mayu, because he refused the soldiers' demands that he come out first.

Others were said to have been shot as they ran away from their burning settlements. The villagers crept back at nightfall, and found everything gone. Then the young men, their own kin from among the SPLA fighters, came to round them up and evacuate them to Ethiopia. The people of the outlying villages nearly all went. A few stragglers were left behind. In one story I was told (but was not in a position to confirm), four elderly women and a small boy who were about to follow the others towards Ethiopia were all shot in front of their houses by the Rufa'a Arabs. The Arabs took what remained of the goats and cattle left in the villages. The soldiers had already shot most of the pigs, though some escaped and are probably living wild in the forest today. In some areas to the south of Uduk country, the Rufa'a took charge of some groups of women and children; what happened to them is unknown.

The people of the Chali church village itself, as mentioned in this account, refused to be evacuated and remained about another month, until they came under direct mortar fire from the garrison. They then decided to accept the invitation of the SPLA and follow the rest of their people to Ethiopia. One of the deep ironies of the situation is that the church leadership and people had throughout signalled their continuing loyalty to the authorities, and tried to distance themselves from the SPLA, but this was not recognized. The garrison, and no doubt its political masters, took the view that the church was behind the people's involvement with the guerrillas, that it was politically motivated and a legitimate target.

The account which follows reflects this clearly. It is a first-hand testimony from a woman who remained with the church group in Chali until they had to leave. As they fled, they were fired on. Another party of women and children who tried to come back to Chali was also fired on. This might have been as a warning, but the effect was to scare the women off; they dropped their belongings and retreated again towards Ethiopia. This party included the wife of the senior church pastor, who was stranded in Khartoum.

In the account below, my informant describes how her own little party eventually managed to return to Chali. Once there, the army insisted they live in the market village near the garrison, and not at their homes near the mission. These homes were later burned and the mission itself was sacked and everything in it stolen or destroyed, including the window-frames. The mission had an old plastic Christmas tree of many years' loyal service. This was taken away, presumably as a trophy, by a senior army officer. Fortunately for the lady whose account follows, her son came from Khartoum in May to collect her and a couple of children. On their journey north they were accused of being 'Garang's people'.

Text 3
(T.K., a middle-aged woman from Chali)

That day when the houses were burned [end of March 1987], the area of Pam'Be and Beni Mayu was burned first, beginning with Pam'Be. As the houses were set on fire, foodstuffs like those which people stored on platforms outside, you have seen them, that sorghum outside was thrown on the fire. They said people would give this sorghum to the guerrillas to eat. [The soldiers] burned people's food, so that hunger would seize them. They burned

153

everything, like the wooden bed you are sitting on, they would take it out
and throw it on the fire. They did this to everything. Then the people fled,
fled, took their children and fled in the bush; and it was extremely hot. It
was March when they did this in Pam'Be first. People took their children to
the bush, to the sorghum fields out there. And the children were seized by
thirst. They stayed, waited, before coming home in the evening. When the
army left and went away, the people came back, looking for dough, dough
burned in the fire, to [boil and] give to the children to eat. They stayed
about five days perhaps, they were hungry, the little children were crying of
hunger.

Then the boys [SPLA] came and said: 'All right, we are going to lead you
away.' And they led them away by night, the people of Pam'Be and Beni Mayu
first. They evacuated them. Later, when they had been away about a month,
they came back again, saying they would take the people of Chali. They came
and we were living at the mission settlement. We didn't know that people had
come to take everyone away. About 7 o'clock in the evening they came: 'We
have come to take you away.' We said we didn't know about this. I got ready.
There were a few cattle, and I said: 'Hassan' — that little boy Hassan who's
now here. There were no grown men — 'Hassan, up you get and untie the cattle.' Hassan untied them, and I put him on the donkey. We went on a little
like that, and the guns fired right over our heads. The guns fired, and the bullets
came over our heads as we went along the path. We went on, and God
[*Arumgimis*] prevented the guns from stopping us, and we went on. We went
on until the moon was high, right into the bush, in the night. We were leading
the children along, on and on until the dawn found us still going. There was
no time for sleep.

Up to the morning we were still awake and going. The children were very
tired, and one of our girls couldn't go on. She collapsed and said: 'I shan't
be able to reach there.' So I said we should go back home. 'If the army are
going to kill us let them kill us.' So I led them, we came back, we got home
when the sun was here in the evening, the day after we had left. We had
been up all through the night. We got back and lay down. They were very
tired indeed, and when we got back to our own homes they lay down and
slept. We had gone on and on, and in the late afternoon arrived back home.
There was water left in the houses of the people who had gone, and I said
we should collect some water from their houses, for our bodies were exhausted
. . . We ate.

Then the army came and said we should leave. 'Where have you come from?
You should sleep at our place' [the market village with the garrison, not the
mission]. They escorted us, to sleep at the market village. A few people were
there. They said: 'All right, we will take in our sister here, she can stay with
us.' We stayed there, and in the morning we went back to the mission. We
went back just that little way. They said: 'You must not sleep there, you must
come back.' So we went back, and we stayed there, for about a month. Then
[her son, who had been in Khartoum] came to find us, for his father said: 'You
should go and find your mother and those with her, and lead them away.' He
came. It rained, and then he took us away, we set off and arrived in Kurmuk.

We had a difficult time on the journey, because they wanted to ask questions
and find a way to arrest [my son]. Saying: 'Those people of Garang, where
are they going? Where are these people of Garang going? You attack people,
and now where are you going?' But we went on, and we stayed at Damazin
until the next month, and then we went on.

The identification of likely 'Garang' sympathizers had been actively pursued in the Blue Nile since the beginning of the year (1987). The Rufa'a militia played a part in this, and certainly were in part responsible for the picking out of supposed suspect ethnic groups among the labourers on the local agricultural schemes. The SPLA did mount attacks and ambushes on the Rufa'a, as they moved through the bush with their flocks and herds, and it seems that revenge was taken a little later in a series of massacres of labourers on the agricultural schemes at But and, I believe, also Ulu. According to one report, labourers were singled out specifically as 'Uduk' and killed. One account I heard described the Rufa'a pointing out those who were Uduk by their characteristic facial or bodily markings — in particular, a cross within a circle. In at least one case I know, help was sought from local police but refused. Survivors fled to the Blue Nile towns and some to the capital city.

My final quotation is from the testimony of one such survivor, whose home was at Borfa. He sought work on the harvest in very early 1987, and accepted a lift from Chali in a merchant's truck going to the cultivation schemes north of Jebel Gule. Not finding any work, he and others were trekking home when they encountered trouble. Suspected by local 'Bunyan' (Bertha- and Arabic-speaking merchants) of being connected with a recent SPLA attack, they were taken in a party of eight to the police. But the police wanted nothing to do with them. Their escorts then consulted with some of the Rufa'a Arabs, who questioned the boys. Although some Arabs spoke up for their innocence, it was decided they should be dealt with. Realizing this, four escaped, but the other four had their hands tied, and were pushed off into the bush to walk to Damazin. They were met by armed Rufa'a who murdered three. The fourth was my informant, who untied his hands and got away. After wandering several days in the bush and finding the southern route blocked by Arabs, he returned to the schemes looking for other Uduk, eventually finding a friend and making his way to Khartoum. He told me his story.

Text 4
(G.H., a young agricultural labourer)

We were very poor at home, and I needed some money to buy a few things to wear and so on, and that's why we went to seek some money to buy a few things. After a while we would come back home. So we went, and arrived at the hill called Gireiwa about 12 o'clock midday, and we got down to rest. Some people, Nuba chaps maybe, black like us, told us that we should stay a little longer, until we got a permit. Perhaps another day, things would improve, and we could get a permit. But we didn't get a permit. So we thought we would go home and see how people were, because we knew that things were bad at home. So we left, and arrived at But, where we slept, on our way home. Then our brother Sora, Sora Mushwa'd was asked by a Bunyan [a Bertha man]: 'How are you?' Then another came and called him, and they went over there and stopped, and talked and talked and talked. Then he [the Bertha] said: 'Call those people. Call those people to come.' Our brother Sora said: 'Come, we have to call the others.' We went to them [eight in all], we didn't delay, and those people said: 'Their people have killed a neighbour of ours at Dawalla. We should take these people to the government.' They took us away.

They took us away, we went on and on, and then they took our things away; our throwing sticks and spears, the things we were carrying, we gave them up. We rested for a while, and they said they were taking us to the government. The police. We waited on the ground. We waited, and they went to see the government. The government said: 'Ay. We don't want these people. If you want to deal with them, you may do what you wish with them.' They kept us until some nomad Arabs [of the Rufa'a] came. They asked us questions: 'How did you come from your home?' We said that a man called Somolia brought us from our home area, to work cutting sorghum at his place. I told the Arab all about it. The Arab said: 'Really? We know that Somolia brings many Uduk to work at But there. Leave these people, they haven't done anything.' Others saw this. They asked us questions: 'Really, really? Did Somolia bring you?' 'Yes. We went to do some work at Somolia's place, but the money was very little, so we went to another man, called Osman, to cut sorghum at his place and go home.' They moved away and talked, this and that, this and that: 'A man was killed in Wadega.' We decided we should go.

But then, they seized us, though we were not fleeing, we were still there, and they seized us. Some of the chaps saw that they were carrying rope and tying our hands behind our backs. Those fellows ran away. They fled. Four of them fled, and four of us were left. We sat there, and those people brought rope and tied us. They took our things, leaving just a few clothes on. We stayed. About seven o'clock they took us away, pushing us along into the bush there, saying: 'You can go to Damazin on foot. You have been making *siyassa* [Arabic: 'politics'] and you want to kill us.' We went on, obeying their words, we went on into the bush. The Arabs were ahead at a little hill. We went on.

Then we stopped. I said to Sora: 'To tell you the truth, you know I am a Christian and I don't want to die for no reason, without seeing the government face to face. If I see the government face to face, and people kill me, as others killed Jesus for the truth, well then, I will die in front of the police.' He said all right. And then the Arabs appeared rushing along the road, and he said: 'You save yourself, I have something, I shall stay as if I'm dead.' I said good. I didn't want to go, but if I were going to die, I wanted to die over there, I didn't want to die here in the bush, people would really kill us here. I did not want to die in the bush. People would really kill us here. Let us die over there. Then they beat us.

They struck us, and I fell down on the ground, but I got up, I don't know how, and then I saw a small place, I ran a little, I don't know how I got away from there. I thought I was dying, what shall I do, I ran on there, and I saw that I had got away some distance. I stopped. I untied myself and I went on, it was a bright moon. I went on, and I stopped. Then they killed the boys with guns, *do, do*. Two boys. And the other one, they beat him until it was finished with a stick. [Question: Who was shot, Sora?] Sora [Mushwa'd], and Limam [Pisko]. And Nyaha [Karabu], he was killed with a stick.

Then I went on and stopped. The thing overcame me, and I was going unsteadily. I went on. I couldn't see what to do, and maybe I would die alone in the bush. After that I went on. God [*Arumgimis*] led me. Led me on and on, in the bush there. My body was tired, and when I got to the road I lay down. I was very thirsty in the night. I slept a little, then at dawn I went on. I decided I would try to go home. I went on and on and on, I was extremely thirsty, and at six or seven o'clock I found some people who were working at making charcoal. I appeared at their place, and greeted them, *Salaam alekum*. They said: 'Welcome, have some water.' I drank water. I sat down for a bit, and they said: 'Welcome, have some tea.' I drank tea. Then they said: 'Should we make some food for you?' I ate food, stayed there a while, and then I said: 'I am going now, going home over there. Through Samaa there.' They asked: 'Is Samaa near?' I told them yes. I just told them this.

I set off and went on. Then I found a lot of Arabs busy ahead of me. I sat down. It was more than I could cope with. [Not knowing if he would be able move southwards towards home, he decided to retrace his steps.] I went back and found the people who had given me food, and I greeted them and said I had decided to go back, back to But. So I drank water and went back. *Arumgimis* led me again. I went in the deep bush, near the road, and I came to a merchant's business place there, half-way to Gule. I drank water there. They said: 'Welcome, have a rest.' I rested a little, and then they said: 'Are you going? It is straight on to that hill, Gule there.' It was night-time, I had been two nights in the bush. I stopped and slept until dawn, and I arrived at Gule about six. I asked some Meban boys: 'Brothers. Are there any Uduk here?' 'No, there aren't any Uduk. No Uduk,' they said.

So I went on, to Gireiwa, to see if there was any Uduk person at Gireiwa. I went on and on, reached there, and I found an Uduk there, a chap we had left behind, from Pan Gayo. He said: 'Aha, so what is it?' I said: 'Caah. Things are not good.' I told him all about it. How some of our boys were killed, others ran in the bush, I don't know whether they would all have died out there. That group all ran into the bush, and three others were killed. I told him about it. Then I said, you can help me because you have a permit. He said, yes, we have permit, but we are tired and plan to go home.

We talked and talked, and then a Meban sheikh came from Bellila there, called Sheikh [name given]. He came and found me, at Roro there. I told him and he said he would take me to the government, in Roro. He took me to the government [the police station] in Roro, and they asked me questions in Roro there. They asked me, do you know a man called [the chief pastor of the Chali church; an affirmative answer would identify G.H. as an Uduk]. I said yes, I knew him. 'Where is he?' I said he was in Khartoum. They asked where I had come from, and I said I had come from But. The man who brought me said I should explain things in my own words, the truth. Then they said: 'Heh. All of you are *maratin* [Arabic: 'rebels']. You have all become rebels. This is useless talk. You just sit down.'

I sat down, I just sat. 'We are not going to arrest you or take you to Damazin. You can just go and find you own work there. This sheikh of yours can take you there.' I went to the sheikh, but people didn't want me; they didn't want to help me. I was very hungry, they were drinking beer, and they took me to the beer place. I drank some beer, for I was very hungry. I was drinking beer, and they left the beer place, but I didn't realize, they had gone saying that if the Arabs found us they would kill us.

I was left there and I had an idea, I would go back to Gireiwa, and would stay there. I went back, and stayed there 14 days. With the Meban boys there, and an Uduk friend who said: 'Let's go to Singa, because I know Singa, with your money.' I didn't want to go, I said I would lead him home. Our home there. He said: 'I want to buy a gun, and kill people.' I said no, we couldn't do this. We should go on until we found where the other Uduk people were living. He didn't want to go. But he had enough of living with the Meban. The Meban realized something of this, and said he should go. They collected money so that he could go, five reals, and we went in the morning at seven. By car from Gireiwa to Mazmum, five pounds. From there we went on to Singa [he later mentioned this was ten pounds]. We stayed there with some other Meban, with a brother of his. We looked for a place, an opportunity. I knew that God [*Arumgimis*] would help me, I went back to the work of *Arumgimis*. I wanted to understand it, I didn't want to live for no reason. I came to Khartoum, as *Arumgimis* had kept me alive, and I thought I should come and see you [the Uduk Christian community in the capital].

G.H. had not previously been a committed Christian, but he went on to explain his intention to prepare for instruction and baptism.

By mid-1987, virtually the whole of Uduk country was empty and devastated, settled only by a few garrisons and those who had no choice but to seek refuge with them. This was less than a century after the wholesale sacking of the country that took place just before the *pax britannica*.

War entrenched: the refugee camp at Tsore, Assosa (1987-9)

Over the border in Ethiopia, the national authorities and the United Nations High Commission for Refugees (UNHCR) had established a refugee centre at Tsore, in the Assosa District of Wollega Province, by mid-1987. Those displaced from the southern Blue Nile Province of the Sudan, and some others, were received here and given assistance in making a temporary home. Uduk-speakers from all parts of their homeland constituted a majority of the population in the camp, and gained the reputation in aid circles of being 'model refugees'. Having brought some tools and seeds with them, and knowing how to utilize wild foods to feed their children, they co-operated with the authorities in setting up schemes for cultivation, craft workshops and camp committees.

The whole situation seemed fairly stable for two and a half years, with the Uduk appearing to give some kind of leadership to other communities in the camp. They led the way in building shelters for worship — 'churches' of a kind — and there were 17 of these by the end of 1989, using the Uduk and Meban languages. Some help from outside, for example via the Sudan Interior Mission office in Addis Ababa, was channelled through to the camp, but in the main the settlement was supported by the Ethiopian authorities and the UNHCR.

On the other side of the border, the civil war in Sudan moved northwards and southwards, and Kurmuk town was briefly captured twice by the SPLA in 1987 and 1989. Throughout this period the SPLA also maintained its presence in this part of western Ethiopia. With each shift in the military situation across the border, new waves of refugees came across to the Tsore camp. A UNHCR survey of October 1989 gave a total of over 34,000 people in the camp, of whom about 75 per cent described themselves as 'Uduk'. By the end of December 1989, when Kurmuk had just been recaptured for the second time by the Sudanese army, there were reported to be around 42,000 people in the Tsore camp. A fresh disaster then struck. To explain what led up to it, we must recount what had been happening on the Sudan side of the border after the bulk of the Uduk left.

During the rains of 1987, the season when the Rufa'a normally move well away to the north, the SPLA made considerable advances. Chali was directly attacked several times but not taken, although in mid-November the towns of Kurmuk and Geissan were taken. Government forces recaptured these towns by late December, after a major campaign to raise funds and support from within the country and abroad. There is substantial evidence that, on the taking of Kurmuk by the SPLA, there were harsh reprisals against civilians further north, particularly in Damazin. Police and army seized a large number who were identified as 'southerners' and SPLA sympathizers on grounds of racial appearance and sometimes religious affiliation, though their origins were fairly local and mostly within the Blue Nile Province. I know of one Uduk man in Damazin who is said to have been rounded up, tied, beaten, kicked and thrown into the river to drown at this time.

Kurmuk was quickly retaken, roads were improved and reinforcements were sent to garrisons in the region. This persuaded the few remaining people in Chali, including the Omda, to leave for Tsore to rejoin their people. During 1988, the SPLA remained active as a guerrilla force in the southern Blue Nile, but it was not until the late rains of 1989 that Kurmuk fell again to them, and this time it was followed by the outlying garrisons. A triumphant address was broadcast from Chali on the SPLA

radio in late November. The officer who spoke used colloquial
Arabic, but a colleague translated his proclamation sentence by
sentence into the Uduk language. This was the first, and probably
only, time that this language had been heard on radio. It was heard,
if not understood, across Sudan and neighbouring countries, and
the name and image of the Uduk people were carried with it.

A complicating factor in the story of the Sudan war on this
border was the activity of the Oromo Liberation Front (OLF).
It is clear that the OLF had been given indirect support by the
Sudanese authorities for some years. The organization's relief
wing, the Oromo Relief Association (ORA), had set up a large
refugee camp of its own just inside Sudan in the Yabus valley,
and by mid-1989 there was free movement for OLF–ORA parties
down from Khartoum, through Kurmuk and the garrison at
Chali, to the Yabus. The OLF played a part in keeping the roads
open for the Sudanese forces based in Kurmuk, and there was
a series of confrontations between them and the SPLA. The
SPLA itself later attacked the ORA camp, dispersing the people
and presumably the OLF forces, and relations between the two
movements were very poor indeed by late 1989.

It was in this context that the SPLA were able to take Kurmuk
for the second time, in October 1989. They held it only until late
December. Following this, the OLF forces overran large parts
of Assosa District in Ethiopia in December 1989–January 1990.
They sacked the refugee camp at Tsore, killing many people and
burning the buildings. They even took Assosa town briefly, but
the Ethiopian authorities reacted quickly and reasserted control.
The UNHCR was left powerless to do very much about the situation, and could only state that there would be no rebuilding of
a camp in an area which had become so insecure.

Renewed dispersal of the Uduk, 1990

As of March 1991, it was impossible for me to gain a clear
picture of where the Uduk were. Even the UNHCR officials in
Addis Ababa confessed they had no idea. Because the refugee
population in Assosa were scattered in the border region, they
seemed to fall between stools. They were not the clear responsibility of agencies dealing with international problems, or of
nationally based agencies on either side of the border. Survivors
of the 42,000 who were dispersed from the Tsore camp in early
1990 were now in many different localities. Individuals were
widely scattered. Sudanese soldiers found some Uduk children

wandering in the bush near Geissan after the sacking of Tsore, and picked them up for questioning. They were later returned to relatives in Damazin and Khartoum.

For most of the Uduk and Meban, one of the initial movements from Assosa was south-westwards into the Upper Nile Province of Sudan, where protection was sought from the SPLA. As their numbers grew, such protection was no longer possible, and the SPLA escorted the majority to the neighbourhood of existing UNHCR camps in the Gambela region. Most were forced to trek all the way down to the very large camp at Itang on the Baro. Numbers of Uduk seem also to have settled on their own in the Daga valley and hill country to the north. There were unconfirmed reports that some of the ex-Assosa people had settled down as agricultural labourers in western Wallega province of Ethiopia.

The military and political situation in Ethiopia and Sudan changed radically in 1991, as a result of the change of regime in Ethiopia, and the refugee population along the border went through a further series of upheavals. Refugees from the camps in the Gambela region left *en masse* for the southern Sudan when security broke down in the area following the collapse of the military regime in Ethiopia in late May. Some 23,000 Uduk who had been registered at Itang by early 1991 were among those who moved, under SPLA pressure, downstream to Nasir, in eastern Upper Nile, where a United Nations relief operation was mounted in June.

In August 1991, a section of the SPLA based at Nasir rebelled against the movement's leadership, and the factional clashes that resulted exacerbated regional insecurity and uncertainty over relief planning. The predicament of the Blue Nile people in Nasir, all of whom tended now to be regarded as 'Uduk', made them once again 'visible' as an ethnic category — in this case to the SPLA and the aid agencies. The latter were anxious to give special help to them and other vulnerable groups, and at the same time had to work with the local Sudan Relief and Rehabilitation Association, an SPLA affiliate, which naturally resented any favouritism. Until mid-1992, the 'ex-Assosa' returnees remained stranded near Nasir, where their safety was further jeopardized by the launching of a major Sudan government offensive into the heartland of the south. When conditions at Nasir became unbearable, the Uduk set off for Ethiopia once again to find refuge with the UNHCR. In midsummer 1992, about 13,000 were reported to have arrived in Gambela to enter a new phase of their epic story.

161

Concluding comments

The verbal testimonies I have quoted, especially the last, indicate how the external definition of the Uduk as an ethnic group identified with the SPLA was strengthened during the current civil war. The church community were pointed to as 'people of Garang' even while handing over to the government authorities lists of youngsters who had joined the movement and later resisting evacuation by th SPLA. Questions of thnic identification in such a context have become matters of life and death, and there is evidence that this tension has contributed to a growing sense of collective ethnic identity among the people themselves, as well as a related commitment to the Christian faith.

Of course, individual accounts of the experience of civil war are always harrowing, and certainly there has been widespread suffering as a result of recent events all over north-east Africa. In most cases, however, it is fairly clear where the political and emotional allegiances of a group lie, and therefore there may seem to be some kind of causal account possible, a rationale behind the tale of death and suffering to give the story some point. For the Uduk, however, and other small communities that gained 'ethnic visibility' as a result of finding themselves caught involuntarily in the conflict, no such coherent account can be given.

The contemporary image of the Uduk as a homogeneous group, marked by all the signs of being SPLA supporters, masks many ambiguities. For a start, their own tradition identifies the Nuer and the Dinka, the core support groups of the SPLA, as the most feared peoples from whom the Uduk frequently and prudently retreated. Moreover, the Uduk played almost no part in the first Sudanese civil war, and for a good part of that period. lived in some fear that what they labelled 'Nyor Dhamkin', or the 'Nilotic Aggression', would spread into their homeland. They were fully prepared to retreat for protection to the government authorities, having already been disarmed by them. Specific local patrons in everyday life tended to be local merchants supporting the Umma party, and those Uduk who voted in elections in the 1960s tended to vote Umma. Moreover, during the heyday of the Christian mission station at Chali, most of the Uduk-speaking population had very little interest in the church. Relatively few were converted. However, the first civil war led to the deportation of the missionaries in 1964 and the breakdown of central mission authority. It was in this context, amid the growing pressure of Islam, that interest in the Christian religion began to grow. This interest was further stimulated later in the setting up of the Tsore camp, under Ethiopian protection.

The main irony of the present situation is that many Uduk are dispersed through the towns of the Sudan, relatively invisible as a distinct group. They are employed in most trades and occupations, and dress and behave in much the same way as most other urbanized Sudanese. It is especially important to note that a relatively large number, probably a few hundred, have sought a career in the armed forces and are distributed in garrisons throughout the country. Some have even found themselves in garrisons in their own home region, and I know of at least two encounters where they have faced SPLA units that included some of their own people. In one case, classificatory brothers were actually firing at each other. One little-recognized aspect of the wide dispersion of people who still feel themselves kith and kin, even across the divisions of civil war, is the existence of a network of communication between them, which operates surprisingly well. Information circulates between rural communities through links in towns, army garrisons and police stations, as well as through links in the SPLA. People devote their energies to a pragmatic exchange of information, travel and visit each other when possible, even across the front lines, solicit help from available patrons and help their kith and kin where they can. They hold no simple view of the situation based on a particular 'ethnic' point of view, but rather a sceptical attitude towards the arbitrariness of power in all its forms.

Conflicts, especially national or regional, but also local, generate the image of 'ethnicities' in the plural. To what extent these correspond to kin or language communities or moral networks on the ground is problematic. Political conflict in north-east Africa has imposed too many intensely uniform 'ethnic' images, conceptually setting apart whole communities while profoundly dividing the actual people in question. This has led to tragedy for many smaller and previously quite neutral populations lying on the conflict's front-line between Ethiopia and Sudan, or between the northern and southern regions of the latter country. Located on the crossing of these two lines, the predicament of the Uduk is an extreme example of the dilemmas faced by many peoples.

We have seen the role played by the Uduk struggle for survival in promoting their ethnic visibility. 'Visibility' as a distinct ethnic group can bring both advantages and disadvantages, according to whether one is seeking protection and aid, or avoiding attack and victimization. Several other communities of the borderlands have moved in and out of the front line, and in and out of relief agency focus, but without gaining the kind of visibility now carried by the Uduk. Only time can tell what are the long-term consequences of 'visibility' for survival.

References

Colson, E. (1971) Heroism, martyrdom and courage: an essay in Tonga ethics. In T.O. Beidelman (ed.), *The Translation of Culture: Essays to E.E. Evans Pritchard*. London: Tavistock.

James, W. (1977) The Funj mystique: approaches to a problem of Sudan history. In R.K. Jain (ed.), *Text and Context: the Social Anthropology of Tradition*. Philadelphia: ASA Essays in Social Anthropology, no. 2, ISHI.

—— (1979) *'Kwanim Pa: the Making of the Uduk People. An Ethnographic Study of Survival in the Sudan–Ethiopian Borderlands*. Oxford: Clarendon Press.

—— (1988) *The Listening Ebony: Moral Knowledge, Religion and Power among the Uduk of Sudan*. Oxford: Clarendon Press.

III CONFLICT AT THE CENTRE

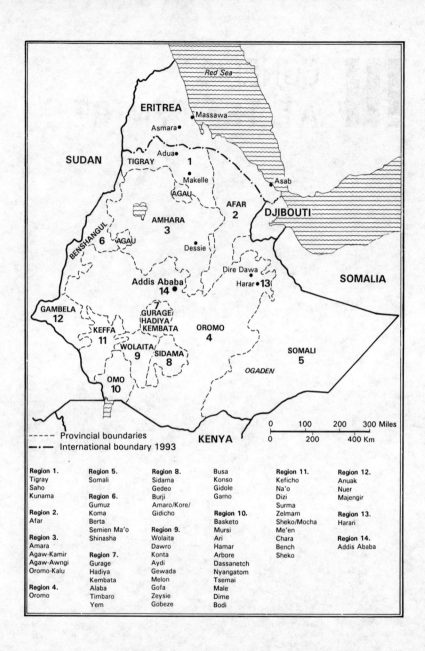

Map 9 *Ethnic groups and regions of Ethiopia (provisional map, 1991)*

166

8 The Creation & Constitution of Oromo Nationality

P.T.W. BAXTER

There are 20 million or so Oromo-speakers, which makes them one of the most populous language groups in Africa. Almost all live in Ethiopia, where they are the largest 'nationality' and make up around 40 per cent of the population. They consist of a number of groups which, until they were incorporated into the Ethiopian empire, were autonomous and frequently in dispute with each other. The best known are the Arssi, Boran, Guji, Karaiyu, Lega, Macha, Afran Kallo, Raya, Tulama and Wollo.

Oromoland varies from parched desert to forested mountains. The different groups have different histories and now demonstrate diversities in culture, ways of life and religion. Many men and some women are now urbanized professionals, craft workers and labourers, and many others are merchants and traders, but most Oromo maintain themselves as cultivators and/or stock-keepers, ranging from densely settled plough farmers to transhumant and nomadic pastoralists. A tiny and diminishing number of Warta still depend on hunting and collecting. Most would describe themselves as Muslims, Orthodox Christians, Roman Catholics, Lutherans or Pentecostals, but the daily religious behaviour of most continues to be rooted in traditional responses. This shows very clearly in the words of hymns and prayers and in ritual forms and demeanour (Bartels, 1983; Van de Loo, 1991). Indeed, whatever variations there may be by group, religious affiliation or education, all Oromo seem to share basic and crucial sets of understandings as to what the proper relations between people, and between people and God, should be. Moreover, any Oromo-speaker, whatever his or her dialect, can be readily understood by any other throughout Oromoland.

167

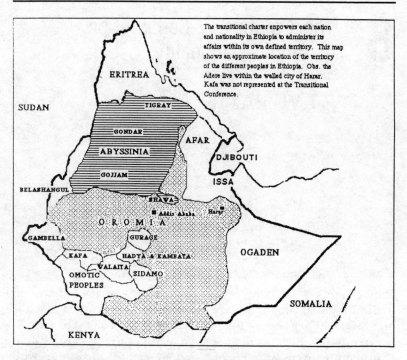

The transitional charter enpowers each nation
and nationality in Ethiopia to administer its
affairs within its own defined territory. This map
shows an approximate location of the territory
of the different peoples in Ethiopia. Obs. the
Adere live within the walled city of Harar.
Kafa was not represented at the Transitional
Conference.

Map 10   Oromia as envisaged by Oromo nationalists
Source: The Oromo Commentary, *Nos 2 and 3, 1991; reproduced*
with the kind permission of the editors.

In my conversations with Oromo, in their homelands and in
exile, few have expressed loyalty to the state which would override
their obligations as Oromo. I think it would be surprising if that
were not so, given our knowledge of the historical experience of
the Oromo. Indeed, many Oromo exiles simply reject Ethiopian
nationality, and some have even argued that Mohammed Hassen
should have dropped 'of Ethiopia' from the title of his pioneering
The Oromo of Ethiopia: a History 1570–1860 (1990a). How deeply
felt Oromo identity is in Ethiopia should become clear if and
when free elections are held there in the future.

It has been reliably estimated (Zitelmann, 1990) that at least half a million Oromo, especially the best educated and most politically aware, have become refugees or *émigrés*. Almost all have the sorts of skills that are so needed in Ethiopia. They live scattered in cities across Africa, the Middle East, the United States and Canada and in London, Melbourne, Stockholm, Amsterdam, Berlin, Hamburg and Rome. With hardly an exception, they have been successful academically and economically. I have been at meetings in Toronto in 1990 and 1991 which were attended by more than a thousand Oromo from across North America, and I could not trace one that was not self-supporting. The same holds for the seven hundred-strong Oromo community in Melbourne. Poor they may be, but none of them are indigent or dependent on charity. But, and most sadly, many thousands are living from hand to mouth in Djibouti, Somalia, Sudan and Kenya. Many of those living both in foreign cities and in the camps had done a stint in the Oromo Liberation Front forces. The Front and the sustained efforts of the exiles, just in themselves, are evidence that a strong national consciousness exists.

The history of the chiefdoms and petty kingdoms which made up Abyssinia is one of 'wars without end', to borrow Reyna's (1990) encapsulation of the history of states in east central Sudan, which were also based on the predatory accumulation of slaves and booty. After centuries of self-sufficient independence, the different Oromo peoples were conquered by Shoa during the last two decades of the last century. The kingdom of Shoa, in effect, became the Ethiopian empire. The empire was created over the same period that the Italians, French, Belgians, British and Germans were carving out their African colonies. The incorporation of the different Oromo peoples took a series of bloody and brutal conquests, which could not have taken place if Menelik had not been able to get arms from the other competing colonial powers (who have constantly been a malign influence on Ethiopia) and if the area of conquest had not been ravaged by severe pestilence and famines. The Oromo were colonized: many were sold into slavery, others were reduced to near serfdom, and much of their land was expropriated (Holcombe & Sissai Ibssa, 1990).

There were a series of local rebellions against oppression and constant endeavours to ease the imperial yoke when it chafed unbearably, which had elements of proto-nationalism, but there was no great national upsurge until some 20 or so years ago (Baxter, 1983). Some older scholars, who got to know Ethiopia only from the centre and before that upsurge, still keep their eyes closed to it, but it is now absolutely clear that Oromo nationality is a political fact which has to be taken into account in all considerations of the present and future of the Horn. The creation of a pan-Oromo consciousness, as distinct from a Boran, Guji or Arssi consciousness, is also, in good measure, a consequence of the colonial experience.

In this respect Oromo responses resemble those of many other African peoples. That they were slower to develop, and may become stronger still in affirmation, could well be because Abyssinian imperialism 'in its degree of oppression apparently surpassed European imperialism' (Braukamper, 1980: 435). Simply, national consciousness has been forced on Oromo as a people and as individuals. Exile after exile with whom I have spoken have attributed their political activism to acts of brutality inflicted on themselves or on members of their families, just because they were Oromo. When your friend has her breasts cut off or your father is beaten to death in prison, myths of empire which you had been taught in school lose whatever little hold they may have had — especially when an alternative Oromo nationalist ideology becomes available, as it did from the early 1960s.

Peasant revolts, like banditry, have been a consistent feature of Ethiopian history. Most have not had an ethnic or a national component; so, for example, Crummey (1986) did not even list Oromo in his index. However, some revolts and rebellions can, in retrospect, be seen to have had proto-national elements. These have been well-enough described, and I do not need to go into them here.[1] The central government's consistent response to rebellion and dissension has been to increase central control and to reduce local autonomy. In this respect the government of Mengistu followed the old imperial policies. It sought to pacify, not to make peace, and continued to try to reproduce a subordinate copy of the north by enforcing the use of the Amharic language and by asserting Amharic cultural values. That meant imposing hierarchy and absolute obedience rather than seeking consensus. From all reports, little changed, even during the last crumbling year of the Mengistu regime. Oromo was tolerated as a 'tribal' language, but not for official use. Publications in Oromo which did not use Amharic script, or were about Oromo culture, were actively discouraged — for example, Bartels's fine study of Oromo religion (1983) and Tilahun Gamta's *Oromo–English Dictionary* (1989).

Most Oromo in exile have been concerned, with varying degrees of passion and commitment, to establish Oromo autonomy. They have not all, of course, agreed about its extent and its form but all, at the least, have wanted to see the Oromo language and Oromo customs given equal status with those of the north, and Oromo to be written and printed in the Roman alphabet. They are simply tired of being patronized and obliged to adopt foreign ways if they want to get on. Others argue that cultural autonomy is not possible without political autonomy, that is, the creation of an independent state of Oromiya, which has been the declared goal of the Oromo Liberation Front.

As part of the creation of a national identity, Oromo intellectuals have been intensely concerned to establish the autonomy, distinctive value and intrinsic worth of traditional Oromo culture. In this respect, as well, they are like other decolonizing people. At the Oromo conferences in which I have been privileged to participate — Berlin, Amsterdam, London, Melbourne, Toronto — the definition and celebration of Oromo culture have been central concerns, the former in passionate discussions and the latter in enthusiastic music-making, dancing, singing and recitations of traditional and contemporary poetry. The less schooled have been prominent in the exposition of tradition, as they would have been if they were at home, while the women, who are much less numerous, have been key performers, again as they would have been at home. Language and folk culture, of course, commonly become symbols of identity for oppressed nationalities, especially among intellectuals, and Oromo are no exception. Oromo patriots would echo Milan Kundera's reflections on the importance of folk culture in the establishment of Czech nationality:

A culture of songs, fairy tales, ancient rites and customs, proverbs and sayings [is the] fragile stem of an unbroken tradition . . . is the sap that kept Czech culture from drying up. . . . My love for it dates back to . . . when they tried to make us believe we had no right to exist, we were nothing but Czech speaking Germans. We needed to prove to ourselves we'd existed before and still did exist. We made a pilgrimage to our sources. (1970: 111)

Thomas Zitelman has reported in a lecture that among the destitute, harassed and insecure in the refugee camps there is also intense concern about the specificity and the worth of Oromo culture: 'There is a culture, and there is a stated fear that one could lose culture and thus fall beyond human dignity' (1990). Chinua Achebe has often said that under bitter stress he experienced his Ibo nationality as part of his very own particular identity. The need to maintain and to renew a sense of cultural identity as part of one's personal identity is probably particularly keen for Oromo because of the particular form their colonial experience took. To succeed they had to Amharicize themselves, not just become proficient in the language. A central tenet of Ethiopian schooling is echoed in Ullendorf's assertion: 'The

Gallas [Oromo] had nothing to contribute to the civilization of Ethiopia; they possessed no material or intellectual culture, and their social organization was at a far lower stage of development than that of the population among whom they settled,' and that they 'are divided into some 200 tribes' (1960: 76, 41). These nonsensical statements are etched in the minds of every schooled, middle-aged Oromo, and are seen as a stigma which devalues their identity and therefore has to be removed.

Oromo have had to put up with the assumption that to be an Ethiopian was superior to being an Oromo, so that the proper and wise course to take was to drop your Oromo identity and become an Ethiopian. Moreover, most European travellers, scholars and diplomats have accepted the view from the centre. Even a scholar as sensitive as Donald Levine could write: 'Where the Oromo culture was fragile, Amhara culture was durable' (1974: 164), without having evidence of any worth to substantiate such a broad generalization. Old-fashioned evolutionist and racist assumptions, mostly unvoiced, have contributed to the belief that a Christian, Semitic culture with Middle Eastern leanings had to be superior to a black African culture. Northern Abyssinian and Shoan cultures have a vast and readily available corpus of chronicles and texts. This has fitted in with the biases of Western historians and classical linguists towards textual study, however dubious some of the texts may be. One of the few exceptions to this was Tutschek, who worked from informants and whose great *Dictionary of the Galla Language* was published in 1844–5. Unfortunately, colonialist arrogance continues to be as set in the minds of many Ethiopians and Ethiopianists as rigidly as it is among the many Europeans who have never become reconciled to the end of empires.

Abyssinians used to stress their Middle Eastern rather than African cultural roots, as is so obvious in the reiteration of the Solomonic legend, taught in schools as history and justification for imperial rule. Just as the expansion of the European empire in Africa coincided with that of the Abyssinian expansion, so the latter took on some of the same sanctimonious assumption of bringing civilization to the savages. Menelik and his courtiers became honorary, if second-class, bearers of the 'white man's burden' in Africa. As Christians, and as members of a socially stratified state headed by an anointed monarch, Shoans could be seen as more civilized than members of the 'primitive' democracies and rudimentary states of the Oromo. Oromo became defined in terms of what they were not, rather than what they were. In similar style, the British in Uganda judged the powerful kingdoms such as Buganda to be more civilized than the 'tribes without rulers', so that a few bossy Baganda were utilized by the British as colonial agents to bring discipline and order to the backward. British policies in Uganda suffered from a cultural myopia brought on by arrogance similar to that of the Shoans, but they did eventually learn and decolonized.

As so often happens, imperial history stood the truth on its head. The victim's reluctance to accept aggressive, civilizing conquest and incorporation came to be interpreted as a wilful resistance to being civilized. Indeed, in popular Ethiopian history the Oromo are represented as savage invaders who had to be repulsed and who, if they could not be kept out, had to be kept down. Mohammed Hassen's recent and innovative history of the Oromo is the first to give an account of events from a non-imperialistic viewpoint (1990a). If the Oromo were denigrated in standard Ethiopian history, the 'Shankilla', the blacks of the west, were placed on a much lower level of civilization still (James, 1990). Sadly, many Oromo are as racist and arrogant about Shankilla as Abyssinians have been of them. Almost perversely, a more recent trend in liberal Western and African thought has contributed to the denigration of Oromo nationality. Nationalism itself is held to be bad and, even worse, assertion of a distinctive ethnic identity within a state has been castigated as tribalism. Since Nkrumah's earliest speeches, it has been held that Africans should be Pan-Africanists and that tribalism is a threat to African unity. Cultural diversity is thought to be a threat to national integration. Recent events in Nigeria, the former Soviet Union and elsewhere have surely demonstrated that ethnic identity cannot be abolished simply by denying it or by asserting that one culture is superior to another. The point I am making is a simple one: the Oromo have as much reason as any African people to be concerned for the proper evaluation of their culture by themselves and by the world.

In the same insightful lecture that I cited earlier, Zitelman writes (1990: from unpaged MS):

Among the Oromo communities in Europe, North America and the Middle East one can find organized circles and individuals who go back into the 'sources of culture', community journals and periodicals are published which inform their readers about different aspects of the aadaa oromoo (Oromo culture) [custom]. Proverbs and tales are collected and published; the puzzle of the venerated age-class and generation system known as gadaa is set together again; or the topic is raised how a woman, according to custom/culture, can choose her future husband herself. The issue of the history of a written language is part of the historical and cultural curricula the Oromo Liberation Front broadcasts into Ethiopia. It may go together with an attempt to retrieve genealogical knowledge, to establish the idea that all Oromo-speakers are kin to each other. Here the question of the aada oromoo is eventually combined with the issue of the saba oromoo, or the Oromo nation. The fear of a loss of culture and history was a constant feature I experienced among Arssi-Oromo in Somali refugee camps in 1988. The written historical texts, distributed through the networks of OLF's mass-organizations, gave a uniform picture of a golden Oromo past, when democracy under the gadaa was flourishing and when Ethiopian colonialism had not yet disturbed the peace of the green pastures. Political activists have openly announced the rewriting of history in the course of the liberation struggle, while people in the camps spoke about their needs to recapture history. (1990)

I do not know what history the activists are producing for political purposes. One suspects that, like most ideologically directed history, it will be intended more to inspire than to enlighten. It would be remarkable in the circumstances if a romanticized, primordial past were not being fabricated. More importantly, at a scholarly level the work of re-evaluating the history of the Oromo-speaking areas of Ethiopia is well under way by Mohammed Hassen (1990a), Negaso Gidada (1984), Jan Hultin, (1987, 1990), Alessandro Triulzi (1986), Ulrich Braukamper (1980) and younger scholars; their work must also cause some of the myths on which pan-Ethiopian nationality is based to be brought into question. Hopefully, they will also diminish the need for those myths of a golden Oromo past, which are being constructed in the camps of the Horn and the college campuses of the United States, as part of the construction of Oromo nationality out of Oromo ethnicity.

Hobsbawm (1992) has suggested that 'nationalism is a political programme' which 'belongs with political theory', whereas ethnicity belongs with social anthropology. It is convenient for me to stick to that division. So I will simply comment on four aspects of pan-Oromo ethnicity which could ease the creation of an Oromo national identity. These are: (i) the common language; (ii) widely shared and deeply felt symbols and values; (iii) ease of incorporation; and (iv) permeable clan structures throughout (and even beyond) Oromo.

All Oromo can understand each other's speech, as I have heard when travelling in different Oromo lands and at conferences of exiles drawn from all parts. I have found some accents impossible to grasp, but my companions never appear to have done so. Of course, to share a language, and even a religion, does not by itself ensure a peaceful and stable nation-state, as is so tragically demonstrated in Somalia, but it must be a helpful precondition for the construction of a nationality. The next step, I would suggest, is to get one standard written form of Oromo spelling accepted. Despite efforts by the Oromo Relief Association, the Lutheran and Roman Catholic churches, and scholars such as Andrezjewski, Tilahun Gamta, Mekuria Bulcha, Mohammed Ali, Rikita Mengasha, Tablino, Venturino, Leus and others, this has still not taken place. The various spellings of *gaada* and *aada* used by the different authors cited below should make this obvious. Next is the need for an efflorescence of popular written literature to supplement the flourishing oral literature and rich bodies of popular traditional music and modern 'pop'.

Following from their common language and early history, Oromo share a common cosmological and philosophical archive, so that a vast fund of words and symbols have pan-Oromo resonances. Rather than enlarge on this here, I find it more convenient to return to this vital component of Oromo ethnicity in the concluding part of this chapter. Oromo have consistently demonstrated a capacity to 'Oromize' the inhabitants of the lands into which they have expanded. Braukamper's comment on the Hadiya could be extended much more widely: 'A considerable part of the Hadiya . . . were absorbed by the expanding Oromo and became actively engaged themselves in expelling their kinsmen who refused to submit to the suzerainty of the Oromo leaders (abba gada)' (1980: 434). Comparisons with the Azande, Abandia and Alur, who also incorporated and assimilated other peoples rather than simply conquering them, spring immediately to mind. Hultin (1987, 1990) has explicated the indigenous metaphor which is used to describe how this process operated. The people spread like the cogorsa grass, 'a runner grass with very deep roots' which is very resistant to drought. He writes from the viewpoint of the Macha Oromo, but I think his imaginative metaphorical analysis can also be applied to Arssi and to other Oromo. But there were, of course, a number of material factors which facilitated Oromo expansion. Frequently the territories into which they infiltrated had been devastated and depopulated by wars, so there was plenty of space. They often offered protection from northern slavers, and they often came as herders, not as settlers.

But this does not explain the ease with which they incorporated the numerous autochtones. When land was not short, the possession of disposable cattle must have been an invaluable asset. So it is a reasonable speculation that Oromo were able to attach herdsmen as clients (*tiisee*) to themselves, or as stock receivers by gift or by loan, just as Boran were doing up to the 1960s in northern Kenya and southern Ethiopia. The descendants of such clients or dependants, if recent practice can be a guide, took the clan of their sponsor and readily, within a generation or two, became Boran. In contrast, in highly stratified Rwanda and Ankole, it was very difficult for a peasant client to become a pastoralist. I would also suggest it was likely that Oromo, being wealthy in cattle, were able to acquire wives in return for bride-wealth cattle from the autochtones without having to transfer Oromo girls in return.

In 1968-9, I found that around a third of the Arssi wives in Kofele on whom I had data had been acquired from Sidamo for bridewealth cattle, but I only heard of a single Arssi girl going as a bride to Sidamo, and that was a political and very atypical marriage. The Sidamo brides soon became Arssi matrons, by what Schlee (1990b) has dubbed 'the process of ethnic reaffilia-tion', as dramatically as Rendille girls become Somali. For Sidamo girls it was a sort of hypergamy. As Hultin (1987) and Bartels (1983) have indicated for the Macha and I can report from Arssi, the adoption of adults, and often all their dependants, used to be a common practice, which thereby incorporated them and their descendants into the family, and hence into the lineage, clan and tribe. These practices, though almost certainly wide-spread and frequent, took place despite the firm ideological con-tention that descent and inheritance were both rigidly patrilineal. Oromo social theory, like most others, was often very flexible in practice.

The several different sorts of incorporation must have varied locally (see Bartels, 1983), but they most certainly worked. In both Kofele and Gedeb districts (*woreda*) of Arussi Governorate, which were areas in which clans of Hadiya origin were highly concentrated, it was irrelevant for almost all purposes in 1969 whether an individual was of Hadiya or of Arssi descent. Braukamper noted that: 'The "Hadiya" clans of the Ar[us]si (pop. 2 million) even outnumber those of the Oromo proper' (1989: 428). But the ethos was an Oromo ethos, and the people referred to themselves as Arssi who spoke the Arssi or Oromo language (*afaan Arssi mo afaan Oromo*). Ethnic identity had become related to symbolic figures, such as Shaykh Hussein (Baxter, 1987; Braukamper, 1989), of religious significance, or in reaction to the oppression of the local colonists (*neftanya*), not to clan histories.

All identities at all levels, from the individual to the congeries of peoples sharing a common name such as Macha, Sibbu, Boran, etc., have been to some extent movable, ambiguous and dependent on context, which is what comparative ethnography would have led us to anticipate. As Mohammed Hassen puts it:

'there is no such thing as a "pure" Oromo tribe derived from a single founding father . . . the history of the Oromo people is . . . a story of fusion and interaction by which all tribes and groups had altered and been transformed constantly' (1990a: 4).

Change of identity, then, could be readily made. Gunther Schlee (1990a) has demonstrated in compelling detail how this could also be done among the pastoral peoples of the southern Oromo borderlands, where identity shifts even spanned Oromo, Somali, Rendille and Samburu divisions. Within Oromo, one consequence of these shifts has been the creation of patterns of similarly named putative descent groups across the whole spectrum of Oromo and at all levels. The presence of similarly named and widely dispersed descent groups has, in its turn, eased and encouraged individual and group movements. There is a solid body of ethnography which supports these contentions, so two simple examples must suffice here for illustration. First, Arssi (Arussi) is the overall name taken by the several million-strong Oromo group whose territories extend from the Rift Valley to the Bale–Ogaden boundary. Among the Boran, the Arssi are one of the clans of the Gona exogamous moiety. Among the neighbouring Gabbra they are a subclan of the Alganna phratry. They are also a Guji subclan. Second, Karaiyu is the name of the largest clan of the Sabho moiety of the Boran. It is also the name of the camel-herding 'tribe' living along the Awash, and of a Guji subclan. Guji is also the name of a Boran clan. The recurrence of a name across a wide range of putative descent groups of varied depths and spans is as much a feature of the Oromo as it is of the interlacustrine Bantu.

Politically active Oromo, the number of whom is increasing very rapidly, seek to create a useful political culture out of shared feelings of ethnicity. In good part, that has required the reconstruction of a powerful, but nevertheless egalitarian and democratic, past which is required to be the opposite of, and therefore morally superior to, that of the Amhara. It has to provide both a charter for the present and a programme for the future. Hence the continuing stress on *gaada* as a symbol of a democratic heritage, which it is. Similarly, there is the reiteration of the relatively high status and respect traditionally accorded to wives and of the unbreakable nature of traditional marriage, both of which are true enough. Both, equally truly, stand in marked opposition to Amhara stress on domination and subservience in economic and political relationships and to the very friable, contractual bases of many Amhara marriages. But these are assertions of cultural superiority and moral superiority which are

177

useful as part of a representation of culture for political use, that is all.

Culture is a tricky word at any time, but when used for political purposes, as Oromo so often do, it is slippery indeed. I shall pause and glance at current uses of the word 'culture' and the use of the word by Oromo writing in English. In both Oromo and in English 'culture' has developed many meanings, so it has become not just one of what Raymond Williams has called 'keywords,' but 'the original difficult word' (1976: 14). In social and cultural anthropology the word has been so over-used that it has become unusable. It is not even a 'budget' term of analysis any more. I do not think that should deter Oromo from using it, any more than it deters anthropologists from using the word in everyday, non-professional contexts — that is, for those bits of past and present artefacts and life ways which cannot easily be given a price and which do not need mercenaries to fight for them.

First is the jumble of ambiguities which lie in the word 'culture', 'one of the two or three most complicated words in the English language' (Williams, 1976: 87). Williams gives many examples of its multivocality and usages. The Oromo word usually translated as 'culture' is *aada* or *ada*. Gragg's dictionary (1982), based on the Oromo of Wollega, gives 'fortune, culture' and *aadaa biyyaa*, 'national culture', as examples. It is worth noting that Gragg's dictionary was not allowed on open sale in Addis Ababa, and that his principal Oromo assistant had to flee the country. 'Culture' has become the modern translation, but I think it is a modernization of an older word. Tutschek (1844–5), whom I have yet to detect in error, I was surprised to find, does not list *aada* in any of its variant spellings, nor in his English section does he list the words custom and culture. Nor do the other older dictionaries. Venturino and Tablino (n.d.) in their dictionary of Boran translate *ada* as 'custom, tradition', and Ton Leus (1988) gives 'tradition, rule, way of life' in his. I would concur with Venturino and Tablino. In the most recent Oromo dictionary which I have seen, Tilahun Gamta (1989) gives *aada*, 'culture, custom'. His example is worth repeating: *sirni abbaa lafaa inni darba aada oromo ballessu barbaada ture*, which he translates, rather freely, as: 'The now defunct feudal regime wanted to destroy Oromo culture.'

Oromo meanings, then, would seem to change with time and circumstance, just as English meanings do, but we should not be surprised by that. My recollections are that both Boran and Arssi usages were closer to what I would translate as 'custom' rather than 'culture', but I was listening in a local field context in which there was no need for a definition of culture. My notes do not lead me to suggest a definition. But the word *aada* was used a great deal, and it was one of the first words for an abstraction that I learned. It was frequently coupled with *seera*, 'laws' or 'rule', as in *aadafi seera keena*, 'our customs or laws', or in reprobation — *kuuni aada nit* 'that is not custom, not proper', even if it is legal under colonial law. Separate *aada* when brought together formed a complex of rules of behaviour which could contain contradictions, but which, as a whole, were *aada Boraana* or *aada Arssi*. It is this whole which, I think, in most contexts, has come to be translated as culture.

I have made this little foray into the meanings of *aada* so that we and Oromo nationalists may come to see that the words *aada* and culture are not simple. They can confuse as much as they can illuminate. Merely to construct an Oromo culture to be presented simply as a morally more attractive alternative to Amhara or Shoan culture is a nothing, if only because there are no cultural absolutes. A re-examination of what Raymond Williams (1976) wrote nearly 20 years ago, just, as it happens, when Oromo nationality was burgeoning, could be useful. As part of his continuous struggle to comprehend British 'society' and 'culture', Williams set out to analyse certain 'keywords' in common English usage:

some of the issues and problems that were there inside the vocabulary, whether in single words or in habitual groupings . . . Of course, the issues could not all be understood simply by analysis of the words . . . some of them cannot even be focused unless we are conscious of the words as elements of the problems . . . The questions are not only about meaning: in most cases, inevitably, they are about meanings . . . We find a history and complexity of meanings; conscious changes, or consciously different uses [as with *aada*]; innovation, obsolescence, specialisation, extension, overlap, transfer; or changes which are masked by a nominal continuity so that words that seem to have been there for centuries, with continuous general meanings, have come in fact to express radically different or radically variable, yet sometimes hardly noticed, meanings and implications of meaning. (1976: 15–17)

There is no reason to think that the Oromo language, in which so much rich verse has been composed, should not have complicated keywords.

Williams started from the inside of meanings and worked outwards, and revelled in the complexities and variations he teased out. These are both poetic and very Oromo ways to work. The simple substitution of an English word for its Oromo equivalent in the dictionary obfuscates by cloaking variation and ambiguity. Basic Oromo would be just as boring as basic English. For the purposes of political discourse and as a component in the

179

formation of Oromo nationality, as distinct from Oromo ethnic self-awareness, the compilation and analysis of a set of keywords, such as *aada*, might be helpful. Indeed, that is what, pragmatically if not analytically, questing Oromo writers are doing. Not surprisingly, in debates over meanings some Oromo get a little heated. Here would not be the place, even if I had the competence, to prepare an inventory of Oromo keywords — that is, those which might be central to the articulation of 'Oromoness'. But I will suggest how such an enquiry might begin.

Gaada is a good example of an Oromo keyword which has been given 'hardly noticed' accretions of meaning over the years. At its most specific it is the sacred condition of a ritually prescribed set of elders who are responsible for maintaining the proper sacrificial relationships between the people and God. Over the years, especially in the writings of scholarly commentators, it has come to be the generic term applied to the extremely complex and varied systems of generation-set cycles based on eight-year time units, first described by Bahrey in the sixteenth century (Bahrey, 1954). Some commentators, including myself, see *gaada* as primarily serving religious purposes, whereas others, including my friend Mohammed Hassen, see its primary purpose as being a political organization. It always has elements of both. For most politically aware Oromo, it is a form of ancient and democratic constitution which could be used as the basis for the constitution of an independent Oromiya, the leap from ancient to modern conferring legitimacy on the latter.

There is a considerable literature devoted to the explication of the complexities of *gaada* as a cyclical generation system. The best-known account of the system and its time reckoning, in its prototypical and renowned Boran form, is that of the Eritrean anthropologist Asmarom Legesse, in his *Gada: Three Approaches to the Study of African Society* (1973). His fieldwork was done and the book published before Oromo nationality had become a prominent issue in Ethiopia. He was more concerned to demonstrate the imaginative and mathematical complexity of *gaada* as an example of the way colonially blinkered observers have under-represented African intellectual capacities, than as a distinctively Oromo (as opposed to Ethiopian) political invention.

Asmarom, a supporter of the Oromo cause, was recently interviewed by a correspondent of the California-based Oromo journal *Qunnamtii* (summer (1990), 14–18). He was asked what were, to the interviewer, clearly the key questions: 'What do you think is the significance of Gada to Oromos and other Africans today?' and 'As Oromos, in our struggle for self-determination, how can we apply the principles of Gada?' I have been asked similar questions myself and know how difficult they are to answer, simply because the questioner is giving a different weighting to the keyword than the listener is. Asmarom is recorded as answering: 'For Oromos I would say that the first place to look when looking for democracy [another of the slippery keywords peeled by Williams] is in their own tradition.' He accepted that there is no reason why Gada should not be used, but that it 'would have to be adapted to modern conditions partly because it is too rigid in the way it is organized traditionally'.

In so far as Gada is thought of in organizational terms, Asmarom is absolutely correct. There is no way that contemporary young freedom fighters who have won power, after years of struggle in the bush, are going to relinquish it when their eight-year term is up, and retire peacefully into ritual elderhood. He went on to answer in terms that his questioner had asked the question, but making the differences between the different meanings of Gada, as used by detached anthropologists and concerned Oromo, absolutely clear to those who had ears to hear. He argued that the underlying values of Gada enshrined universally approved principles and values, and these were an undeniable part of Oromo heritage. Moreover, Gada gave respect to institutionalized generational differences, and what could be more unexceptionably African, and also true, than that? The recognition of generation rather than rank also runs contrary to both imperial and revolutionary Ethiopian orthodoxy. Asmarom goes on to bring the question into the pragmatic realm, and notes 'the *belief* [my emphasis] that the people govern ... In Boran, government appears in the form of the Gumi government. Gumi simply means the multitude, the people ...' A *guumi*, or general meeting, which is open to all office holders and all elders, can be called at any time and not only when a generation set is assembled. Asmarom deftly uses the differences in the meanings given to Gada, and in a very Oromo style, rather than confront the unanswerable question head on.

I suspect that Asmarom's reservations about the contemporary utility of Gada as a political mechanism have not been heeded as much as his faint praise, but I do not think that matters. No one is actually seriously suggesting a return to the strict forms of Gada, any more than any populist politician in England or America is speaking literally when he proposes a return to the Victorian family. The *guumi gaiyo* or *chaffee*, to which Asmarom rightly points as the source of the Boran egalitarian ethos, is the national assembly, or one of a series of dispersed assemblies. It

181

is concerned with laws, customs and external affairs. The last national Boran assembly about which I have information, but not direct observation, was held four years ago in Dirre, southern Ethiopia. I have been told that there was a great assembly of elders, accompanied by a host of foreign observers, and pedlars selling soft drinks and beer — which demonstrates that the assembly was not just a set of greybeards in their *arbora* and *suuri ruufa*[2], but part of ongoing, changing life. The accent there, as in every Boran, and I think every Oromo, assembly was on consensus, agreement and fulfilment.

Nowadays, there are situations in which a consensus between Muslims and traditionalists is just not obtainable. This happened in Kenya after its independence, when there was a referendum and the Muslims voted to join Somalia, and the followers of the traditional religion voted to stay in Kenya. Elders of both sides agreed that the fact there was division was, in itself, a sin indeed, a heinous sin because it led to the spilling of Boran blood by Boran connivance. Boran recognize the times are out of joint, and that such irreconcilable divisions must recur increasingly. But everyone would agree that any differences among Boran should never go beyond the level of words, and that violence should never happen. The maintenance of the 'peace of the Boran' by words, prayers and sacrifice is the work of the elders, and especially those who are participating in the rituals that are the culmination of the *gaada* cycle (Baxter, 1965). So *gaada* is a part of the 'peace of the Boran'. Elders should pray and pray, and should continue to debate and to debate, until some consensus is reached, if only for the present. *Nagaa*, 'peace', is a keyword in Boran and Arssi, and I think throughout Oromo — though it is not in Williams's list as a keyword in English!

As the world changes, so must custom, *aada*. After full deliberation, *guumi* have often changed laws and customs in radical ways, just as *gaada* has changed over the years in organization, if not in voice. Arssi adopted sister-exchange marriage at a *guumi* after the great rinderpest epidemic, and Boran reorganized their military age-set organization radically at a *guumi* the better to confront the Somali. I would concur with Asmarom (1973) that, at the pragmatic level, the example of the *guumi* offered more for the future than did *gaada*. But *guumi* are not embedded in Oromo religion. They are workaday institutions, so not suitable as values to rally round. I think significantly, *guumi* are held under a great, ancient *oda* (sycamore) tree, which is the motif of the flag of the Oromo Liberation Front. The trees are held in veneration both in themselves and because of the prayers and blessings which they generate. There are complexes or 'fans' of key symbols as well as of keywords: *gaada* and *oda* are dominant symbols as well as dominant words.

Of course, there is nothing uniquely Oromo in having a generation-set system. The neighbouring Sidamo and Konso people have one, as do several other East African peoples. What are important about *gaada* are the hold that it has on Oromo imagination and the basic assumptions on which it is based. The mechanisms, in themselves, are unimportant. Indeed, many of the Oromo people gave up the organization decades ago, when confronted by centralizing power in the Gibe states or by Islam in the east. However, most Boran, Gabbra and Guji and some Macha still maintain their cycle of rituals, even if in attenuated forms with reduced sacrifice (Baxter & Almagor, 1978). To argue that *gaada* could be revived and used as a modern political system seems to me as fanciful as suggesting that the United Kingdom could return to rule by the monarch, House of Lords and an unreformed Commons. But values drawn from the past do, nevertheless, have contemporary relevance and a hold on all our imaginations, for better or for worse.

The hold that *gaada* has had and still has on Oromo imagination must already be clear. The shared assumptions are more tenuous and may be more friable. One is that, though earned and properly acquired veneration can endure until even after death, office and power should only be held for specified periods and must be relinquished. Power also should never be used overbearingly and to bully people. In Boran even a slave who is of a generation senior to his master has to be addressed courteously as an elder. This is the opposite of Amhara political values, as Levine (1974) has demonstrated so clearly. For Oromo, at least in theory, power cannot be detached from moral and ritual responsibilities. Oromo despots, such as the kings of Jimma, opposed *gaada* and the *guumi* because they were constrained by them. However, even after they had eroded the traditional sanctions on abuse which were embedded in the *gaada* system, the despots were never able to assume the trappings or arbitrary powers which marked Abyssinian and Kaffan despots (Lewis, 1965).

There are several other keywords, each of which merits a paper to itself. *Nagaa*, 'peace', and its host of derivatives would seem to me to be the most important. Others are *eeba* and *tuufa*, types of blessing; *kadaaca*, 'prayer'; *kalla*, 'sacrifice'; *waaka*, 'God/sky'; *ayaana*, the part of God immanent in persons; the kinship terms and many others. A good deal of work has already been

183

done, notably by Bartels (1983), Hultin (1987, 1990), Hinnant, Kassam, Blackhurst and Bassi (see Baxter 1986). Oral plenitude and variety, cosmological and religious sophistication, and stress on the person and on active human co-operation are embodied in Oromo *aada*, that is, in their customs and culture. They all appear to be resilient. If so, then it is by using their skills as mediators and co-operators that Oromo might best devise the political forms they need as an emergent nation, whether that be in a new Ethiopia or in a new nation-state. Certainly, neither top-down political systems nor top-down development policies have done anything to improve the lives of the long-suffering Oromo, or of Abyssinian peasants, or indeed of any of the millions of ordinary, hard-working African people anywhere on the continent.

Notes

1 Gebru Tareke (1991) describes some recent examples. See also Markakis (1987), Baxter (1983) and Triulzi (1986). For two representative Oromo views, see Gadaa Melba (1980) and Mohammed Hassen (1990b).
2 *Arbora* are ivory armlets, only worn by men who have killed a man or a big-game trophy. *Suuri ruufa* are red, black and white turbans worn by elders at rituals. They commemorate the first *Kaallu* (divine leader), who was found as an infant swaddled in such a cloth.

References

Asmarom Legesse (1973) *Gada: Three Approaches to the study of African Society*. New York: Free Press.
—— (1990) interview in *Qunnamtii*, issue no. 2. Daly City, California.
Bahrey (1954) History of the Galla. In C.F Beckingham & G.W.B. Huntingford (trans., eds), *Some Records of Ethiopia 1593–1646*. London: Hakluyt Society.
Bartels, L. (1983) *Oromo Religion: Myths and Rites of the Western Oromo of Ethiopia — an Attempt to Understand*. Berlin: Dietrich Reiner.
Baxter, P.T.W. (1965) Repetition in certain Boran ceremonies. In M. Fortes & G. Dieteren (eds), *African Systems of Thought*. London: Oxford University Press.
—— (1983) The problem of the Oromo, or the problem for the Oromo? In I.M. Lewis (ed.), *Nationalism and Self-Determination in the Horn of Africa*. London: Ithaca Press.
—— (1986) The present state of Oromo studies. In *Bulletins des études africaines de l'Inalco*, 7.2.
—— (1987) Some observations on the short hymns sung in praise of Shaikh Nur Hussein of Bale. In Ahmed el Shahi (ed.), *The Diversity of the Muslim Community*. London: Ithaca Press.
Baxter, P.T.W. & Almagor, U. (eds) (1978) *Age, Generation and Time*. London: Hurst.

Braukamper, U. (1980) *Geschichte der Hadiya Sud Athiopiens*. Wiesbaden: Franz Steiner.

—— (1989) The sanctuary of Shaykh Husayn and the Oromo-Somali connections in Bale (Ethiopia). *Frankfurter Afrikanistische Blatter*, 1.

Crummey, D. (ed.) (1986) *Banditry, Rebellion and Social Protest in Africa*. London: James Currey.

Gadaa Melba (1980) *Oromia: a Brief Introduction*. Finfine, Ethiopia.

Gebru Tareke (1991) *Ethiopia: Power and Protest. Peasant Revolts in the Twentieth Century*. Cambridge: Cambridge University Press.

Gragg, G. (1982) *Oromo Dictionary*. Michigan State University.

Hobsbawm, E.J. (1992) Ethnicity and nationalism in Europe today. *Anthropology Today*, **8** (4).

Holcombe, B. & Sissai Ibssa (1990) *The Invention of Ethiopia: the Making of a Dependent Colonial State in Northeast Africa*. Trenton, New Jersey: Red Sea Press.

Hultin. J. (1987) The long journey: essays on history, descent and land among the Macha Oromo. Ph.D. thesis, Uppsala University.

—— (1990) The conquest of land and the conquest of fertility: a theme in Oromo culture. In A. Jacobson-Widding & W. van Beek (eds), *The Creative Communion: African Folk Models of Fertility and the Regeneration of Life*. Uppsala: Studies in Cultural Anthropology, no. 15.

James, W. (1990) Kings, commoners and the ethnographic imagination in Sudan and Ethiopia. In R. Fardon (ed.), *Localizing Strategies: Regional Traditions of Ethnographic Writing*. Edinburgh: Scottish Academic Press.

Kundera, M. (1970) *The Joke*. Harmondsworth: Penguin Books.

Leus, T. (1988) *Boran-English Dictionary*. Yabello: Catholic Church, Dadim.

Levine, D. (1974) *Greater Ethiopia*. Chicago, Illinois: Chicago University Press.

Lewis, H.S. (1965) *A Galla Monarchy: Jimma Abba Jifar, Ethiopia 1830–1932*. University of Wisconsin Press.

Markakis, J. (1987) *National and Class Conflict in the Horn of Africa*. Cambridge University Press.

Mohammed Hassen (1990a) *The Oromo of Ethiopia: a History 1570–1860*. Cambridge: Cambridge University Press.

—— (1990b) Why did it take so long for the Oromo to be politically mobilised? Toronto: Proceedings of the Conference of the Oromo Nation.

Negaso Gidada (1984) History of the Sayyo Oromo of the south western Wollega, Ethiopia from about 1730–1886. Ph.D. thesis, Johan Wolfgang Goethe University, Frankfurt am Main.

Reyna, S.B. (1990) *Wars Without End: the Political Economy of a Precolonial African State*. Hanover: University Press of New England.

Schlee, G. (1990a) *Identities on the Move: Clanship and Pastorialism in Northern Kenya*. Manchester: Manchester University Press.

—— (1990b) Holy Grounds. In P.T.W. Baxter & Richard Hogg (eds), *Property, Poverty and People: Changing Rights in Property and Problems of Pastoral Development*. Manchester International Development Centre, University of Manchester.

Tilahun Gamta (1989) *Oromo–English Dictionary*. Addis Ababa.

Triulzi, A. (1986) Centre–periphery relations in western Ethiopia: the case of Nagamte. In W. James & D. Donham (eds), *The Southern Marches of Imperial Ethiopia*. Cambridge: Cambridge University Press.

Tutschek, K. (1844–5) *Dictionary of the Galla Language*. Munich.

185

Ullendorf, E. (1960) *The Ethiopians: an Introduction to Country and People*. Oxford University Press.

Van de Loo, J. (1991) *Guji Oromo Culture in Southern Ethiopia*. Berlin: Dietrich Reiner.

Venturino, B. & Tablino, P. (n.d.) *A Boran–English: English–Boran Dictionary*. MS.

Williams, R. (1976) *Keywords: a Vocabulary of Culture and Society*. London: Fontana.

Zitelman, T. (1990) Oromo culture, nationalism and refugee communities. The Elizabeth Colson Lecture, Institute of Refugee Studies, Queen Elizabeth House, Oxford, 24 October.

9 The Ideology of the Dinka & the Sudan People's Liberation Movement
M.A. MOHAMED SALIH

The majority of the Dinka in Sudan live in the Bahr al-Ghazal and upper Nile regions in the south, and the southern part of Kordofan region in the north. The expansion of the Sudanese economy earlier, and war and famine recently, displaced large numbers of Dinka people, many of whom migrated to northern Sudan in search of employment or to Ethiopia to seek refuge from war and famine. Demographically, the Dinka represent the largest ethnic group in Sudan. The 1955 population census, the only one which classifies Sudanese according to ethnic origin, put the Dinka population at 1 million representing about 10 per cent of the total population of Sudan. Modest estimates put the total number of Dinka today at about 2 million. Dinka subsistence economy is based on cattle, goat and sheep husbandry, and the cultivation of various food (millet, maize, cow-peas) and cash crops (cotton, ground-nuts and sesame). The Dinka are industrious farmers and subsist most of the year on millet porridge mixed with sour milk. Gathering of wild edible plants is common during the rainy season. By Dinka standards fishing is considered the poor man's source of livelihood, but they resort to it whenever grain shortages are experienced.

According to various sources (Seligman & Seligman, 1932; Lienhardt, 1958, 1961; Deng, 1972; Southall, 1976) the Dinka are particularly devoted to their cattle. Ownership of large herds is a source of pride and prestige. Owners of large herds perform rituals and participate actively in public life, and are praised for their ability to marry often and produce many children to protect the family and look after the herds. Dinka interest in cattle is rooted in their ecology, which favours animal husbandry, while

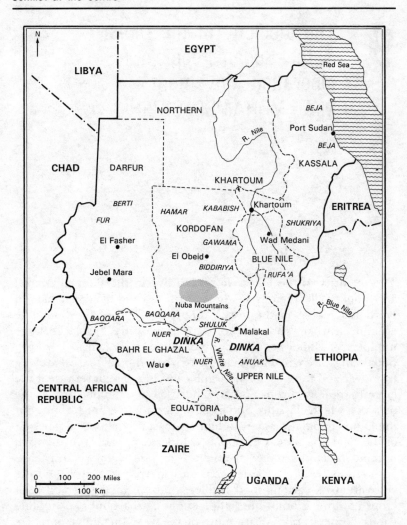

Map 11   The Dinka in Sudan

cultivation is plagued by seasonal floods, heavy soils, endemic pests, termites and thick, tall grass cover.

Seasonal variations in rainfall and pasture determine the rhythm of the agro-pastoralist way of life led by the Dinka. While the young men follow the herd, the rest of the population live in homesteads built on high ground to avoid the floods, but not too far from the rivers, where water is accessible during the dry season. During the dry season, which lasts five to six months, the young men take the herds to the river banks away from the village. They return to their villages during the rainy season to assist in handling labour-intensive agricultural operations, such as weeding and harvesting. Economic activity among the Dinka and other Nilotes is carried out between the village and the camp, a span that can be seen as a continuum of complementary activities defining two spheres of production, one dealing with animal husbandry and the other with grain production. The trade-off between these two defines the Dinka properly as agro-pastoralists, despite their devotion to cattle.

Even though they share an ethnic identity, a common culture and a language, the Dinka do not constitute a political entity, although they may appear so to outsiders. Warfare among the Dinka clans is as common as warfare against other Nilotes. Moreover, given the high incidence of intermarriage with other Nilotes, especially the Nuer, there is nothing like a pure Dinka (Seligman, 1913; Lienhardt, 1961; Southall, 1976). None the less, the Dinka overshadow other ethnic groups in the south and play a prominent role in Sudanese political life, a fact explained by their sheer demographic dominance, relative wealth and better access to modern education since colonial times, rather than their affinity or influence with their fellow Nilotes.

In common with other ethnic groups in southern Sudan, Dinka historical experience with intruders from the north — slave-traders, ivory hunters, colonialists — was an unhappy one, and their relationship with the northern Sudanese, before and after independence, has been uneven. The Dinka have been under continuous pressure from predators who sought to force them to come to terms with new but harsher ways of life. Reading through the history of Dinkaland from pre-colonial times to post-independent Sudan, one has the impression that they have always been at war (Seligman & Seligman, 1932; Deng, 1972). Their ethnocentric sense of pride is symbolized in the phrase *monyjang* ('masters of men') used to describe themselves, while all non-Dinka are called *jur* ('the other', or 'foreigner').

Dinkaland, along with the rest of southern Sudan, has been a theatre of savage civil war from 1955 to 1972, and from 1983 to the present. Out of 34 years of Sudan's independent existence, the south has spent 24 years at war. The price paid by the Dinka and other Nilotes has been heavy. Past accounts describing Dinkaland as a land of plenty, where 'threatening relatives with the prospect of leaving Dinkaland was seen as little short of suicide', and the Dinka as the richest cattle-owners in Africa, who could pay up to 200 head of cattle for bridewealth (Deng, 1972: 3–6), are no longer true. Today the Dinka are a society struggling to survive war and famine. Hundreds of thousands of Dinka are living in appalling conditions in northern Sudan, many others fled their homes to seek refuge in Ethiopia and in areas of the south under the control of the Sudanese People's Liberation Movement (SPLM), while others joined its military wing, the Sudanese People's Liberation Army (SPLA). Those who remain in the villages and cattle camps of Dinkaland live under constant fear of attack by the Sudanese army, the Baqqara militia or hostile southern ethnic groups like the Nuer, Mandari and Fertit.

This chapter examines the Dinka response to the changing nature and magnitude of war, and the manner in which they incorporated modern warfare values into traditional institutions entrusted with self-defence. It also highlights latent contradictions between Dinka ethnic ideology and the SPLM's advocacy of socialism.

War and Dinka society

The debate among social anthropologists concerning warfare in Africa has focused on three themes which depict patterns of association between social organization and war. The salient features of these three themes are the following.
1 War and the level of social organization among East African pastoralists is a theme elaborated by Fukui & Turton (1979), who point out that certain elements of social organization mediate to heighten or moderate the intensity of conflict. They argue that warfare among East African pastoralists 'has more in common with raiding . . . than with the large-scale, set piece or pitched battles of European history' (p. 7). However, an increasing tendency towards the Europeanization of war amongst East African pastoralists has narrowed the distinction between war and raiding. Nevertheless, the distinction serves to define two different levels of armed conflict. One is determined by socially accredited values and beliefs, while the other is an individual

or small-group act with limited, or without, societal approval.

2 Baxter & Almagor (1978) elucidate the theme of war and age organization, which encompasses social and political roles used to distinguish between warriors and the rest of the society. Baxter & Almagor recognize firstly that quite specific political, military, legal and ritual responsibilities are often vested in age sets on behalf of the community, and secondly that there are certain consequences emanating from being a member of an age set for the interactive social relationships in which the member is involved. War is only one such relationship, which involves a certain social category of population based on age.

3 The warrior tradition is placed by Mazrui (1977) at the meeting point between culture, war and politics, and is linked with the issue of the origin of the state in Africa. A related theme is the relation of this tradition to military factors in historical evolution. Unlike Fukui & Turton (1979), Mazrui (1977) plays down the distinction between raid and war. He asserts that 'the warrior tradition underlines all those other issues linking pre-colonial combat to modern warfare, mediating between culture and politics, affirming the individual's obligations to society, and constantly drawing the boundaries between war and peace in human experience' (p. 4).

These three approaches provide a basic framework for delineating the relationship between war, society and ideology. It is important to note from the beginning that war is not the preoccupation of the whole Dinka society during normal years. Moreover, like any other society, the Dinka have developed through the centuries institutions entrusted with the role of defending people against intruders and potential enemies. Therefore, it is important to treat war and society with careful consideration of the socio-political context within which people go to war. Of relevance to war among the Dinka is what Lienhardt (1961: 9) refers to as Dinka political theory, which is based on the

> nuclear lineage of a warrior subclan, which provides its war-leaders as the nuclear spear-master lineage provides its priests. In inter-tribal warfare one of the several masters of the fishing-spear, and one of the several war-leaders, emerge as master of the fishing-spear and war leader of the whole tribe. The theory, then, is of the dual control of war-leader and priest, in the subtribe and in the tribe.

Lienhardt has depicted the essence of Dinka ideology, which is based on a defined structure of beliefs, ideas and values, consciously or unconsciously used to handle war. This theory, however, is better understood with reference to the role of age

191

organization in Dinka society, and here lies the importance of the distinction between war and raiding: not as a dichotomy between war as modern and raiding as a traditional phenomenon, but as a contrast between war, on the one hand, and routine conflicts between individuals and groups, on the other.

Every Dinka is a member of an age group with a ritually conferred name. Age organization is socially recognized as one determinant of status. Dinka men pass through socially defined age grades — newly born, child, youth, adult, elder — and these have an intimate association with status/role responsibilities as defined by society. These and other features of age organization are meticulously depicted by Baxter & Almagor (1978) in their work on age, generation and time.

The transition to youthhood is celebrated by the Dinka and festivities are held in appreciation of it. The ceremonies marking the transition to youthhood take place on a subtribal basis, when the initiates are between 16 and 18 years of age. A set of initiates bears a name of its own, has a spokesman and appears as a corporate group until death. Each initiate receives seven to ten long cuts on the forehead and has to show courage and valour during the operation. Deng (1972: 73) reports

the period following initiation is supposed to be one of training not of serious fighting for the youth. Immediately after their initiation, they are forbidden to drink beer, not only to keep them physically fit but also to make them less unruly. They retire into the wilderness with their age-set father who instructs them in the art and ethics of war. They must not provoke, they must defend; and when they fight a just war, they are to rest assured of ancestral support and the blessing of God.

There is, therefore, a period of training and preparation for war before engagement in real combat. As Baxter (1977) has argued, the initiates do not represent a specialized army in the modern sense; they take up their new role as a routine activity through which every adult member of the society passes.

In contrast to the military role of youth, the transition to adulthood is indirectly celebrated through marriage. An adult is a settled family man, participates in public life and can attend the courts to voice his opinion and take part in the decisions which affect the whole society. Old age is an extension of adulthood, but the elder is listened to with much respect and is less challenged, and his views have much more weight than those of an adult or a newly married man. Hence, the role of the elders is to counterbalance the aggressive and military orientation of youth. If children, adults and old people are not directly involved in warfare, it is not logical to claim that the political ideology of the whole society is based on aggression because it pays attention to the military role of the youth.

The point of departure here is that no society takes up war as a routine activity unless it is forced to do so by internal or external circumstances. Moreover, there is no reason to claim that Dinka society is warlike, aggressive and violent without understanding the factors which lend themselves to the creation of such attributes. The use of negative terms such as 'violent' or 'warlike', I suggest, is a way of creating an enemy image and using it as an ideological justification for counter-aggression. Nevertheless, I am intrigued by the manner in which Deng (1972: 6) describes the Dinka, his own people, as

> an exceedingly violent society, and from very early age one of the central values in a boy's education is valour and physical strength. Determination and readiness to fight for one's honor and right against anyone of whatever strength merit high esteem in children and youth. Fighting with clubs between individuals and local groups leaves many Dinka with scars on the head; and fighting with spears between tribal segments leaves many a feud to continue in perpetuity.

One wonders whether Deng conforms to the common image which the Dinka have of themselves, or is responding to the European readers by reinforcing the image they have of Dinka society. Deng claims. that youth are socialized and trained for war, and that Dinka social structure has two forms of leadership, one for war, and another for conflict resolution and peace making. Yet the fact that every country has a military establishment does not mean the whole society is routinely involved in war. The existence of institutions built on aggression, such as the defence systems of Western nations with their sophisticated weaponry, shows that these nations are not less prepared for war than the Dinka.

The transition from traditional to modern warfare

Before and during the Turco-Egyptian (1821–81) conquest, southern Sudan was known as a source of slaves (Crabites, 1933). Arab slave-traders came to Sudan through Egypt, across the Red Sea and across the Sahara from North Africa, to settle alongside the Nile and the hinterlands. They established Islamic kingdoms with close connections with Egypt and the Hijaz. Soon after their southward expansion, and the rise of the Funj kingdom, the Arabs acted also as middlemen for European slave-exporters (O'Fahey & Spaulding, 1974). The fifteenth century was described as a 'dark age' in Sudan, when slave-raiding was rampant and people in the rural areas feared for their lives and property. The same applies to Dar Fur kingdom, which played a central role in regulating the slave-trade through licences granted by its sultans (O'Fahey, 1973).

The history of the Dinka since the early seventeenth century is a history of war and raids by many intruders: Arabs, Europeans, Egyptians, Turks and others. The eighteenth century was particularly infamous for the atrocities committed by slave-raiders, a fact which according to Crabites (1933) contributed to an international outcry for putting an end to the horrors of the slave-trade. The slave-trade reached its apogee in the nineteenth century. According to one source, 'it has been estimated that during the 19th century Arab slavers carried off about two million blacks from the Southern Sudan' (cited in O'Balance, 1977: 20). The Turco-Egyptian colonial rule is remembered in Dinkaland as a tragedy, when people were enslaved and sold like cheap commodities or given to the government in payment of taxes. Collins (1971: 32) describes how,

under European direction, the Arab intruded by force, not only inland from Bahr al Jabal, but also up Bahr al-Ghazal to Mashara ar-raqq and the plains beyond. Here the Arab established stations, seized wives and slaves from among the neighbouring African tribes, and collected ivory in the heartland of Southern Sudan.

The rule of the Mahdiya (1881–98) was no better; its troops penetrated deeply into the south, using firearms captured from the defeated Turco-Egyptian army, and many Dinka suffered the same fate. Those who espoused Islam were conscripted to fight in the black *jahadiyya* battalions of the Mahdiya army.

The Nilotes were not enslaved without resistance. The Shilluk organized an army which advanced northward during the second half of the sixteenth century to attack the bases of the slave-raiders, but were repulsed by the Funj Islamic kingdom, which amassed an army several times larger and better armed than the Shilluk (Mercer, 1971). The Dinka did not have a centralized state like the Shilluk, and lacked a strong military organization to confront the advancing slave-raiders. They and other Nilotes used rudimentary weapons consisting of throwing spears, stabbing spears, knives and clubs made of elephant tusks. There was no comparison with the weapons used by the European and Arab slave-raiders, especially during the Turco-Egyptian period, when the slave-trade intensified through the use of firearms.

Within the misfortune of colonial rule, there were some positive aspects related to the administration's efforts to eradicate slavery. While ethnic groups claiming Arab origin were disarmed, those of African origin were allowed to possess firearms to protect themselves. Spaulding gives an account of 260 slaves whose ethnic identity was determined between 1910 and 1930 (1988: 30). Only five of them were Dinka, and the majority were from diverse ethnic group such as Oromo, Berti, Koma, Nuba and Fur, who constituted 88.8 per cent of the total sample. There were even nine Arab slaves, which means there may have been more Arab than Dinka slaves in central Sudan at that time. By 1930, the Anglo-Egyptian administration had succeeded in the struggle against slavery in the south, and the northern Sudanese war-lords were eliminated.

Sudan began its independence from colonial rule in 1956 with bloodshed; the civil war between north and south was already one year old. Although the war began in Equatoria Province, in Sudan's southern borders with Uganda and Zaïre, the Dinka joined the rebel Anya-nya movement in concert with their fellow southerners against the domination of the Muslim Arab north. It is estimated that about 2,000,000 southerners lost their lives in the first civil war (1955–72). When it began, many southerners were already in possession of firearms. Many of the soldiers who took part in the Torit mutiny defected with their arms, and formed the nucleus of the Anya-nya guerrilla army. In 1965, a mass of Congolese soldiers defected to the southern Sudan with their arms. The war created a thriving market for weapons, and many villagers in the south began to have access to modern fire-arms, including sub-machine-guns. The importation of modern weapon systems by the Anya-nya became the order of the day until the Addis Ababa Agreement was signed in 1972. Reportedly, not a few southerners were dissatisfied with the terms of the agreement and did not hand over their arms to the government (SPLA/SPLM, 1983; Khalid, 1987; Alier, 1990).

The second civil war began in 1983. Three factors contributed to the rise and wide acceptance of the SPLA/SPLM in the south (Mohamed Salih, 1985, 1990). Firstly, there were the redivision of the south into three regions, and the undoing of the Addis Ababa Agreement, which established southern Sudan as one region, within the boundaries inherited from the colonial regime. While Equatorians supported redivision in fear of Dinka domination, the Dinka perceived it as an act designed by the Nimeiri regime to weaken the bargaining power of a united South. Secondly, there were the redrawing of the borderline between north and south in order to put the newly discovered oil sites in southern Sudan inside the north, and the decision not to build an oil refinery in Bentiu in the south, but to build a pipeline that would take the crude oil to the north. Thirdly, there was the imposition of the Islamic Sharia laws on all sectors of the Sudanese population, Muslims, Christians and animists alike. Although Sharia was not applied in the south, southerners living in the north were among its first victims.

These precipitating factors can be added to the underlying basic issue of the gross disparity in material and social development between north and south, and the historical legacy of fear and suspicion. John Garang de Mabior, a former colonel in the Sudanese army and an economist with a doctorate from the University of Iowa, was never in favour of the Addis Ababa Agreement, and was among the few Anya-nya officers who argued for the continuation of the first civil war. Garang, a Dinka, became the leader of the Sudan People's Liberation Movement, and the Dinka became the dominant ethnic group in the Sudan People's Liberation Army. It might be said that, with the beginning of the second civil war in 1983, the transition from traditional 'raiding' to modern 'warfare' was completed.

Dinka ideology and the SPLM/SPLA

Ideology plays an important role in defining societal interests and justifying social and political goals. Gould & Kolb (1965: 225) define ideology at the most general level as 'a pattern of factual and normative beliefs and concepts, which purport to explain complex social phenomena with the view of directing and simplifying socio-political choices facing individuals and groups'. Hence, cultural values based on historical experience are important parts of any ideological orientation, whether in the pursuit of peace or war. According to Bell, 'ideology is the conversion of ideas into social levers . . . For the ideologue, truth arises in action, and meaning is given to experience by the "transforming moment"' (1960: 370).

Ideology in societies in which the social hierarchy, or access to individually owned but collectively claimed resources, is based on a social contract, the borderline between group and individual ideology is so thin that shared values are always given prominence over individual interests. All the more so in a situation of war. The merger between individual and group ideologies can be explained by the fact that ethnic groups are not political parties which may have ethnically heterogeneous membership. The cultural meaning of group ideology and its organizational principles are factors that distinguish one ethnic group from another.

War ideology, in both class-based and ethnic-based societies, has a much wider meaning than individual ideology, and may sacrifice the individual's life in pursuance of common security. War ideology is perpetuated through the advocacy of the image of an enemy to justify the need to eliminate the threat he poses, and the obligation to endure suffering for the interest of the whole group or 'nation'. However, although bellicose attitudes against an enemy can be fostered, the 'public good' justification can be challenged on the grounds that interest groups or individuals rather than the whole society benefit from war. These questions pertain significantly to the relevance of the SPLM ideology for Dinka people and their perception of the present war.

The ideology of the SPLM is different from that of Anya-nya, who fought the first civil war (1955–72). It also differs from the ideology of a smaller rival southern movement, called Anya-nya II. The SPLM is perceived by its leaders as a national, that is all-Sudanese, movement. While the political wing of Anya-nya II is called the Southern Sudan People's Liberation Movement, that of the SPLA is called the Sudan People's Liberation Movement. The SPLM claims its aim is not to separate the South from the north, but to build a united socialist Sudan. If ideologies can be explicated in any form, manifestos and political charters present features that are believed will gain popular support for the movement. According to its *Manifesto* (1983):

The SPLA/SPLM is convinced of the correctness of its socialist orientation. The SPLA/SPLM programme is based on the objective realities of the Sudan and provides a correct solution to the nationality and religious questions within the context of a United Sudan, thereby preventing the country from an otherwise inevitable disintegration.

The ultimate objective is the creation of the 'New Sudan'. According to the SPLA/SPLM (1989: 84),

the 'New Sudan' as a concept, therefore, strives to establish a new cultural order in the country. It takes as its point of departure the notion that human beings in any society have equal rights and obligations regardless of race, beliefs, colour, etc. The establishment of the new Sudan cultural order demands of necessity a radical restructuring of state power to establish genuine democracy and to follow a path of development that will lead to far-reaching social change.

The *Manifesto* of the SPLA/SPLM encompasses five of the features which Young (1982: 101) refers to as characteristic of a populist socialist doctrine based on five pillars.

197

First, intensive nationalist tendency, second, radical mood, third, anti-capitalism, fourth, an exaltation of the people hence populism where ideology is pervaded with a moralistic celebration of the virtues of mass, above all the rural mass, and fifth, socialism — though not orthodox Marxism — becomes a diffused but important component of the syndrome.

The most glaring aspect of the SPLM tendency towards populist socialism, both in its ideology and in its vision of a new Sudan, is its advocacy of mass participation through a national democratic alliance, which is synonymous with the one-party system for mass mobilization.

Apparently the revolutionary situation in the country has attained the peak of maturity. This is so because the intensity of the present overall crisis indicates that the Sudan can hardly become more ungovernable than it is already today. . . . The reality calls for joint efforts to make the objective factors necessary to success prevail. Specifically a qualitative higher level of political organization of the democratic forces and the broad masses is needed. In this sphere the formation of a broad-based National Democratic Alliance as a framework for fusion of the armed forces and the mass: political action appears a matter worthy of consideration [*sic*]. (SPLA/SPLM, 1989: 90)

While according to its ideology the SPLM is a national movement, it is perceived by many Sudanese as a Dinka movement inspired by traditional Dinka concerns and aspirations. Some of the other ethnic groups in the south are said to have joined the movement out of fear of being attacked by it, or after actual military defeat. Shilluk and Nuer defectors from the SPLA have complained of discrimination in promotion to higher ranks, and claimed they were used as ethnic tokens to give the movement a national character.

Elsewhere I have suggested that traditional war values can easily be incorporated into modern military institutions, albeit with considerable modification of their content, form and structure (Mohamed Salih, 1990: 170). The infusion of Dinka ideology into SPLM ideology can be attributed to other factors as well. For instance, over 90 per cent of the Dinka are illiterate and have little awareness of ideological concepts like socialism, or political notions like the democratic alliance. For many Dinka the present war is essentially not different from other wars they have fought against intruders over the centuries. It is a war for survival against aliens in whose hands they suffered slavery in the past, and more recently suffered neglect, poverty and famine. No one has expressed this Dinka feeling of continuity better than chief Makuei Bilkuei, who is quoted by Deng (1978: 75):

The suffering of the people is such that even as we sit here today, it has not ended. It will not end. But if people continue to endure this, suffering will one

198

day come to an end. The ancient world has not been abandoned. To abandon it is what brings disaster.

There is little doubt that most Dinka regard the SPLA as the carrier of their own concerns and aspirations. Dinka ideology accommodates the political programme of the SPLM as a strategy for survival, not as a substitute for traditional values derived from historical experience. For the ordinary Dinka, the enemy remains the north, the region the SPLM claims it is fighting to liberate from a corrupt ruling class. No matter what the motives and ideology of the Dinka leaders of the SPLM are, the Dinka people identify with them only as long as they do not openly abandon traditional Dinka values and beliefs in favour of populist socialism and an abstract vision of a 'New Sudan'. The Marxist belief that 'ideology includes not only the theory of knowledge and politics but also metaphysics, ethics, religion and indeed any "form of consciousness" which expresses the basic attitudes or commit-ments of a social class' (Lane, 1969: 321) ignores the fact that in war ideology transcends class and magnifies common sentiments beyond social and economic stratification. It is no wonder that the Dinka ideology plays a greater role in defining the nature of the war in southern Sudan than the universal appeal of the SPLA/SPLM.

Conclusion

Societies in transition combine traditional and modern values in their economic and political life. I presume this holds true also for war, which is a violent expression of societal conflict. Social change, therefore, is bound to be affected by the nature of war. Consequently, the transition from tribal to modern warfare cannot be seen as a dichotomy between the simple-traditional and complex-modern type of conflicts (Mohamed Salih, 1990). The incorporation of traditional values related to war in modern warfare has much in common with the response of traditional institutions to the agents of modern change. In this context, the dividing line in perception between war against the state and war against ethnic groups which dominate the state is too thin and difficult to demarcate. The average Dinka may not perceive the difference between fighting against the traditional predator from the north and fighting against the kind of state that not only permits but also encourages such depredation against its subjects. In that sense, Dinka ideology and SPLM ideology coincide.

However, Dinka and SPLM ideology is not identical. For the individual Dinka, the group membership binding effect is strengthened by defining the north as the common enemy. However, it is questionable whether the Dinka masses share the modern ideology of their élite who command the war and their vision of 'socialist transformation'. The modern political élite are accepted by the Dinka only when their political rhetoric in the battlefield is charged with 'ethnic sentiments' and explained in terms of traditional ideology. In this case, uttering seemingly uniform popular aspirations disguises an inherent contradiction between traditional and modern political values.

References

Alier, A. (1990) *Southern Sudan: Too Many Agreements Dishonoured.* Exeter: Ithaca Press.

Baxter, P.T.W. (1977) Boran age-sets and warfare. In D. Turton and K. Fukui (eds), *Warfare among East African Herders.* Osaka: Senri Ethnological Foundation, National Museum of Ethnology.

Baxter, P.T.W. & Almagor, U. (1978) Introduction. In P.T.W Baxter & U. Almagor (eds), *Age-Generation and Time: Some Features of East African Age Organization.* London: C. Hurst.

Bell, D. (1960) *The End of Ideology; On the Exhaustion of Political Ideas in the Fifties.* New York: The Free Press of Glencoe.

Collins, R.O. (1971) *Land Beyond the Rivers: the Southern Sudan, 1898–1918.* New Haven, Connecticut: Yale University Press.

Crabites, P. (1933) *Gordon and Slavery.* London: George Routlege.

Deng, F.M. (1972) *The Dinka of the Sudan.* New York: Holt, Rinehart and Winston.

—— (1978) *Africans of Two Worlds: the Dinka in Afro-Arab Sudan.* Khartoum: Institute of African and Asian Studies, University of Khartoum.

Fukui, K. & Turton, D. (eds) (1979) *Warfare Among East African Herders.* Osaka: Senri Ethnological Foundation, National Museum of Ethnology.

Gould, J. & Kolb, W.L. (eds) (1965) *A Dictionary of Social Science.* Glencoe: Free Press.

Khalid, M. (1987) *Garang Speaks.* London: Kegan Paul.

Lane, R.E. (1969) *Political Thinking and Consciousness: the Private Life of the Political Mind*, Chicago, Illinois: Markham.

Lienhardt, G. (1958) The western Dinka. In J. Middleton & D. Tait (eds), *Tribes Without Rulers.* London: Routledge & Kegan Paul.

—— (1961) *Divinity and Experience: the Religion of the Dinka.* Oxford University Press.

Mazrui, A. (ed.) (1977) *The Warrior Tradition in Modern Africa.* Leiden: E.J. Brill.

Mercer, P. (1971) Shilluk trade and politics from the mid-seventeenth century to 1861. *Journal of African History,* **12** (3).

Mohamed Salih, M.A. (1985) Some methodological problems in the study of nationalism and nation building in the Sudan. *Bayreuth African Studies Series*, **1**.

—— (1990) The Europeanization of war in Africa: from traditional to modern warfare. In V. Harle (ed.), *European Values in International Relations*. London: Pinter Publishers.

O'Balance, E. (1977) *The Secret War in the Sudan*. London: Faber.

O'Fahey, R.S. (1973) Slavery and slave trade in Dar Fur. *Journal of African History*, **14** (1).

O'Fahey, R.S. & Spaulding, J.L. (1974) *Kingdoms of the Sudan*. London: Methuen.

Seligman, C.G. (1913) Some aspects of the Hamitic problem in the Anglo-Egyptian Sudan. *Journal of the Royal African Institute*, **43**.

Seligman, C.G. & Seligman, B.Z. (1932) *Pagan Tribes of Nilotic Sudan*. London: Routledge.

Southall, A. (1976) Nuer and Dinka are people: ecology, ethnicity and logical possibility. *Man*, **11** (4).

Spaulding, J. (1988) The business of slavery in the central Anglo-Egyptian Sudan, 1910–1930. *African Economic History*, **17**.

SPLA/SPLM (1983) *Manifesto*.

SPLA/SPLM (1989) On the New Sudan. In A.M. Ahmed & G. Sorbo (eds), *Management of the Crisis in the Sudan*. Bergen: Centre of Development Studies.

Young, C. (1982) *Ideology and Development in Africa*. New Haven, Connecticut: Yale University Press.

10 The Social Bases of Regional Movements in Sudan 1960s-1980s
YOSHIKO KURITA

Sudanese politics since the 1960s have witnessed the emergence of several 'regional movements'. At first sight this does not seem surprising, since Sudan is a vast country with great cultural diversity, bound together only by the artificial boundaries imposed upon it by alien rulers (Egyptian and British). The emergence of regionalism as a political factor, however, is a relatively recent phenomenon, and should be analysed against its particular historical background. In the 1940s and 1950s, it was the 'national' parties, the Umma Party, the National Unionist Party and the People's Democratic Party, that called the tune in the political arena. In the 1960s, this system began to crumble, and Sudan witnessed the emergence of regional movements. After the collapse of the military regime in 1985, there was another upsurge of political activities based upon the aspirations of particular regions. However, we can observe a considerable change in the social significance of the regional movements in the 1960s and 1980s.

Regionalism is not the natural product of some self-evident 'regional identity' whose content is understood a priori, but is a social and political movement which emerges at a particular stage in the process of structuring and restructuring the state. This chapter will try to analyse the social factors which have led to the emergence of regional movements in Sudan, and will try to locate these movements in the broader context of Sudan's modern historical experience as a colonial and independent state.

Before regionalism: the rural areas in the traditional political framework

Regional movements have appeared in the relatively backward rural areas of Sudan: Kordofan, Nuba Mountains, Dar Fur, the Red Sea region and the south. Before analysing the nature of these movements in the 1960s, it is necessary to have a look at the general situation in the rural ares of Sudan before independence.

As is well known, during the Anglo-Egyptian condominium period, the rural areas of Sudan were under the native adminis- tration system. This was a system introduced by the British in the 1920s, and was designed to devolve administrative functions to the 'natural leaders' of the various communities, that is, to the tribal chiefs. It has often been pointed out that Sudanese society, especially in the north after the experience of the Mahdiya, was no longer a 'tribal society' (Daly, 1980, 1986). This did not bother British officialdom, however. What was needed were 'tribal chiefs' with sufficient political powers, rather than 'tribes' as natural social units. In other words, they needed elements inside Sudanese society that would collaborate with the colonial administration. In order to bring into existence these 'tribal chiefs', and to support their authority morally and materially, 'tribes' were reconstructed and, in some cases, invented.[1]

In his work on the Kababish in Kordofan, Talal Asad (1970) vividly demonstrates how the Kababish 'tribe' was artificially constructed by the British administration. The whole tribal system, including genealogy and 'tribal' territory (*dar*), was created and manipulated in order to support the paramount chief (*nazir*) and his close relatives. The same phenomenon can be discerned in the case of al-Humr Baqqara in southern Dar Fur, and al-Hassaniya and Rufa'a al-Hoi in the Gezira area (Abd-al Ghaffar Muhammad Ahmed, 1974; Mohamed Ahmed Abbas, 1980; Deng,1982). Sometimes, especially in the south and in some parts of the Nuba Mountains, the British encountered societies which were, unlike northern Sudanese society, unmistakably 'tribal', but totally different from the ideal 'tribe' the British had in mind. They lacked a tribal chief, an asset essential in the eyes of the colonial administrators. They were examples of what Evans-Pritchard called a 'stateless society', a society presumably lacking any form of government. Undaunted, the British adminis- trators managed to invent 'tribal chiefs' in these cases as well.

It is worth noting that in many cases throughout the country, the most effective measures for the creation of 'tribes' and 'tribal chiefs' seemed to have been the institutionalization of the payment

203

of 'tribute' to the chief, and the standardization of the amount of blood money paid by the different groups which were supposed to constitute a tribe (Talal Asad, 1970). It is also interesting to note that, in the case of 'stateless societies' in the south and the Nuba Mountains, the chiefship was often given to those who happened to have contact with the outside world, that is, with the northern riverain society, and had acquired through this contact a knowledge of the Arabic language and of trade, firearms and so on (Stevenson, 1984; Deng, 1986). Thus, paradoxically enough, the tribal chiefs, who were supposed to represent pure tribal tradition, were often those who had the strongest links with the outside world.

The tribal chiefs thus created rapidly amassed power and wealth, as a result of the 'devolution of power' to them. While formally restricted, such power was enhanced in practice. Establishment of a 'native administration' entailed the establishment of 'native courts', 'tribal police', 'native administration bureaucracy' and 'native administration budget'. In some cases, the tribal chiefs were empowered to assess and collect taxes. Those who belonged to the chief's lineage were exempted from taxes (Bakheit, 1965; Abd-al Ghaffar Muhammad Ahmed, 1973). In other cases, the tribal chiefs were entitled to allot pieces of land to the members of the tribe. They were also in charge of construction and maintenance of roads, wells and ponds. All these privileges enabled the tribal chiefs to turn into potential rural bourgeoisie.

The *shaykh* of the Rufa'a al-Hoi accumulated wealth through the allotment of gum-tree fields among his tribesmen. The *shaykh* of al-Hassaniya succeeded as the owner of an agricultural scheme in the Gezira area after the building of the Jabal al-Awliya' dam. Among the Beja of the Red Sea district, the power of the tribal chiefs grew side by side with the introduction of irrigated cultivation and the development of gum production. In the Nuba Mountains, some of the cotton-growing agricultural schemes were concentrated in the hands of the *meks* (Henderson, 1953).

In the eyes of the British officials who were putting the native administration policy into practice, it was desirable that each tribal territory (*dar*) included the members of the tribe in question only. Since the tribe was conceived as the framework inside which the tribal chiefs were allowed to have their own way — monopolizing resources and allotting them arbitrarily — justified by tribal authority, it was inconvenient if the tribal territory included people whose tribal affiliation was different from that of the chief. Under these circumstances, many people were compelled to move ('return') to the places which were supposed to be their original *dar*. It was feared that, if they continued to live outside their *dar*, they would not have access to resources, and would live as second-class citizens of the host tribe.

Without doubt, this kind of emigration had a significant effect on Sudanese society. Especially in the case of the areas where the 'Arabs' and the 'blacks' formerly used to live together, the effect was far reaching. We read about the southern districts of Kassala Province, where the 'black elements were formerly included under an Arab *nazir* and vice versa', but in the late 1920s, as a result of the 'success' of the native administration policy, the blacks began to 'sort themselves out of the former mosaic of Arab and Sudanese villages, and to carry themselves and their homes into the nazirate appropriate to them'.[2] Thus, the demarcation of tribal territories widened the fateful divide between the 'Arab' north and the 'black' south.

The tribal chiefs in the rural areas were not the sole indigenous basis of colonial rule. After all, the agricultural and pastoral products which were produced and collected at a low cost inside the tribal framework had to be transported to the market. For this purpose, the British administration had to gain the collaboration of the merchants in the towns. Especially in the late 1930s and the 1940s, when it became necessary to fully mobilize Sudan's economic potential in order to fight the Second World War successfully, the British administration tried to conciliate the merchant class. The Local Government Ordinances (1937–8) were issued, and the Sudanese merchants and the *effendiya* (Sudanese functionaries in the colonial service, an important component of colonial Sudanese society) were invited to take part in local government through the elected town and village councils. A Baqqara *nazir* complained about these developments, fearing that the participation of the new forces would cause a 'financial loss' to him and to his relatives.[3]

These developments, however, did not necessarily undermine the status of the tribal chiefs. Rather, the two forces — the tribal chiefs on the one hand and the merchants and officials on the other — entered into an alliance, forming two pillars of the economic foundation of the colonial state. It was this alliance of classes which was ultimately consolidated through the formation of the 'national' political parties, such as the Umma Party (Umma = nation in Arabic) and the various 'Unionist' parties which were eventually integrated into the National Unionist Party and the People's Democratic Party. As is well known, two religious dynasties, the House of the Mahdi and the House of Mirghani, mediated the conclusion of these alliances.

The House of the Mahdi, which became the core of the Umma Party, operated a successful agricultural enterprise by this time, and had attracted around it ambitious merchants and officials. At the same time, this family developed a close relationship with tribal chiefs in the Gezira region and western Sudan, such as the al-Hassaniya and al-Kawahla chiefs, mainly through marriage. The Unionist parties generally drew support from groups of merchants and intellectuals, who were considered more progressive than the groups supporting Umma. These groups eventually rallied around the Sufist House of Mirghani. This family, however, also had close connections with tribal chiefs in many areas of Sudan, and thus served as a liaison between the urban élite and the rural ruling class.

To summarize, rural society in colonial Sudan was strictly regulated by the native administration system, and this system itself was woven tightly into the emerging national political process. This system was preserved in the post-colonial period.

Challenges to the traditional system: Sudanese politics and regionalism in the 1960s

Sudanese society in the 1950s and 1960s was characterized by the progress of peripheral capitalist development. A new bourgeoisie began to emerge in the sectors of import and export, internal commerce, large-scale mechanized agricultural production, and so on. The social significance of the working class and the peasants who worked as tenants in large-scale agricultural schemes also increased with capitalist development. Independence entailed a large increase in the number of Sudanese employed in the state apparatus and public sector, and these groups began to exert considerable influence in society. As a result of these developments, post-independence politics came to be characterized by growing criticism aimed at the established political parties. The authority of these parties was challenged in the rural areas as well, and the legitimacy and effectiveness of the native administration system itself was called into question.

An early sign of this challenge can be observed in the policies of General Ibrahim Abbud's regime (1958–64). Needless to say, this regime was by no means a progressive one. To begin with, it was the Umma Party itself that invited General Abbud to assume power through the pretence of a *coup d'état*. However, it was under this regime that the traditional parties' control of local government was first challenged. In fact, one of the main factors which led to the deterioration of the relationship between the regime and the Umma Party was the introduction of new local councils (*al-majalis al-mahalliya*) (Bechtold, 1976). When Umma demanded the repeal of this decision, the regime responded by claiming that this was its way of 'applying democracy from the bottom', while Umma's parliamentary democracy was 'democracy applied from the top'.[4]

It is noteworthy that, while the Umma Party boycotted the government elections of local councils in April 1963, the Sudanese Communist Party chose to take part. Although the Communist Party was strongly opposed to the military dictatorship, it perceived a positive element in these elections. It argued that this could prove a step towards the liberation of the rural masses from the native administration system. It also described the Umma's boycott of the elections as an expression of the traditional party's desire to 'detain the masses in political and social backwardness'.[5]

The period after the collapse of the Abbud regime in 1964, known as the October Revolution, witnessed a full-fledged challenge to the traditional political system. It is true that the traditional parties also took part in the Revolution, but it was the workers, students and especially the urban professionals — engineers, doctors, lawyers, university teachers — that played the major role in overthrowing the regime. These groups not only were opposed to the military dictatorship, but were also critical of established party politics. There was a feeling that Sudanese society was on the verge of a great social revolution, and in this political atmosphere the abolition of native administration became one of the central issues of the day.

If we turn again to the analysis the Sudanese Communist Party, whose influence was greatly enhanced during this period, particularly among progressive intellectuals, the success of the revolution depended on the outcome of two kinds of struggle. One was the struggle carried out by the 'masses of the modern sector' and the other was a struggle to be carried out in the 'traditional sector' (the rural areas) of the country. The latter was supposed to consist of a series of movements which would pursue the reform of local government and the abolition of the tribal chiefs' power — in other words, the abolition of native administration itself.[6]

In this context, the various regional movements which came into existence in the 1960s were regarded as potential allies for the revolution. Sudanese politics after the October Revolution witnessed the emergence of several regional movements, including the General Union of the Nuba Mountains (*Ittihad 'Amm Jibal al-Nuba*) and the Beja Congress (*Mu'tamar al-Bija*). There were other movements demanding autonomy for the south as well, i.e. the Sudan African National Union and its military counterpart, the Anya-nya. All these movements were regarded by the Communist Party essentially as forces for reform in the traditional sector. In fact, the Party's literature of those days described the struggle for the reform of local government and the abolition of native administration as 'a form of agrarian reform' and one of the 'bases of non-capitalistic development' in Sudan, which eventually would lead to socialism.[7]

This became the common attitude of the progressive political forces towards the regional movements. The Socialist Party (*al-Hizb al-Ishtiraki*), which was founded in 1967 by a group of intellectuals and tenants of the Gezira scheme, adopted a similar view of the future social revolution. It recognized the importance of the struggle waged by the regional organizations, and admitted the necessity of autonomy for some areas of Sudan.[8] The positive attitude shown by the progressive forces towards regional aspirations was in sharp contrast with the negative attitude assumed by some of the ruling parties. The National Unionist Party, for example, criticized the regional movements as 'racist' (*unsri*), ones opposed to the national unity of Sudan.

When we turn to the actual state of things in the 1960s, however, we find a rather different situation. Although the true victims of native administration without doubt were the tribal masses, the call for the abolition of native administration was taken up not by these people, but by the local merchants and owners of mechanized agricultural schemes, the groups which had experienced rapid growth as a result of capitalistic development since independence. As Abd-al Ghaffar Muhammad Ahmed (1973) has shown in his study on the Rufa'a al-Hoi, they tried to use the slogan of the abolition of native administration as a political tool in their competition with the tribal chiefs over local control.

A similar tendency had already been observed earlier in the result of the elections to the local councils introduced by the Abbud regime. Contrary to the rather idealistic assumption by the Communist Party that these elections would give the tribal masses a chance to liberate themselves from social and political backwardness, those who were actually elected to these councils were retired officials, merchants and some tribal chiefs who chose to side with the military regime rather than with the established parties.[9]

To a considerable extent, the same applies to the regional movements. These movements were not created by the rural masses. Rather, they were launched by the elite of rural society.

Many of the leaders of these movements were professionals or former officials who had the privilege of being educated at Khartoum.[10] Thus, those who spoke in the name of the 'periphery' were, in fact, those who had the closest links to the 'centre'. At the same time, they were often the sons of tribal chiefs or local merchants, and thus belonged to a particular social class in rural society which had exceptionally strong ties with the outside world. There were cases where the local leader and champion of regionalism (and often anti-Arabism) turned out to be the descendant of an Arab merchant long settled in the region.[11]

This is not to deny the fact that regional movements had a popular basis to some extent. For example, the General Union of the Nuba Mountains found support among the ordinary people from the Nuba Mountains in Khartoum — former soldiers, hospital workers and so on. Its demand for the abolition of the poll tax reflected the desire of the people in the Nuba Mountains. Possibly encouraged by the activities of the Nuba Mountains Peasant Union, which was founded in the 1950s in close contact with the tenants' movement in the Gezira scheme, the General Union had a provision concerning land in its programme.[12] Nevertheless, it seems its popular support in the 1960s was relatively small compared with the situation in the 1980s.

The essentially élitist nature of the leadership of the regional movements is best reflected in their participation in the so-called Congress of New Forces (*Mu'tamar al-Quwa al-Jadida*) towards the end of 1967. This was an odd political alliance, consisting of the Umma Party (the Sadiq al-Mahdi wing), the Islamic Charter Front (Muslim Brotherhood), the Beja Congress, the General Union of the Nuba Mountains and the Sudan African National Union (William Deng wing). At first sight, it seems as if the coexistence of these forces in one political body is impossible. While the Beja Congress and the General Union of the Nuba Mountains demanded a degree of autonomy for their respective regions, and the Sudan African National Union claimed federal status for the south, the Islamic Charter Front called for the application of the Islamic laws (Sharia) and the building of an Islamic state in Sudan.

However, these contradictory political forces had something in common with respect to their social background. The leadership of these groups consisted of a new generation of former officials, merchants and petty bourgeois intellectuals (notably in the case of the Muslim Brotherhood), truly 'new forces' which had come to the foreground of Sudanese politics thanks to the progress of capitalistic development and the transformation of Sudanese society since independence. At the core of this alliance was the Sadiq al-Mahdi wing of the Umma Party. This wing represented the 'modernist' tendency inside the Umma Party, and was eager to broaden the party's base among the urban intellectuals. Unlike the Imam al-Hadi wing of the party, which continued to rely on the tribal chiefs to rally support in the rural areas, the Sadiq al-Mahdi wing tried to enter into an alliance with the new élite, who were advocating reform in this sector.

Thus, far from the the Communist Party's assumption that the reform of local government constituted one of the bases of non-capitalistic development in Sudan, the 'Congress of New Forces' was an attempt to unite and reorganize the rapidly expanding Sudanese bourgeoisie into one political body, after the failure of the traditional parties became manifest. It is worth mentioning that, in the framework of this congress, even the Sudan African National Union and the Islamic Charter Front were, in a sense, supporting each other. It has been reported that the former was ready to accept the application of Sharia and the turning of Sudan into an Islamic state, provided that federal status for the south was guaranteed (Fawzy-Rossano, 1981).

Beyond regionalism: the Nimeiri regime and its aftermath

Under the Nimeiri regime (1969–85), which came to power through the *coup d'état* of May 1969, native administration was finally abolished, at least in the north. It seemed then as if Sudan was entering an age of genuine social revolution under a regime which called itself 'the successor of the October Revolution'. As is clearly demonstrated by the abolition of native administration, the Nimeiri regime, at least in its early days, portrayed itself as a government of the progressive forces, whose ultimate goal was the liberation of Sudan from dependency, and the adoption of 'the non-capitalistic path to development'.

However, the regime soon shifted into a clearly capitalistic direction, especially after the famous confrontation with the Communist Party in 1971. In this renewed era of capitalistic development, the petty bourgeois intellectuals — bureaucrats, technocrats, army officers — played a leading role, while the traditional parties were banned and their social base undermined to a great extent by the abolition of native administration. The People's Local Government Act was introduced in the place of native administration in 1971. Under the new system, the local councils had power to impose local taxes, to distribute resources, including land in some cases, and to manage social services. Thus the new local government system, needless to say totally dominated by the Sudan Socialist Union — the sole political organization under the Nimeiri regime, established in 1972 — rapidly turned into a means for capital accumulation by the new bourgeoisie, as well as a tool for mass mobilization.

As a result of the failure of its development policy, the accumulation of foreign debt, and the interference of international financial institutions, the latter half of the regime's reign (approximately 1978–85) witnessed a rapid deterioration of the economy and the standard of living of the people. The situation was especially grave in rural areas such as the Nuba Mountains, Dar Fur and the south. Shortages of basic goods and the deterioration of public services were more serious in these areas than in the northern riverain region. Exploitation through the local government apparatus also intensified. The peasant was oppressed by the establishment of publicly owned large-scale mechanized agricultural schemes. Leases of these schemes were often obtained by local and central government officials, and merchants financed by the 'Islamic banks' which began to flourish at this time. Sometimes the local peasants were even deprived of their own land (Elhassan, 1988).

The disintegration of rural society led to an influx of people into the local towns and the national capital, Khartoum, where they constituted a stratum of low-paid labourers, the jobless and the homeless, known as *shammasa* ('children of the sun'). In its last days, the Nimeiri regime often evicted the *shammasa* from Khartoum, and drove them back to their 'place of origin' (Abd al-Latif, 1985). The same policy was pursued in local towns of the south, where the unemployed were requested to return to the rural areas. Again, when the regime introduced the so-called 'Islamic' penal code in September 1983, many of its victims happened to be *shammasa*.

Although the regional political organizations were disbanded along with all other political parties, the regime and the leaders of these movements were on relatively good terms for some time. Many of the former champions of regionalism came to occupy important posts in the Sudan Socialist Union. In fact, this political organization succeeded in uniting various factions of the new bourgeoisie in the country, and bears a considerable resemblance to the 'Congress of New Forces' of the 1960s. It is well known that southern regionalism as embodied in the Anyanya, turned out to be one of the regime's strongest props after the signing of the Addis Ababa Agreement in 1972. The so-called 'decentralization' policy under the Nimeiri regime (Regional Government Act, 1980) was to a certain degree a result of lobbying by the leaders of the regional movements (Markakis, 1990: 293, n. 12). At the same time, it was an expression of the regime's desire to divide the people's resistance and to deflect popular discontent from the central government (Khalid, 1985: 205). It seems that up to a certain point there existed a subtle balance between the regime's interests and those of the élite whose influence relied upon the aspirations of particular regions. Indeed, this élite was part of the regime.

The situation began to change in the 1980s. As a result of accelerating social changes in the rural areas, the regional movements began to acquire new social dimensions. A comparison of the movements that emerged, or re-emerged, after the overthrow of the Nimeiri regime by a popular uprising in 1985, with their predecessors in the 1960s can be misleading at first sight. As in the 1960s, their leadership is in the hands of the educated élite. However, the demands and claims they make reflect the actual grievances of the people in the 1980s. For example, a clause in the charter of the General Union of the Nuba Mountains, which was reorganized after 1985, demands that 'the freedom of movement and residence inside the Sudan should be guaranteed unconditionally to all the Sudanese' (Salah Abd al Latif, 1985: 163). Without doubt, this refers to the policy of evicting people from urban centres, known as *kasha*, to which many people originally from the Nuba Mountains were subjected. Similar criticisms of this policy are found in the speeches of Philip Abbas Ghabashi, a leader of the General Union of the Nuba Mountains in the 1960s, and founder of the Sudanese National Party (*al-Hizb al-Qawmi al-Sudani*) after 1985.

The Sudan African National Union (SANU) in the 1960s was essentially élitist in nature and sometimes showed a sort of opportunism in dealing with the northern political parties. Even the reconstructed SANU after 1985 seemed to retain this characteristic to some degree. Still, in its 1986 manifesto there is severe criticism of agricultural schemes in the south, owned by 'absentee landlords resident in Khartoum, Medani, Kosti, Port Sudan, etc.', which are oppressing the life of the local inhabitants. Concern for the plight of the peasants who were deprived of their land is even keener in the case of the General Union of the Nuba Mountains. After the fall of Nimeiri, the Union demanded not only the 'elimination of the feudalistic relations and the feudalistic agricultural policies' — no doubt a reference to the remaining power of the *meks* — but also an end to the building

212

of mechanized agricultural schemes in the Nuba Mountains, and proposed that the existing schemes which were built by appropriating land from the inhabitants should be transformed into co-operatives for the landless.

It seems that, as a result of the appalling situation in the rural areas, and the emergence of new urban social strata like the *shammasa*, which actively participated in the uprising that toppled Nimeiri's regime in 1985, the élitist leadership of the regional movements was compelled to voice popular grievances. Indeed, a document published by the General Union of the the Nuba Mountains hails the entry of the rural masses and the urban poor on to the political stage as an essential player.[13] After the fall of Nimeiri, 13 political bodies, including the General Union of the Nuba Mountains, the Beja Congress, the Front for the Renaissance of Dar Fur (*Jabha Nahda Dar Fur*), the Southern Sudan Political Association, and the Sudan African Congress assembled to found the 'Alliance of Rural Forces' (*Tadamun Quwa al-Rif al-Sudani*). This differed from the Congress of New Forces in the 1960s in that the regional movements no longer sought to ally themselves with the traditional parties, but rather chose to co-operate with certain labour unions and socialist groups.[14]

At this point, we might consider another important issue, that is, the significance of the activities of the Sudan People's Liberation Army/Sudan People's Liberation Movement (SPLA/SPLM). Despite the SPLM's assertion that it is not a regional, but a national and progressive popular movement, entirely different from SANU and the Anya-nya in the 1960s (Khalid, 1987), it would not be difficult for a critically minded observer to refute these claims. The SPLA/SPLM began its activities in the south and, despite its eagerness to play a national role in Sudanese politics, it has been understandably influenced by the local situation in that region. As to its social basis, an élitist tendency can be easily noted. In fact, the career of John Garang, the SPLA/SPLM's leader, bears a strong resemblance to the career of Joseph Lagu, the leader of the Anya-nya. Both were Sudan army officers who had the chance to receive the higher education unavailable to most southerners. Moreover, many of the SPLM's leaders are members of the military and civil élite and former officials of the Sudan Socialist Union. Indeed, the SPLM's inclination to socialism, which was very conspicuous in its early years (1983–5), may be partly attributed to the fact that, given their experience with Nimeiri's socialism, the leaders of the SPLM were well versed in 'socialistic' rhetoric.[15]

Looked at from another viewpoint, however, the reasons for

213

the impact of the SPLA/SPLM on the political scene become clear. The movement's activities are important because it appeals potentially, not only to those who are in direct contact with the armed struggle in the south, but also to the people from the south, the Nuba Mountains and Dar Fur who are scattered throughout Sudan, living as *shammasa* in the towns of the north. When the SPLM speaks of the poor *shammasa* who are being evicted from their own national capital by the 'apartheid-like' *kasha* policy, it is no longer speaking on behalf of one region, but of the whole of Sudan (Khalid, 1987: 26). Unlike SANU in the 1960s, which was ready to accept the building of an 'Islamic state' in the north in exchange for federal status for the south, the SPLM rejected any attempt to divide Sudan in accordance with ethnicity, language, religion, etc.[16] The significance of this apparently idealistic attitude is clear, if we call to mind the problem of the *shammasa*. Indeed, the plight of the Sudanese people in the 1980s could no longer be resolved by old-fashioned regionalism. Hence the need for the supra-regional (national) approach adopted by the SPLM. Interestingly, there seems to be a tacit approval for this approach even on the part of the other regional movements. Between 1985 and 1988, the various regional movements were generally in favour of the SPLM, and eager to establish links with it.[17]

We may conclude by saying that nowadays, as a result of the intensive breakup of rural society, unmistakably a national phenomenon, the regional movements are assuming a national character. Paradoxically, while the 'regional' movements are demanding a united Sudan free of any kind of discrimination among its citizens, successive 'national' regimes have been pursuing policies that divided its people. The infamous *kasha* policy introduced by the Nimeiri regime in its last stage, was taken up by the governments after 1985, and greatly intensified by the Muslim fundamentalist military regime that seized power in 1989. This policy resembles the colonial practice of forcing people to return to their 'place of origin', to their own 'tribal territory'. Moreover, there were attempts after 1985 to restore native administration and return power to the tribal chiefs. The recent practice of arming tribal militias to combat the SPLA is a step in the same backward direction.

It seems, that after more than 30 years since independence, the post-colonial state is trying to cope with its crisis by reproducing structures designed by the colonial regime, contrary to the avowed determination to wipe out all vestiges of colonial rule from national life. Whether this approach is appropriate for contemporary Sudanese society is still to be seen.

Notes

1 For the spirit of native administration see Lugard (1923: 196–7, 214–18). Among students of native administration in the British empire, there is a tendency to contrast its application to Sudan and northern Nigeria. It should be noted, however, that even in northern Nigeria Lugard was not simply using existing 'tribes', but was also reconstructing and inventing them.

2 *Command Paper 3403, Sudan, No. 2 (1929), Report on the Sudan in 1928*, pp. 116–17.

3 *FO 371/69251, 1314, Sudan Political Intelligence Summary*, No. 1, January 1948, p. 6.

4 Concerning the details of the negotiations between the Abbud regime and the Umma Party, see Sudanese Communist Party (n.d.: 241–6).

5 Ibid., pp. 391, 393.

6 Sudanese Communist Party (1987: 134–49): resolutions adopted by the fourth congress of the Sudanese Communist Party in 1967.

7 Ibid., pp. 147–9, 158–9, 173. Lecture given by 'Abd al-Khaliq al-Mahjub, Secretary General of the Sudanese Communist Party at the University of Khartoum.

8 *Roz al-Yusuf*, No. 2014 (16/1/1969, No. 2065 (8/1/1968). The Socialist Party was founded after the ban of the Communist Party in November 1965, and it is thought that the membership of these two parties overlapped to some extent. In the early days of Nimeiri's rule, many former members of the Socialist Party collaborated with his regime.

9 For the results of the elections see Niblock (1987).

10 In this context, it is worth noting that in the early 1960s the dormitories of the University of Khartoum were divided according to the students' region of origin. This might have contributed to the development of regional consciousness among the students.

11 For the programme and activities of the General Union of the Nuba Mountains, see Abbas (1973). For the Beja Congress see Niblock (1987: 147). Data concerning the social origins of the leading members of these movements were obtained by the author through interviews with spokesmen of the General Union of the Nuba Mountains and SANU in 1986.

12 See Mukhtar Ahmad Ali (1974), cited in Markakis (1990). For the Nuba Mountains Peasant Union, see Markakis (1990: 80–1).

13 The General Union of the Nuba Mountains (1986: 2).

14 The other participants in the Alliance of Rural Forces were: the Union of Northern and Southern Funj, Organization for Socialist Action, Union of National Democratic Forces, General Union for the Funj Area, National Act Party, Trade Union Block for the Upper Nile District, Trade Union Block for the Bahr al-Ghazal District, Block of the Trade Union Leadership at the National Capital.

15 See the careers of SPLM members in Khalid (1987). Among the northerners who also joined the SPLM, there were several former high officials of the Nimeiri regime, such as Mansour Khalid and Uthman Khalil.

16 A more south-orientated tendency has been developing in the SPLA/SPLM since the internal split in August 1991.

17 In contrast, the SPLA/SPLM was anxious to distinguish itself from the regional movements and was cool towards what it described as 'regionally based and possibly regionally biased' organizations (Khalid, 1987: viii).

References

Abbas, P. (1973) Growth of black political consciousness in northern Sudan. *Africa Today*, **20** (3).

Abd al Latif, Salah (1985) *Ashara Ayyam Hazzat al-Sudan (The Ten Days that Shook the Sudan)*. Cairo.

Ahmed, Abd-al Ghaffar Muhammad (1973) The Rufa'a al-Hoi economy. In

I. Cunnison & W. James (eds), *Essays in the Sudan Ethnography*. London: Hurst & Co.

—— (1974) *Shaykhs and Followers: Political Struggle in the Rufa'a al-Hoi Nazirate in the Sudan*. Khartoum: Khartoum University Press.

Bakheit, M.A. (1965) British administration and Sudanese nationalism, 1919–1939. Ph.D. Dissertation, Cambridge University.

Barnett, T. & Abbas Abdel-Karim (eds) (1988) *Sudan: State, Capital, and Transformation*. London: Croom Helm.

Bechtold, P.K. (1976) *Politics in the Sudan*. New York: Praeger.

Cunnison, I. & James, W. (eds) (1973) *Essays in the Sudan Ethnography*. London: Hurst & Co.

Daly, M.W. (1980) *British Administration and the Northern Sudan, 1917–1924*. Istanbul: Nederlands Historisch-Archaeologisch Instituut.

—— (1986) *Empire on the Nile: the Anglo-Egyptian Sudan, 1898–1934*. Cambridge University Press.

Deng, F.M. (1982) *The Recollections of Babo Nimr*. London: Ithaca Press.

—— (1986) *The Man Called Deng Majok: a Biography of Power, Polygyny, and Change*. New Haven, Connecticut: Yale University Press.

Elhassan, Abdalla Mohammed (1988) The encroachment of large scale mechanised agriculture: elements of differentiation among the peasantry. In Barnett & Abbas Abdel-Karim (eds), *Sudan: State, Capital, and Transformation*. London: Croom Helm.

Fawzy-Rossano, D.D. (1981) Le Soudan: problèmes du passage de la création de l'état à la libération de la nation. Dissertation, University of Paris VII.

General Union of the Nuba Mountains (1986) *Towards Peace and Progress for the Building of the Sudanese Nation: Participation of the General Union of the Nuba Mountains in the National Dialogue*. (Arabic). Khartoum: GUNM.

Henderson, K.D.D. (1953) *The Making of the Modern Sudan: the Life and Letters of Sir Douglas Newbold*. New Haven, Connecticut: Greenwood Press.

Khalid, M. (1985) *Nimeiri and the Revolution of Dis-May*. London: Kegan Paul.

—— (ed.) (1987) *John Garang Speaks*. London: Kegan Paul.

Lugard, F.D. (1923) *The Dual Mandate in British Tropical Africa*. London: Blackwood.

Markakis, J. (1990) *National and Class Conflict in the Horn of Africa*. London: Zed Books.

Mohamed Ahmed Abbas (1980) *White Nile Arabs: Political Leadership and Economic Change*. New Jersey: Athlone Press.

Mukhtar Ahmad Ali (1974) Communalism in northern Sudan. Diploma thesis, Institute of African and Asian Studies, Khartoum University.

Niblock, T. (1987) *Class and Power in Sudan*. London: Macmillan.

Stevenson, R.C. (1984) *The Nuba People of Kordofan Province*. Khartoum: University of Khartoum.

Sudanese Communist Party (n.d.) *Thawra al-sha'b* (People's Revolution). Cairo.

—— (1987) *Al-Marksiya wa Qadaya al-Thawra al-Sudaniya* (Marxism and the Problems of the Sudanese Revolution), 2nd edn. Khartoum.

Talal Asad (1970) *The Kababish Arabs: Power, Authority and Consent in a Nomadic Tribe*. London: Hurst.

11 Ethnic Conflict & the State in the Horn of Africa

JOHN MARKAKIS

'Ethnic' conflict in the Horn of Africa is a many-sided, violent struggle waged at several levels. It involves nations, regions, ethnic groups, clans and lineages, and is fought between and within states, regions and ethnic groups. As commonly defined, ethnicity certainly is a factor in the conflict, since in nearly all cases the opposing parties belong to groups with different ethnic and clan identities. Whether such differences in themselves are sufficient cause for conflict is debatable, and to define the conflict a priori as 'ethnic' is questionable. This chapter adopts what Enloe (1973) called a 'situational perspective', which focuses on objective factors in the social setting that act as catalysts to endow ethnicity with the potential for political conflict. It examines various dimensions of conflict in the Horn of Africa, but highlights two factors it considers catalysts in this context. These factors are: (i) competition for resources in conditions of great scarcity, and (ii) the role the state plays in controlling the allocation of such resources.

Because it controls the production and distribution of material and social resources, the state has become the focus of conflict. Access to state power is essential for the welfare of its subjects, but such access has never been equally available to all the people of the Horn, and to many it has never been available at all. Since those who control the state have used its power to defend their own privileged position, the state has become both the object of the conflict and the principal means by which it is waged. Dissident groups seek to restructure the state in order to gain access to its power, or, failing that, to gain autonomy or independence. The ultimate goal of most parties to the conflict, of course, is to enlarge their share of the resources commanded by the state. This is the real bone of contention and the root cause of the conflict in the Horn, whether it is fought in the name of nation, region, religion, ethnicity or clanship.

The contribution of nature and history

As noted, the intervention of the state occurs in conditions of resource scarcity that lead to intense competition among groups and individuals. Such conditions are the product of nature and history, which can be said to have set the stage for the current conflict. The natural endowment of the Horn of Africa is meagre and unevenly distributed, and large parts of it are not fit for settled human habitation. Man's adaptation to it was premised on movement, and the history of the area is marked by extensive migrations and population shifts, the constant jostling and shoving of peoples in search of land, pasture and water. Mobility was specially noted among the pastoralists who inhabit the Horn's arid expanses, and the epic migrations of the Arabs from Egypt to Sudan, the Oromo from the tip of the Horn to the Ethiopian plateau, the Somali from the Gulf of Aden to the foothills of the East African highlands, and the Beja into Eritrea are well-known instances (Paul, 1954; Lewis, 1955; Yusuf Fadl Hasan, 1973). Agriculturalists moved as well. The Abyssinian movement from the northern plateau southward over the centuries is the best-known instance (Jones & Monroe, 1935).

Scarcity remains a harsh fact of life in the Horn. Partly, this is due to the meagre natural endowment. The bulk of the region is lowland and has an arid regime with an average precipitation rate of less than 500 mm and a moisture index of minus 40 to minus 50. In the Horn, soil and climatic conditions set a high water requirement for cultivation. Whereas in Europe a mean annual precipitation of 750 mm is sufficient for most crops, it is insufficient for most crops here. More than 50 per cent of Ethiopia's land falls in this category, and the figure for the Sudan is 66 per cent, for Kenya 72 per cent, for Somalia 75 per cent, and for Djibouti 100 per cent. This regime is insufficient for regular cultivation, and only wandering pastoralists find a livelihood here. The Horn is home to the highest concentration of traditional pastoralists in the world. Sudan, Somalia and Ethiopia rank first, third and fifth respectively in the world in terms of pastoral population size, and more than one-third of Djibouti's inhabitants are pastoralists.

218

Nature's parsimony in the region is accentuated with a pattern of recurring drought that invariably results in massive famine. A rough collation of recorded incidents over the past 100 years suggests that major drought occurs every 10 years on the average (Markakis, 1987: 4). In the past two decades, drought has been nearly continuous. It caused famines of biblical dimensions in the 1970s and 1980s (Johnson & Anderson, 1988), and struck several areas of the region in the early 1990s. Drought afflicts all countries, and threatens to turn formerly fertile land to desert. Such land is already under great human and animal population pressure. Although the Horn is not a crowded region, it has one of the highest rates of human population growth in the world. Sudan's rate is 2.8, Somalia's 3, Ethiopia's 3.1, Djibouti's 3.5 and Kenya's 4. The mass of the population in each country is concentrated in limited areas of cultivation. For instance, in Ethiopia cultivated land accounts for less than a quarter of the total land surface. Animal population numbers have increased at a very rapid rate in all four countries. The combined pressure on land cultivated without benefit of fertilizer or fallow periods has diminished productivity throughout the region and accelerated soil erosion. In conjunction with drought, it is threatening some areas with desertification.

Mobility is increasingly constrained, but the need for it remains as valid as ever. This is particularly true of the pastoralists, for whom mobility is an economic imperative, and they continue to shift about and press against their neighbours in a constant search for pasture and water. The restiveness of the pastoralists is aggravated by the proliferation of constraints placed upon their movements by state borders, provincial boundaries, grazing zones, game parks, quarantine restrictions and the massive incursion of cultivation into their habitat. Nor have agriculturalists ceased to move away from infertile and overcrowded areas. Cultivators from the Ethiopian plateau have been moving down its slopes, while others found seasonal employment in the cotton plantations of the Awash valley, the coffee-producing region of the south-west and the commercial farms of the Humera district in the west, until the 1975 land reform outlawed hired labour. Afterwards, in the grip of famine, hundreds of thousands were moved to the west and south-west by the resettlement programme of the 1980s. In Sudan, hundreds of thousands of impoverished peasants from the west migrate seasonally to work in the cotton plantations of the Gezira.

Scarcity and mobility make conflict inevitable, and the Horn has never been a peaceful place. The major migrations of the past

219

gave rise to endless strife, memories of which continue to nourish contemporary hatreds. To this day, pastoralist movement generates conflict without end, among the herders themselves and with cultivators. Occasionally, such conflict is enmeshed with major confrontations and escalates out of control. For example, the traditional Baqqara–Dinka conflict has been woven into the civil war between north and south in Sudan (Mohamed Salih, 1989). The Ishaq–Ogaden conflict over the prized Haud pastures is similarly woven into the perennial confrontation between Ethiopia and Somalia, as well as into the current civil war in Somalia (Markakis, 1987). An attempt by the Ethiopian government to stem the Somali drift into the southern part of Sidamo province in the early 1960s sparked off a rebellion there and in the adjacent province of Bale. This was to become a factor in the mid-1970s Somali invasion of Ethiopia (Gebru Tareke, 1991).

Pastoralists also clash with cultivators, and occasionally such clashes are also enmeshed into larger conflicts. Peasants from the eroded and overcrowded northern Ethiopian plateau moving down its flanks often collide violently with pastoralists who graze their animals there. In the Awash valley, the Afar Liberation Front made its début in 1975 by massacring the highlanders who had moved to the valley. Further to the north, conflict between Saho pastoralists and highlanders was woven into the internecine war between the rival Eritrean liberation fronts in the 1970s. At present, in western Sudan, a confrontation between the Baqqara pastoralists and Fur cultivators is entangled into a local war that involves, among others, Libya and the parties to the civil war in Chad.

The role of the state

The emergence of modern states with expansionist tendencies is another historical phenomenon with a crucial bearing on the current conflict. It coincides with the imperialist intrusion in the last quarter of the past century, when the existing state framework in the Horn was established. The expansion of Abyssinia into the empire of Ethiopia occurred at the same time. In nearly all instances, borders between states were drawn through the lowland pastoralist habitat, fragmenting ethnic groups and cutting communities off from their pastures, markets, kinsmen and places of worship. The Somali were partitioned among no less than five state units during the colonial period: Ethiopia, (French) Djibouti, (British) Somaliland, (Italian) Somalia and (British)

Kenya. Their Afar neighbours were claimed by Ethiopia, Italy (Eritrea) and France (Djibouti). The Beja were split by the border between Eritrea and Sudan, while the Boran found themselves on both sides of the Ethiopia–Kenya border. The partitioning of the pastoralist domain proved permanent, and the fragmentation of pastoralist communities has not healed. The economic viability, social integrity and political efficacy of pastoralist society were gravely impaired as a result, and pastoralist groups were gradually relegated to a marginal position, alien and alienated in a changing world. The decline of pastoralism and endemic conflict in the lowlands of the Horn are closely related phenomena (Markakis, 1993).

The emergence of the modern state in this corner of Africa was characterized by a strong expansionist trend. During the scramble for the Horn, Ethiopia and the European colonial powers competed strenuously for territory. The British moved into southern Sudan to prevent it becoming a French or Ethiopian possession, and for practical reasons attached this region to their colony in the north. They also pushed the borders of Kenya into the north-eastern lowlands, until they were stopped by the Ethiopians and the Italians, who were both busily extending their respective domains in that area. Having established themselves in Eritrea in the north, the Italians invaded Ethiopia, only to be violently repulsed. Expansionist trends did not cease with the decline of colonialism. A new round began at the end of the Second World War, with the disposal of Italy's former colonies. Seeking an outlet to the sea, Ethiopia at one time laid claims to all parts of Somalia, and succeeded in annexing Eritrea. In turn, when it gained independence in 1960, the Somali Republic laid claims against all its neighbours, and the pursuit of these claims became a source of perennial conflict in the region. Ethiopia and Somalia both claimed Djibouti, and the enclave has survived intact to this day only thanks to the protection of France.

In many parts of the Horn, the goals of expansion — effective control and integration — were never fulfilled. Many of the territories and peoples incorporated into the state domain, especially the pastoralist lowlands, were never fully integrated, due to the resistance of the population. It was not until the late 1950s that the imperial regime in Ethiopia attempted to make its presence felt in the lowland periphery of the state, where it immediately encountered violent resistance, and the rebellions of the 1960s in the Ogaden, Bale and southern Sidamo provinces were the result. The same thing happened when the military regime sought to impose its fiat on the Afar in 1975. Likewise,

221

the imposition of direct rule in Eritrea sparked a revolution in the early 1960s, which had its start in the western lowlands.

In the colonial period, southern Sudan was administered separately from the north, and Islamic and Arab influence was minimized, while Christianity and the English language were promoted. It was not until after independence in 1956 that the nationalist regime based in the north sought to exert its authority in the south. Southern resistance had become manifest even earlier — in the 1955 mutiny of southern Sudanese troops at Torit — and a full-scale rebellion was to follow (Mohammed Omer Beshir, 1968). In 1960, the former British colony of Somaliland in the north joined the former Italian colony of Somalia in the south to form the Somali Republic. Union was effected by common consent, but the sparsely populated, predominantly pastoralist north was weary of being dominated in a centralized state by the more populous and agriculturally developed south. In a referendum held soon afterwards, the north rejected the constitution of such a political system, which was adopted nevertheless with a massive vote in the south. An attempted *coup d'état* by a group of military officers in the north, aiming at separation, followed, and relations between that region and the central government in Mogadisho have remained volatile ever since (Lewis, 1961). Similarly, Kenya's independence in 1963 was followed by a rebellion in the Somali-inhabited Northern Frontier District, whose Somali inhabitants preferred to join the Somali Republic. In all the areas mentioned above, as well as others, the state has been able to maintain only a military presence, proof of the failure of integration (Markakis, 1987).

Expansion brought into intimate contact peoples of different nationalities, ethnic groups, religions and languages — social and cultural features which readily become rallying symbols of group mobilization in times of conflict. The expansion stored great potential for conflict in the nature of the relationships formed between those who controlled the state and those who became its subjects through incorporation. Simply put, these relationships were both unequal and iniquitous. They defined positions of superiority and inferiority, domination and subjugation, and translated into the oppression and exploitation of many ethnic groups by a few others. A system of what Horowitz (1985) calls 'ranked' ethnic groups emerged, and an explosive combination of ethnic and class contradictions was the result, creating the potential for massive conflict. Ethiopia and Sudan are the clearest examples of what Mazrui has called the 'ethnocratic' state (1975).

Not surprisingly, they also have the longest record of ethnic strife in the region.

This potential matured quickly in the post-colonial period, ironically due to measures taken by the states to prevent this from happening. One of these measures was the centralization of state power, a familiar trend throughout Africa, designed to protect the monopoly of power acquired by nationalist cliques with independence. The constitutional models bequeathed to Africa by the departing colonial powers were soon scrapped, legislative and judicial controls of the executive were eliminated, and the nationalist regimes quickly moved through the one-party system and the lifetime presidency to authoritarian rule, with increased reliance on force as an instrument of government. Reliance on force required the strengthening of the military and security apparatus of the state, and it was these repressive branches that expanded inordinately in Africa, despite the economic malaise that afflicted most of the continent.

Centralization was promoted vigorously in Ethiopia by an imperial regime unhampered by constitutional, legal or political constraints. Indeed, centralization is considered the outstanding achievement of Haile Selassie's reign. Militarization was another achievement, with Ethiopia boasting the largest army in black Africa in the mid-1960s. Civilian rule in Sudan did not last long enough to go through the intermediate stages. Military rule was imposed there within two years of independence, and the build-up of the Sudanese army and security forces began soon afterwards.

In Somalia, the nationalists managed to impose a unitary constitution despite strong opposition from the north and the Sab group in the south. Despite its vaunted homogeneity and national consciousness, however, the predominantly pastoral Somali society did not provide a solid base for the state that came into existence in 1960. Clan strife pervaded political life during the period of civilian rule (1960-9), weakening a nationalist regime mesmerized by the vision of expansion to incorporate other lands inhabited by Somali in the Horn. This vision led to hostility and clashes with all three neighbouring states: Ethiopia, Kenya and Djibouti. The resulting tension in the region promoted an arms race, with the Soviet Union sponsoring Somalia, the United States supporting Ethiopia, Britain backing Kenya and France providing protection for Djibouti. Militarization also sealed the fate of civilian rule in Somalia, where soldiers seized control of the state nine years after independence.

Centralization, militarization and authoritarianism signified

223

the determination of ruling groups to maintain the status quo with all its iniquities, using the power of the state. Demands for political reform were invariably rejected, and the most serious conflicts in the region were the immediate result of such rejections. The civil war in Sudan was preceded by the rejection of a southern demand for a federal system of government, and the Eritrean revolution began when a federal arrangement there was scrapped by Addis Ababa. Rebellion became endemic in Ethiopia when the military regime that came to power in 1974 proved more centralized and authoritarian than its imperial predecessor. The internecine struggle of the Somali clans was foreshadowed soon after independence, when the northern region decidedly rejected in a referendum the unitary constitution that was favoured in the south.

Uneven development

Uneven development among regions and groups is another basic ingredient of the conflict in the Horn of Africa. Uneven development was a major feature of the colonial economy, when capital and modern technology were brought together to create a new mode of production, that is, cultivation of export crops, in areas where suitable land, labour and water were available. The growth of an urban sector was promoted simultaneously to provide the required services and administration. Little was done elsewhere, and nothing at all in the pastoralist domain. The resulting unevenness translated into gross disparity in the development of the productive forces in different regions and in the standard of living of their inhabitants. Investment in infrastructure and social services was concentrated in areas of modern economic development, and only nominal development in this regard appeared elsewhere.

Notwithstanding the fact that the colonial economy followed the capitalist model, the prime mover in its development was the state. The state either owned, managed or effectively controlled the modern economic sector. Accordingly, the state became the determining factor in the production and distribution of material and social resources. It was this function that endowed the state with overwhelming predominance in colonial society. As a result, access to the state became essential for the welfare of its subjects. Lack of access meant exclusion from the processes of production and distribution of material and social resources.

Little changed in this regard in the post-colonial period, when

224

the state took upon itself the task of economic development. Economic policy followed the colonial blueprint, directing capital and technological innovation to commercial cultivation, while also trying to build a productive capacity in the urban sector. Hardly anything was done for subsistence cultivation, and nothing at all for pastoralism. Consequently, the disparity between regions and ethnic groups inherited from the colonial period was not diminished; rather, in many cases it was exacerbated, and the resulting tension was a catalytic element in the political conflict that followed. The state's control of the economy reached its apogee under the pseudo-Marxist military regimes that ruled Sudan (1969–85), Somalia (1969–91) and Ethiopia (1974–91), when the state actually took over the processes of production and distribution. It now became quite impossible to redress disparity without recourse to the power of the state. Not surprisingly, conflict proliferated in that period.

It is not surprising that the areas and groups most wanting in development are also the ones that have the least access to state power. These are also the areas where dissidence and rebellion flourished, and the connection is not hard to perceive. One needs only to list them to make the point: southern and western Sudan, northern Kenya, northern Somalia, Ogaden, Bale, Danakil, Tigrai, western Eritrea. Needless to say, most are pastoralist regions. Highland Eritrea is the exception that proves the rule. Inflated during the last phase of Italian rule and the wartime boom of the 1940s, the Eritrean economy collapsed afterwards, forcing many Eritreans to seek jobs abroad.

Cultural oppression

The propagation of what may be called 'state nationalism' in the guise of 'national integration' was one political initiative taken by ruling groups in an attempt to reinforce the shallow foundations of the state. Understandably, their perception of national identity was the mirror-image of their own ethnic and cultural ego. Thus, the language of the Amhara and Christianity became the salient features of Ethiopian nationalism, and the Arab language and Islam of Sudanese nationalism. Consequently, integration was premised on assimilation into what was presented as the superior culture of the ruling ethnic group. In Ethiopia, no other indigenous language was allowed to be printed, broadcast or spoken in public functions, and attempts to study the culture and history of other groups were decidedly discouraged.

The ban also applied to the sister language of Tigrigna, spoken in Tigrai province and highland Eritrea. Ignoring the religious needs of Muslims, the imperial regime limited the teaching of Arabic to a handful of privately maintained schools. Although Muslims make up a very large section of the country's population, their religion was ignored by the state, whose official religion was Christianity.

In Sudan, it was Christianity that was handicapped, and this affected southern Sudan, where a sizeable part of the population had espoused this faith during the colonial period. Northern Sudanese regimes made no secret of their desire to Islamize the south, and they proceeded by taking over missionary schools soon after independence, making Friday the weekly day of rest, and expelling all missionaries in 1964. A plan for educational reform adopted in 1961 was premised on thorough Arabization.

Predictably, forced assimilation not only was rejected by subordinate groups, but also encouraged them to invoke their own cultural symbols, most often religion and language, in the propagation of what may be called 'dissident nationalism'. Language, for instance, became a rallying symbol for dissident movements, which claimed to be fighting an attempt to deracinate their people. Religion, an even more emotive subject, is as often invoked, especially among pastoralists, for whom secular ideologies have little appeal. As a result, the conflict often appears to be a sectarian or communal struggle lacking objective causes.

However, appearances can be misleading. On the one hand, cultural elements are often used as rallying symbols to mobilize groups in conflicts that have an objective material basis. For example, when asked who their enemy is, Muslim pastoralists in south-eastern Ethiopia readily reply 'the Kaffirs' (Arabic, 'infidels'), meaning the Abyssinians. However, the conflict is not about religion, although that is a related factor, and to focus exclusively on such symbols risks missing the substance of the issues at stake. On the other hand, cultural elements themselves can have a material dimension in a given situation. For example, language often mediates access to power and privilege. Members of a group whose language is not recognized by the state will find themselves at a distinct disadvantage in competing for access to education and employment. In resisting assimilation, the southern Sudanese intelligentsia appeared to be defending the colonial heritage, with the English language and Christianity becoming the salient cultural features of an emerging southern Sudanese identity. In fact, southerners were defending an educational asset, since the first generation of educated southerners were virtually unemployable in a system where Arabic prevailed. Religion may have similar significance attached to it. In imperial Ethiopia, for instance, it was easier for a non-Christian who also did not speak Amharigna to pass through the eye of a needle than to enter the charmed circle of power and privilege. The same applied in Sudan to a non-Muslim who also did not speak Arabic.

The role of the various factors mentioned above in the generation of conflict in the Horn of Africa is illustrated by the examples sketched below.

Regional movements

The two most serious and enduring conflicts in the Horn occurred in Eritrea and southern Sudan. The origins of both can be traced to the early 1960s. The dissident movements that emerged in both cases are regional in character, that is, they are coalitions of ethnic groups sharing a region. Like nearly all political movements that emerged in Africa during the period of decolonization, their frame of reference is a territorial unit carved out by colonialism. Both regions first acquired a vague identity under colonial auspices, neither having existed as a distinct entity before. In other words, there was nothing known as Eritrea or southern Sudan earlier. Neither region is ethnically or culturally homogeneous. Quite the opposite: they are highly diversified along these lines. Moreover, this diversity is strongly manifested in their political development. The history of the Eritrean nationalist movement is replete with internal strife, in which ethnic, sectarian and sectional divisions are prominent. The same is true of the history of the southern Sudanese movement. Nevertheless, these divisions were transcended in a determined effort to resist absorption and subordination of their region into a state controlled by ethnic groups with a monopoly of power and resources. In the course of a long struggle, regional solidarity evolved into a consciousness of distinct identity that is akin to a national consciousness, most apparent in the case of the Eritreans.

The roots of the conflict in both regions can be traced to the manner in which they were incorporated into larger states without reference to the wishes or interests of their inhabitants. In Sudan the issue was settled even before the south had time to mobilize in order to represent its people. As Sudan approached independence in 1956, the southern region had changed little since pre-colonial times, while the north had one of the most highly developed economies in black Africa and a sophisticated political party system. It was clear that the south was destined to play a marginal role in a unitary Sudanese state. To avoid that, the very first political organization that appeared in the south called for regional self-government in a federal system of government. This became a catholic and persistent call in the south, but it was not seriously considered until the Anya-nya rebellion forced the Nimeiri regime to the negotiation table in Addis Ababa in 1972. The Anya-nya movement was riven with internal divisions along ethnic lines, but managed to contain them and maintain regional unity in the war against the north. The Addis Ababa Agreement gave the south regional autonomy to run its own affairs and, as long as it was respected by the north, it appeared to satisfy southern aspirations (Mohammed Omer Beshir, 1975).

The Agreement was violated in the early 1980s by its own author, Nimeiri, as he sought political support from the Muslim Brotherhood, the most implacable opponent of southern Sudanese political aspirations. A new struggle then began in the south, led by the Sudan People's Liberation Movement (SPLM). In contrast to the Anya-nya, the SPLM adopted a national (Sudanese) rather than a regional (southern Sudanese) posture, claiming to represent the underprivileged and powerless people of the whole by Sudan, and defining as its goal the transformation of the Sudanese state and society on the basis of socialism. Its potential appeal to the impoverished non-Arab communities in the north was regarded as a real threat to the ruling class, and the civil war continued during the interlude of civilian rule in Khartoum in 1986–9. The new military regime that seized power in 1989 sealed an alliance with the Muslim Brotherhood, declared Sudan an Islamic republic and redoubled the effort to subdue the SPLM.

The regime in Khartoum had some success when the guerrilla movement lost its bases in Ethiopia due to the change of regime there in 1991. It also benefited from an internal crisis in the SPLM, which produced a split and a challenge to its leadership. The fact that the split followed ethnic lines was not surprising, since ethnic aspirations were submerged but not eliminated within the SPLM, as Mohamed Salih argues in his contribution to this volume. The rebel faction demanded that the SPLM drop its national posture and its goal of transforming Sudan, and opt for secession and independence for southern Sudan. While the avowed aim of the rebel faction was to assert the regional nature of the southern movement, the initial result was to promote ethnic strife within the south.

Eritrea was initially linked to Ethiopia in a federal arrangement

228

(1952–62). This was arranged by the Western powers through the United Nations, as a compromise between Ethiopia's claims for annexation and the desire of a large section of Eritrea's population for independence. Independence appealed mainly to Muslims in Eritrea, who, for obvious reasons, were opposed to any link with Ethiopia. Many Christians, on the other hand, favoured the Ethiopian connection as a guarantee of their own political predominance in Eritrea. Both groups accepted the compromise of federation, but the imperial regime in Addis Ababa did not. Within a few years it had deprived Eritrea of meaningful autonomy, and in 1962 abolished the federation altogether and annexed Eritrea as a province into the imperial domain.

The same year witnessed the founding of the Eritrean Liberation Front (ELF), which initially was a purely Muslim affair. The loss of autonomy and demise of a fledgling democracy, direct and heavy-handed imperial rule, the banning of their language, and the stagnation of the local economy gradually turned most Christian Eritreans against Ethiopia as well and, when the second nationalist movement, eventually to become known as the Eritrean People's Liberation Front (EPLF), was formed at the beginning of the 1970s, it attracted a majority of Christian followers. While struggling against the Ethiopians, the rival Eritrean movements also waged a civil war against each other. Ethnic, sectarian and sectional factors were involved in this intra-regional struggle, as well as ideological differences and conflict between generations. The internal struggle ended after 10 years with the elimination of the ELF. From then on, the nationalist movement acquired a solid regional base.

Independence was the goal of the Eritrean movement from the beginning. With the collapse of the military regime in Ethiopia in 1991, the EPLF gained complete control of Eritrea, a situation that was acknowledged and accepted by the new regime in Addis Ababa, led by the Tigrai People's Liberation Front, an old ally of the EPLF. The future of Eritrea was decided in a referendum held in 1993, and independence was the result. The outcome of a conflict that began on a parochial basis, therefore, is a new state with a multi-ethnic population whose 'national' (Eritrean) consciousness was forged in a bloody struggle that lasted three decades.

Ethnic movements

The movement that played the leading role in the overthrow of the military regime in Ethiopia in 1991 represents an ethnic constituency in Tigrai province of northern Ethiopia. Tigrai is the junior branch of the Abyssinian family, closely related to the Amhara, the former rulers of Ethiopia, from whom they are distinguished only by their language. The inhabitants of this impoverished and famine-stricken province have long resented and resisted the domination of the Amhara in the imperial state. A particularly deep source of resentment was the proscription of the Tigrai language, along with all others, in favour of the Amhara tongue. Tigrai was completely bypassed by economic development under the imperial regime and, when that regime collapsed in 1974, there was not a single factory in the entire province. The people of Tigrai, especially the intelligentsia, whose members were compelled to find work outside their homeland, were inclined to link their province's destitution to its political impotence, and blamed the Amhara regime for directing investment capital to the central and southern regions of Ethiopia. When the imperial regime collapsed, hopes flourished for political reform that would provide fair representation and equal access to the power of the state for all groups. Such hopes were soon dashed by the successor military regime, which opted for even greater centralization and rule by coercion. The result was the formation of the Tigrai People's Liberation Front (TPLF) in 1975.

After a period of ambivalence, when the TPLF appeared to entertain the option of secession from Ethiopia and independence for Tigrai, it proclaimed its intention to remain within a democratic, pluralistic, decentralized Ethiopian state, if such could be attained. Once that decision was made, the TPLF sought to devise a strategy that could enable it to play a role beyond the bounds of Tigrai province. To begin with, it formed a political party called the Marxist Leninist League, which, it was hoped, could affiliate with similar organizations to be founded in other provinces of Ethiopia and form a national party. Later, it formed a coalition with several minor dissident groups of varied ethnic affiliation labelled the Ethiopian Peoples Revolutionary Democratic Front (EPRDF), and it was in the name of this coalition that the TPLF took over the reins of power in Addis Ababa in May 1991.

Another movement that represents an ethnically homogeneous constituency is the Oromo Liberation Front (OLF). The Oromo are one of the largest and most widely dispersed ethnic groups in the Horn, ranging from northern Kenya to northern Ethiopia. Dispersion, adaptation to varied ecological conditions and mingling with other ethnic groups resulted in considerable differentiation among the numerous Oromo communities. Those who found themselves in the arid zone retained the traditional pastoralist vocation of their ancestors, while the rest took to cultivation on the highlands. Traditional Oromo socio-political organization was modified extensively, with some groups developing stratified societies and monarchical political systems that contrasted strongly with the egalitarian Oromo tradition. Many Oromo, including all the pastoralists, espoused Islam and developed an affinity with their Somali neighbours, while others were converted to Christianity and were partially assimilated by the Abyssinians who conquered their lands in the second half of the last century.

In the wake of the conquest, the Abyssinians expropriated a major part of the land and turned the majority of Oromo peasants into their tenants. Such a conjunction of ethnic and class divisions created the potential for mass discontent, the kind that can be readily exploited by ethnic political movements. Indeed, this was the target of the OLF when it was formed in 1975. However, the opportunity to exploit it was lost when the sweeping land reform of that year gave the land to the peasants in usufruct and dispossessed the alien landlords. As a result, initially the OLF appeal elicited little response from this class.

Like almost all dissident movements in the Horn, the OLF is the creation of the intelligentsia, whose efforts to define the Oromo ethnic identity and reclaim its culture are discussed in this volume by Paul Baxter. The OLF's efforts to rally urban Oromo to its avowed goal of an independent Oromo state were hampered by the considerable extent to which the urban Oromo have integrated into the national economy. Oromo workers, traders, professionals and others became dependent for their economic welfare on the economy whose foundation is the state of Ethiopia. Other Oromo who made careers in the civil and military branches of the state are directly dependent upon the state. Consequently, the response of the Oromo to the call of ethnicity was limited initially.

The collapse of the state's centre following the defeat of the military regime changed the situation dramatically. The construction of a new political system on the basis of ethnic autonomy was launched by the EPRDF, and ethnicity became the dominant principle of political mobilization in Ethiopia. Ethnic political organizations proliferated, and a new constitution sketched a

231

highly decentralized federal system of government with autonomous ethnic regions and districts as its constituent units. The OLF chose to take part in this experiment, thereby abandoning, at least temporarily, its goal of independence. This, and the fact that people were now obliged to mobilize politically on the basis of ethnicity, gained the OLF increased following and made it potentially one of the most important political movements in Ethiopia.

In Sudan, both the north and the south provide fertile ground for ethnic movements, which often appear as supporting actors in the major civil conflict described in the preceding section. The nature of such movements in the north is described by Kurita in her contribution to this volume. She also refers to the paradox presented by Sudanese regimes which promote such movements and ethnic conflict in their effort to defeat the southern rebellion. An example in the north is the arming of a Baqqara militia force, which has been raiding their Dinka neighbours. The same technique has been used in the south. An example there is the dissident Nuer guerrilla movement, which called itself Anya-nya II, and was active in that region before the founding of the Sudanese People's Liberation Army. When it refused to merge with the SPLA, it was attacked and partly absorbed by the latter. The remnants of Anya-nya II then accepted Khartoum's offer to serve as a militia force against the SPLA.

Clan movements

Ethnic conflict waged on the level of clans and subclans is raging in Somalia, ironically the only state in sub-Sahara Africa that boasts ethnic homogeneity. Here also state power is the bone of contention. Clan strife is part of Somali tradition, and it permeated the body politic of the Somali state after it attained independence in 1960. The dominant nationalist party, the Somali Youth League, represented a coalition of clans wide enough to ensure a measure of stability, until it was undermined by clannishness and corruption. Among the pledges made by the military regime that seized power in 1969 was a promise to eliminate clannishness and corruption. In fact, it did the opposite. After a few years, the erosion of public support forced the regime to cultivate the loyalty of clans related to the head of the regime, General Siad Barre. Soon the state came under the control of a coalition of three clans (Marehan, Ogaden and Dulbahante), which, one Somali wrote, divided among themselves the wealth of the country, 'the lion's share going to the Marehan, the leopard's share to the Ogaden, and the hyena's share to the Dulbahante' (Said Samatar, 1983: 6).

Other clans reacted accordingly. Militant opposition was mounted first by the Ishaq, the dominant clan in northern Somalia, a region with precious few resources and no sign of development, despite the fact that it produced the animals that were the country's main export. The Ishaq were not part of the Somali Youth League, and remained outside the centre of power after independence. In their struggle against the military regime in Mogadisho, they violated an imperative of Somali nationalism by accepting Ethiopian assistance, in return for which they assisted the Ethiopians to suppress the efforts of another clan, the Ogaden, who were fighting to join the Somali Republic. On their part, the Ogaden clan assisted the Siad Barre regime to devastate northern Somalia. For some decades, the Ishaq and the Ogaden had been conducting their own feud over contested pasturelands, and they now proceeded to weave that conflict into the broader confrontation between north and south in Somalia and between the Somali and Ethiopian states (Markakis, 1989).

Other clans excluded from the ruling coalition in Mogadisho took up arms against the regime. The final offensive that put Siad Barre to flight in January 1991 was launched by the Hawiye, the dominant clan in the Mogadisho area. By this time, nearly all Somali clans had organized military contingents to take part in the general struggle for power that broke out when the Hawiye sought to monopolize power at the centre. The centre itself collapsed when the Hawiye clan split into two subclan factions, which fought each other savagely for control of the capital. As clan warfare became general throughout the south, the rebel movement in the north declared the region's independence. Three decades after independence, the Somali state had dissolved into its clan components and anarchy reigned.

Interestingly, the Ogaden clan in Ethiopia, who have long fought to join their ethnic kinsmen in the Somali Republic, now shifted their sights towards Addis Ababa, where ethnicity had become legitimate as the principle of group recognition and political mobilization. Organizations claiming to represent the Ogaden participated in the transitional government in Addis Ababa, which experimented with the ethnic alternative. This implied that the goals of the ethnic movement were shifting from irredentism to regional self-government.

Class conflict and ideology

Conflict of the sort described above is not the only kind of social struggle waged in the Horn. The instability of regimes and states was exacerbated by class tension within the ruling ethnic groups. Class contradictions reached an explosive point in Ethiopia and were the immediate cause for the collapse of the imperial regime in 1974. In Sudan, the authority of the ruling class of merchants, bureaucrats and religious leaders was weakened by a confrontation with workers, tenant farmers and a disgruntled intelligentsia. In both countries, the intelligentsia adopted a radical political posture associated with Marxism, and sought to rally workers and peasants against the ruling classes.

In seeking support among the underprivileged and disaffected, the radicals were tempted to make common cause with other dissident movements. In Sudan, the Communist Party supported the demand of the south for regional autonomy, and in Ethiopia the radical student movement supported the Eritrean liberation struggle. The combined pressures emanating from regional, ethnic and class confrontations disabled the nationalist regime in Sudan and caused the collapse of the imperial regime in Ethiopia, while clan strife undermined the nationalist regime in Somalia. Ultimately, military rule, the epitome of centralization and reliance on force as the instrument of government, was imposed in all three states. Military rule is the logical outcome of the trend towards the monopolization of political power begun earlier. It represents the ultimate effort to preserve the state, if not the regime, in its existing form.

While the seizure of state power by the military in these circumstances is anything but surprising, the espousal of Marxism by military regimes in all three countries shortly after the seizure of power was a surprising development (Markakis & Waller, 1986). In retrospect, it appears to have been an attempt to deploy this ideology in defence of the regime and the state. Lacking a political constituency, the soldiers needed to rally support among the opponents of the regimes they had overthrown, and they found it at the start among the radical intelligentsia. Accordingly, the Nimeiri regime allied itself initially with the Sudanese Communist Party, and the Siad Barre regime rallied the handful of radicals that were to be found in Somalia in 1969. The tortuous manipulation of the radical left in Ethiopia by the Mengistu regime is a well-known story. In all cases, having consolidated their hold on the state, the soldiers got rid of their radical allies and formed their own political organizations.

Marxism was also invoked to reinforce the legitimacy of the state. 'State nationalism' had proved a weak ideological prop, and it was now blended with socialism in the hope of producing a new political consensus to underpin the sagging foundations of the state. The contribution sought from socialism in this context was twofold. First, it aimed to undermine dissident movements based on regional and ethnic differences by focusing on class. Second, it sought to deny legitimacy to these movements, on the grounds that ethnic contradictions have no objective existence once class contradictions are resolved. Moreover, socialism sanctioned the centralization of the state and the use of force against dissidents. Socialism was also the vogue among regional, ethnic and clan movements, which used it to endow their parochial cause with universal attributes. Thus, class ideology, which derived its appeal from the real cleavages and tensions of stratified social structures, became a weapon in the conflict between the state and its opponents.

Conclusion

On a certain level, analysing the conflict in the Horn of Africa appears a fairly simple task. Given the clear differences of ethnic identity that characterize the rival groups, and their own claims to cultural distinctiveness and autonomy, it is understandable why the label 'ethnic' is commonly attached to it. Undoubtedly, ethnicity is an element in the conflict, but is it a sufficient cause for it? The assumption that it is a sufficient cause has still to find a logical explanation, yet it remains a common assumption. The argument of this chapter is that other factors provide sufficient cause for ethnic conflict, and for the most part these have an objective nature and are therefore discernible.

Competition for resources in conditions of increasing scarcity is the process that shapes the confrontation between groups and individuals in the Horn of Africa. The mediating role the state plays in it renders this process intrinsically political, and this means only groups can compete. Competition takes place not in the economic but in the political realm, and the immediate object is access to power, the key to the acquisition of material and social resources. The question that is frequently posed then is: why are groups formed on an ethnic basis, or, to put it differently, why is ethnicity the preferred and most efficient basis for political mobilization?

From a situational perspective, the answer can only be framed in the regional context sketched in this chapter. It was noted that a dominant feature of the situation there is the 'ethnocratic state', whose mediating role in the competition for resources is decisive. In that situation, ethnicity is an imperative embedded in the foundations of the political order and functions as a controlling factor in the political process, long before an ethnic movement appears to challenge that order. It is precisely because ethnicity is intrinsically political in that setting that ruling groups go to great lengths to exorcise its spirit with invocations of 'nation-building' and 'national unity'. In the 'ethnocratic state', as one would expect, ethnicity is also the ruling principle of economic and social differentiation. This means that this principle divides, along ethnic lines, groups that confront each other in the process of competition for material and social resources.

Consequently, there is a manifold sense of commonality among members of an ethnic group, a sense of sharing the same material and social prospects. As an activating force in political terms, this is probably more important than ethnic identity because, as several contributors to this volume intimate, this identity is itself defined in the process of interaction — co-operation, competition, confrontation, even war — among groups. In other words, the ethnic group as a political actor is a product of the situation, not of history, and what mobilizes its members to take collective action is concern for future prospects, not an atavistic attachment to the past. As a potential political actor, the ethnic group already exists in that setting, before conflict erupts. Therefore, the familiar question as to why political groups are formed on an ethnic basis is beside the point.

Moreover, ethnicity is not always the basis upon which ethnic groups mobilize. The sense of commonality mentioned above may exceed the bounds of ethnicity, and a wider framework may be used for purposes of political mobilization, as was the case with the regional movements described in this chapter. The future prospects of the inhabitants of southern Sudan seemed common to all, regardless of ethnic identity, and mobilization there occurred on a regional basis, as was the case in Eritrea for the same reasons. Furthermore, concern for future prospects can lead to the abandonment of what are usually considered primary symbols of ethnicity. For example, Eritrea's Muslims chose Arabic as the language of education for their children, even though it is not the native tongue of any ethnic group there. The same holds true for English in southern Sudan.

References

Enloe, C. (1973) *Ethnic Conflict and Political Development*. Boston, Massachusetts: Little Brown.

Gebru Tareke (1991) *Ethiopia: Power and Protest: Peasant Revolts in the Twentieth Century*. Cambridge: Cambridge University Press.

Horowitz, D. (1985) *Ethnic Groups in Conflict*. Berkeley: University of California Press.

Johnson, D. & Anderson, D. (eds) (1988) *Ecology and Survival: Case Studies from Northeast African History*. London: Lester Crook.

Jones, A.H.M. & Monroe, E. (1935) *A History of Abyssinia*. Oxford: Clarendon Press.

Lewis, I.M. (1955) *Peoples of the Horn of Africa*. London: International African Institute.

—— (1961) *A Pastoral Democracy*. Oxford University Press.

Markakis, J. (1987) *National and Class Conflict in the Horn of Africa*. Cambridge: Cambridge University Press.

—— (1989) The Ishaq–Ogaden dispute. In A. Hjorn & Mohamed Salih (eds), *Environmental Stress and Security: Ecology and Politics*. Uppsala: Scandinavian Institute of African Studies.

—— (ed.) (1993) *Conflict and the Decline of Pastoralism in the Horn of Africa*. London: Macmillan.

Markakis, J. & Waller, M. (eds) (1986) *Military Marxist Regimes in Africa*. London: Frank Cass.

Mazrui, A. (1975) *Soldiers and Kinsmen in Uganda: the Making of a Military Ethnocracy*. Beverly Hills, California: Sage Publications.

Mohammed Omer Beshir (1968) *The Southern Sudan: Background to Conflict*. Khartoum: Khartoum University Press.

—— (1975) *The Southern Sudan: from Conflict to Peace*. Khartoum: Bookshop.

Mohamed Salih, M.A. (1989) Tribal militias, SPLA/SPLM and the Sudanese state: new wine in old bottles. In Abdel Ghaffar & G.M. Sorbo (eds), *Managing the Crisis in the Sudan*. Bergen: University of Bergen.

Paul, A. (1954) *A History of the Beja Tribes of the Sudan*. Cambridge: Cambridge University Press.

Said Samatar (1983) Somalia into the 1980s: problems and definitions of social transformation. Paper presented to the Second International Conference of Somali Studies, University of Hamburg, August.

Yusuf Fadl Hasan (1973) *The Arabs and the Sudan*. Khartoum: Khartoum University.

Index